Bottom Line's
GREAT
BOOK OF
HUGE
TAX
LOOPHOLES

Bottom Line
Books

www.BottomLineSecrets.com

ISBN 0-88723-373-2

Bottom Line® Books is a registered trademark of Boardroom® Inc.
281 Tresser Boulevard, Stamford, CT 06901

Printed in the United States of America

Table of Contents

Section 1: Retirement and Estate Planning 1

Estate Planning Loopholes...3

Renovate Historic Buildings for Fun, Profit and Tax Breaks............7

Sell Your Company to Your Employees...and Avoid Capital

      Gains Tax 10

Stop Uncle Sam From Stealing Your Retirement Dollars 14

Limiting Your Tax Hit...18

Tax Traps to Avoid in Retirement Plan Distributions 19

Tax-Wise Retirement: The Best States for You 23

The New Tax Law and Your Retirement—How to Make It

      Work Best for You...27

Smart Bequest to Charity Saves Income Taxes for Heirs...............31

The Best Ways to Take Money Out of Your Retirement Plan...

      Early 32

Best Retirement Plans for Small-Business Owners 36

Estate-Planning Update for Your Family Business...........................40

Tax-Smart Way to Hold "TIPS" for Retirement...............................44

Tax Break for Inherited IRAs..45

How Non-Spouse Beneficiaries Can Stretch Out an Inherited

      Retirement Account 46

Good Gift for a Child: Roth IRA...50

The Importance of IRA Tax Basis 51

Estate Tax Loopholes 52

SIMPLE Retirement Plans: Act Now to Catch the
 October Deadline...55

Use an IRA to Be Charitable...and Still Leave More
 To Your Heirs 60

Revised IRA Trust Rules Can Hurt Clients and Pros....................64

Retirement Plan Tax Traps that Business Owners Must Avoid......68

IRA Withdrawal Opportunity for Business Owners.......................72

IRA Protection 73

For the Self-Employed—Great Flexibility with
 One-Person 401(k)s 74

You Can Buy Real Estate with Your IRA 79

Surprisingly High Taxes on Social Security Benefits....................83

A Cascading Beneficiary Plan for Maximum IRA Tax Deferral......85

401(k) Alert—The Rules Have Changed 90

Retirement Plan Loopholes for Business Owners..........................95

The Three Kinds of Joint Ownership...98

Section 2: Tax Strategies and Savings...99

Don't Miss These Tax Savers 101

Key Midyear Tax-Planning Moves for Your Business...................106

Like-Kind Exchange Loopholes 109

Tax Traps and Tax Savers for Gamblers 112

No Records? No Problem—You Can Still Rescue
 Big Deductions 116

For Richer or For Poorer—Tax Planning with
 Marriage in Mind..120

Bankruptcy Rules...124

Best Strategies for Joint Ownership of Real Estate...

    Bank Accounts...Cars...Other Assets... 125

How to Shelter Your Income from the IRS.................................129

How to Reduce Gain When Selling an Investment Property..........133

Money-Saving Tax Moves to Make Now.....................................134

Shrewd Ways to Use Your Home as a Tax Shelter.......................138

Very Valuable Tax Deductions Even If You Don't Itemize..............141

Converting an IRA to a Roth IRA 144

Enjoy the Tax Rewards of Charity, Club and

    Union Memberships...145

Estimated Taxes...The Very Costly Trap for

    Those with Nonwage Income 149

How to Squeeze the Most Tax-Free Profit from

    Selling Your Home...154

Use Voluntary Withholding to Beat Penalties............................157

Don't Let Your Corporation Own Real Estate.............................158

Section 3: Charitable Contributions and Helping the IRS.................159

Charitable Contribution Loopholes...161

Charitable Contribution Loopholes Part 2 164

How to Protect Your Charity Deductions....................................167

Make Charity Sweeter with Innovative

    Donation Techniques...168

Year-End Charitable Strategies..173

New Auto Donation Rules and Exceptions.................................177

Selling Your Company? Use a Charity to Sweeten the Deal..........178

A Boost for Your Heirs 183

Charitable-Gift Annuity..184

How to Turn In a Tax Cheat..185

Section 4: Business 189

Much Wiser Tax Return Filing for Business Owners 191

Loopholes in Working Abroad.....................................195

Advertising Loopholes...198

The Too, Too Common Mistake Made with Employer Stock...

    How to Keep More Profit 201

When to Lease Business Equipment...and When To Buy.............205

Loopholes for Foreigners Working In the US.....................209

How to Get a Bigger Tax Refund for Your Business 212

The Key Information Returns for Your Business........................216

Avoid the Tax Bite When You Pay for Employees' Meals 220

For Free Answers to Your Business Tax Questions...

    Look On-Line 224

FUTA and SUTA—The Ins and Outs of Unemployment

    Taxes for Small Business 229

Cut Your Company's Building Costs With Clever Use of the

    Tax Code 233

Business Owners: Tax-Saving Moves to Make Before Year-End....237

Why It's So Useful to Set Up Your Business as an LLC.................241

A Microbusiness Can Create Tax-Sheltered Wealth, Cut Other

    Taxes and Help You Start a New Career, Too.......................245

12 Easy High-Tech Ways to Simplify Business Tax Chores..........249

Beware: Incentive Stock Option Trap 253

Risks and Benefits of Borrowing From—or Lending to—

    Your Own Company..254

Independent Contractors Are Still Under IRS Scrutiny—How to

    Protect Your Business...258

Challenge for Businesses...Collecting Tax On On-Line Sales 262

AMT Protection for Employees...................................266

Section 5: Family Loopholes..................................267

How to Save Big On Taxes If You're Divorced or Separated..........269

When It Pays to File Separate Returns................................273

Dependency Exemptions for Parents and Nonrelatives 277

Defensive Divorce—Avoid the Tax Traps..........................279

Hidden Risks of Tax-Favored College Savings..............................283

Six Ways to Save On Taxes When Children

　　　Move Back Home 287

Tax Traps and Opportunities in Making Loans to Your Kids........291

"Family Support" Payments Qualify as Deductible Alimony..........295

Shift Income for Tax Savings......................................296

Generous Tax Breaks that Help You Support

　　　Your Aging Parents 301

Protect Against Spousal Liability.................................306

Section 6: Real Estate and Investment Loopholes..........................307

Get the Most Tax-Free Gain When You Sell Your Home...............309

Pros and Cons of Home Loans and Margin Loans 313

Protect Your Family for Generations with a Dynasty Trust..........317

Deducting Worthless Enron Stock................................321

Tax-Free Exchange Loopholes—Swapping for Bargains...............322

Tricks to Avoid Taxes When Buying and

　　　Selling Mutual Funds 325

Tax-Sheltered Alternatives to Mutual Funds...............................328

Investors: Take Losses Now for Tax Benefits Tomorrow.............333

Cut Your Taxes by Investing In Low-Income Housing Deals.........337

Gigantic Tax Breaks for Real Estate Investors 341

Year-End Tax Moves for Investors.................................346

Investors: Get Big Deductions By Qualifying as a "Trader"..........350

Section 7: Deductions, Deductions, Deductions................................353

The Overlooked Trillion Dollar+ Income Tax Deduction................355

Best Way to Lower Your Property Tax.....................................359

Best Tax Return Filing Strategies for a Bigger Refund................360

Loopholes in Tax Return Preparation.....................................365

Biggest Tax Preparation Mistakes to Avoid..............................368

Special Purpose Trust Loopholes 373

Giving Stock vs. Collectibles 376

How to Shelter Your Income from the IRS................................377

Mutual Fund Tax Saver 381

Nine Ways You Can Save Money Under the New Tax Law 382

Frequently Overlooked Deductions for Legal Fees.......................385

Lock in Business Expense Deductions With an

Accountable Plan...386

Deduct Fun from Your Taxes..391

Smartest Ways to Deduct Business Start-Up Costs.....................395

Protect Small Business Deductions...That the IRS Looks at

Every Time 400

Section 1: Retirement and Estate Planning

Estate Planning Loopholes 3

Renovate Historic Buildings for Fun, Profit and Tax Breaks 7

Sell Your Company to Your Employees...and Avoid Capital Gains Tax 10

Stop Uncle Sam from Stealing Your Retirement Dollars 14

Limiting Your Tax Hit 18

Tax Traps to Avoid in Retirement Plan Distributions 19

Tax-Wise Retirement: The Best States for You 23

The New Tax Law and Your Retirement—How to Make It
    Work Best for You 27

Smart Bequest to Charity Saves Income Taxes for Heirs 31

The Best Way to Take Money Out of Your Retirement Plan...Early 32

Best Retirement Plans for Small-Business Owners 36

Estate-Planning Update for Your Family Business 40

Tax-Smart Way to Hold "TIPS" for Retirement 44

Tax Break for Inherited IRAs 45

How Non-Spouse Beneficiaries Can Stretch Out an
    Inherited Retirement Account 46

Good Gift for a Child: Roth IRA 50

The Importance of IRA Tax Basis 51

Estate Tax Loopholes 52

SIMPLE Retirement Plans: Act Now to Catch the October Deadline 55

Use an IRA to Be Charitable...and Still Leave More to Your Heirs 60

Revised IRA Trust Rules Can Hurt Clients and Pros 64

Retirement Plan Tax Traps that Business Owners Must Avoid 68

IRA Withdrawal Opportunity for Business Owners 72

IRA Protection 73

For the Self-Employed—Great Flexibility with One-Person 401(k)s 74

You Can Buy Real Estate With Your IRA 79

Surprisingly High Taxes on Social Security Benefits 83

A Cascading Beneficiary Plan for Maximum IRA Tax Deferral 85

401(k) Alert—The Rules Have Changed .90

Retirement Plan Loopholes for Business Owners 95

The Three Kinds of Joint Ownership .98

Section 1: Retirement and Estate Planning

Chapter One

ESTATE PLANNING LOOPHOLES

Take advantage of these smart ways to reduce your estate and gift tax bill. Changes in the US estate tax laws have created additional planning opportunities.

Loophole: You can give up to $12,000 a year free of gift tax to an unlimited number of individuals—$24,000 tax free for married couples that "split" gifts.

Even better: No dollar limits apply to tax-free gifts that cover tuition or medical costs, as long as you write the check directly to the school or the medical services provider.

Loophole: The top estate tax rate goes down in 2006 to 46% from 47%, reducing the tax bill of estates that owe estate tax. The top tax rate is reduced to 45% in 2007 through 2009.

The estate tax is completely eliminated for 2010 but resumes in 2011 with a 55% top rate and an additional 5% tax on certain estates over $10 million.

Loophole: The estate tax exemption threshold is $2 million in 2006. The threshold increases to $3.5 million in 2009. This has a major effect of reducing the number of estates subject to estate tax.

Trap: The gift tax exemption remains $1 million. Gifts over that amount will be subject to gift tax while amounts up to $2 million will escape estate taxation.

Loophole: The generation skipping transfer (GST) tax exemption is now equal to the estate tax exemption. Transfers to skipped generations (grandparents to their grandchildren) will not be subject to the GST tax (at the highest estate tax rate) until they exceed the exemption amount—$2 million in 2006.

Loophole: Inherited assets receive a "stepped-up basis" equal to the value of the asset at the time of death. People who inherit assets receive a stepped-up basis, even if the estate itself is not taxable.

Example: Your parents die and leave behind a house. They paid $40,000 for the property, which has increased in value to $200,000 by the time of their deaths. Your parents had no other assets and no estate tax return is required to be filed. Their beneficiaries inherit the house estate tax free. The beneficiaries' basis in the property is $200,000, meaning that if the house is sold for $200,000, no capital gains tax will be due.

Comment: The step-up in basis only applies to capital gains items and not IRAs and other ordinary income items.

Note: In 2010, the step-up of basis rules change. In 2011, the rules revert back to the original rules.

In 2005, the state death tax credit was replaced by a deduction for state death taxes actually paid. A deduction from income or assets is not worth as much as a tax credit, which is subtracted directly from your taxes.

The federal estate tax top rate was increased under the "estate tax reduction" law. Before, the top federal rate was 55% minus a 16% state tax credit, leaving a 39% net federal tax rate.

Now: The new federal law has a 45% tax rate with a state tax deduction worth 45% of the 16% paid to the state...so the new effective top tax rate equals 37.8% (45% − 7.2%).

Loophole: "Crummey letters" make gifts to a trust to pay life insurance premiums eligible for the annual gift tax exclusion. If donees do not waive their rights to their portion of the gift by using the Crummey letter, the gift will be subject to gift tax by the donor. These letters should be prepared in accordance with the terms of the trust agreement.

Loophole: The valuation and terms in business buy-sell agreements will be honored by the IRS for estate tax purposes if they reflect arm's-length negotiations and market conditions. These should be periodically reviewed with regular valuation updates.

Alternative: Use a formula that recognizes changing values and situations.

Loophole: Disclaimers of inheritances must be made within nine months of the donor's death. Note that the beneficiary could not have gotten any benefit from the asset being disclaimed. Assets that are disclaimed by a beneficiary go to the next named beneficiaries. IRA and pension account disclaimers require an acceptable contingent beneficiary to have been designated before death.

Example designations are...

Primary beneficiary: Spouse.

First contingent beneficiary: Each child per stirpes.

Second contingent beneficiary: Family charitable foundation or charity.

Caution: When the alternate, secondary, tertiary or contingent beneficiaries are in the form of a trust, this must be provided in the document designating the beneficiaries.

Loophole: When you plan an estate that includes an IRA, and the IRA has a trust as a beneficiary, a copy of the trust agreement must be given to the custodian. Where there are multiple beneficiaries that will share in the IRA, you can consider picking a percentage of the IRA or pension you would be comfortable leaving "outright" to each beneficiary and note the percentage on the designation of beneficiary forms instead of fixed dollar amounts.

Strategy: IRA accounts can be split among the account beneficiaries after the death of the participant up until September 30 following the year of death.

IRA beneficiary designations can be changed by disclaimers. However, no new beneficiaries can be added—the primary beneficiaries can be removed and the contingent beneficiaries promoted.

Loophole: Living trusts can be used to ease and speed up the probate process. In many cases, these are substitute wills and should be treated with some care. To be valid they must be funded.

Caution: Many people set up living trusts but then neglect to follow through with the proper funding.

Note: Living trusts do not save tax—either income tax or estate tax—but are nonetheless an important part of the estate planning process. Living trusts are easy to administer, and it is not necessary to obtain a federal identification number nor does any tax return have to be filed. The grantor should use his/her own Social Security number and report the transactions on his individual tax return.

Living trusts become irrevocable upon the death of the grantor/trustee. Upon the death of the grantor/trustee, the alternate trustee immediately becomes the trustee and assumes complete control of the trust.

Source: Edward Mendlowitz, CPA, shareholder in the CPA firm WithumSmith+Brown, 120 Albany St., New Brunswick, NJ 08901. He is author of *Estate Planning* (Practical Programs).

Chapter Two

RENOVATE HISTORIC BUILDINGS FOR FUN, PROFIT AND TAX BREAKS

The market for historic buildings has heated up. This is partly because of the "new markets credit" created by the federal *Community Renewal Tax Relief Act of 2000*, intended to encourage development in low-income communities. This credit, when combined with federal and state credits for rehabilitating historic structures—plus the potential for capital appreciation—makes investments in historic properties highly attractive.

Historic buildings defined

For you to obtain special funding and tax breaks, your building must be listed—or be eligible for listing—on the National Register of Historic Places or a state historic register. Listing is not dependent on the age of the building. It depends only on its historical significance.

Designation as historic also dictates, to some extent, the types of changes you can and cannot make to the structure.

To learn whether a structure has national designation—nearly 79,000 already do—go to the National Park Service Web site at *www.cr.nps.gov/nr*.

To learn whether a structure has state designation, contact your state's agency for historic preservation, commerce, or community development.

To get a building listed: If you believe that a property is of historic significance, apply for designation before you start renovating.

Key: A historic listing does *not* require you to open your property to the public or receive permission from the federal or state government to make renovations.

Requirements, restrictions

When working with a historic building, you face special restrictions in addition to current building code and legal requirements, such as those in the *Americans with Disabilities Act.*

Any work on the building must conform to historic preservation restrictions. The National Park Service has two helpful publications—*Secretary of the Interior's Standards for Rehabilitation* and *Illustrated Guidelines for Rehabilitating Historic Buildings* (both available free at *www.cr.nps.gov/hps*).

When you renovate, an old building must be brought up to local building code requirements. Check your local building and fire code laws.

If the building has public access (a commercial building, for example), you must also comply with the *Americans with Disabilities Act,* a federal law setting standards for handicapped accessibility. State law may also impose public access rules for the handicapped. However, federal and state laws may provide alternatives for compliance—for example, a steeper ramp or a secondary entry.

Tax credits

Designation as a certified historic structure entitles you to financial assistance for renovations. This can come in the form of loans, grants, and tax credits...

• Rehabilitation credit. There is a 20% federal tax credit for the rehabilitation costs of a certified historic structure—residential or nonresidential. However, to qualify for this credit, you must use the building commercially.

The credit applies only to renovation costs, not to such things as painting. "Renovation" includes things like heating, ventilating and air-conditioning (HVAC), roofing, and masonry. To qualify for the credit, you must incur at least $5,000 in rehabilitation expenses or spend at least the amount of your adjusted basis (generally, the purchase price, not including land, plus any additions) in the building, whichever is greater. There is no dollar limit on the amount of the credit.

Important: To claim the federal tax credit, you must pay a fee to the National Park Service of $250 to $2,500, depending on the projected amount of qualifying expenditures. This fee covers submission of your application that includes your plan for renovation, something that needs National Park Service approval.

The credit is claimed on IRS Form 3468, *Investment Credit*. It is subject to two further limitations...

☐ Tax liability limitation of the general business credit. (See IRS Form 3800, *General Business Credit*.)

☐ Passive activity restrictions. (See Form 8582-CR, *Passive Activity Credit Limitations*.)

• New markets credit. This credit, designed to encourage investments in community development entities (CDEs)—entities that provide investment capital for low-income communities—is 39% of investment. The credit is spread over seven years. It is 5% of the stock or capital interest in a CDE for each of the first three years and 6% annually for the final four years.

Important: Both the rehabilitation credit and the new markets credit may be claimed for the same investment.

• State tax credits. Your state may also provide tax credits designed to encourage rehabilitation of historic structures—almost half the states do. Maine and North Carolina, for example, offer a 20% credit to an owner who qualifies for the federal 20% credit, for a total credit of 40% of renovation costs. Missouri and Virginia have a 25% credit, for a total credit of 45%. New Mexico has a credit of up to 50% of costs up to $25,000. Iowa's credit, 25%, is restricted to historic barn renovation.

Source: Daniel J. Smith, CPA, partner in the San Francisco–based accounting firm Novogradac & Company LLP, which has expertise in the real estate sector, especially housing tax credits, *www.novoco.com*. His office is in Dover, OH.

Chapter Three

SELL YOUR COMPANY TO YOUR EMPLOYEES...AND AVOID CAPITAL GAINS TAX

When you start to think about a succession plan for your business, consider setting up an employee stock ownership plan (ESOP).

Selling your company to your employees can benefit your company as well as yourself. You'll get a fair price for your business, and you can ease your way out as well as avoid crippling your company. With proper planning, you can defer—and perhaps avoid altogether—paying tax on the capital gains on the sale to the ESOP.

How it works

Example: You're 56 years old, the sole owner of XYZ Co., valued at $9 million. You would like to cut back your ownership stake and fully retire by age 62.

After creating an ESOP, XYZ Co. borrows $3 million from a bank or other financial institution. XYZ Co. then lends the $3 million to the ESOP. The ESOP uses the money to buy one-third of your stock.

Key: An appraisal from a reputable third-party appraiser is necessary to set the price the ESOP will pay for your shares.

Repaying the loans: After the stock purchase, XYZ Co. continues to do business as usual. Assuming it is profitable, the profits can be used to make a contribution to the ESOP.

The ESOP, in turn, can use those funds to repay the loan from XYZ Co., and XYZ Co. can repay the original bank loan.

Loophole: An ESOP is a qualified retirement plan. Therefore, contributions XYZ Co. makes to an ESOP are tax deductible, up to 25% of payroll per year.

Result: After the money flows from XYZ Co. to the ESOP, then back to XYZ Co. and to the bank, the effect is to repay the loan, principal, and interest, with pretax funds.

If XYZ Co. is in the 35% tax bracket, it is essentially repaying the loan with 65 cents on the dollar. Yet you wind up with a full dollar in your pocket from the sale of your shares.

Note: There are various ways to structure leveraged ESOP transactions. This example shows one approach that can result in major tax advantages.

Over and over

Once the original $3 million loan has been repaid, in the above example, another $3 million can be borrowed to purchase more of your shares. When that loan has been repaid, the final block of stock can be sold to the ESOP.

Advantage: If you wish, the entire transaction could be handled with one loan. However, that would increase the interest XYZ Co. owes for the larger loan.

If XYZ Co. already has some debt, additional interest payments would reduce profits and make it more difficult to pay down the ESOP-related debt. A gradual approach may be better.

Bottom line: At the end of the process, you have cash from selling your shares to the ESOP.

Happy ending

You probably have a low cost basis in your company's shares so a sale normally would generate a substantial capital gains tax.

Loophole: When you sell shares to an ESOP, no capital gains tax is due.

Required: The ESOP must own at least 30% of the company after the purchase. The company must be a C corporation, and you must have held the shares for at least three years before the sale.

In addition, the sales proceeds must be reinvested in stocks or bonds issued by US corporations. The reinvestment in such "qualified reinvestment property" (QRP) must take place within 12 months of the sale to the ESOP.

Tactic: You can start up a new company or purchase another business. The stock of such a company will be considered a QRP, so you can invest your sales proceeds there and defer tax on your prior gains.

Benefit: As long as you hold onto the QRP, the tax on the sale to the ESOP will be deferred.

Endgame: You can give away your QRP, if that's part of your estate plan. Alternatively, you can hold the QRP indefinitely.

Under current law, if you die holding the QRP, your heirs inherit with a basis equal to the market value at date of death. The deferred capital gains tax need never be paid.

Trap: Selling any of the QRP will trigger the deferred tax on the portion of the QRP that was sold. The same is true if bonds that you hold are called or redeemed.

Strategy: For an extended deferral, you can buy long-term ESOP notes from highly rated US corporations. ESOP notes are available through major brokers.

With long-term maturities, it's doubtful you'll outlive your ESOP notes.

Key: ESOP notes are low-yielding in today's environment. If you want higher returns, you can borrow against your ESOP notes and reinvest in other securities.

Example: After investing the $9 million from selling your XYZ Co. shares in ESOP notes, your brokerage firm allows you to borrow $7.65 million (85%), using the ESOP notes as collateral. You then reinvest that money in a diversified portfolio of stocks, bonds, and mutual funds.

Borrowing against the ESOP notes doesn't trigger any tax. Nor does buying and selling the securities that you acquire with the loan proceeds, other than gains on those securities. You actively manage the $7.65 million portfolio and never pay tax on your original sale to the ESOP as long as you retain the ESOP notes.

Control factors

Despite all of these advantages, few companies use ESOPs in succession planning.

Myth: Many business owners think that a sale to an ESOP means relinquishing control of everyday operations. They believe that their employees will give themselves big raises, and run the company into the ground.

Reality: An ESOP trustee administers the plan. The trustee, in turn, is selected by the corporation's board of directors.

Often, the trustee is an entity that includes a financial firm or a professional adviser. You can be a trustee, along with the key officers and managers of the company.

Management of the company remains in the hands of key executives. If you stay with the company, you may be able to direct its operations, if you wish.

Trap: Any shareholder owning 25% or more of company stock can no longer receive new interests in the ESOP while deferring tax under the QRP rules described above.

Myth: Many business owners believe that they must share the company's financial statements with ESOP participants.

Reality: There is no legal requirement to do so. Many companies do share some financial information in order to foster an ownership culture within the company.

Key: Creating and maintaining an ESOP can be complex, so you must work closely with advisers who have experience in setting up ESOPs.

Source: Michael D. Cohen, CPA/ABV, CFE, partner at the accounting and consulting firm Singer Lewak Greenbaum & Goldstein LLP, 10960 Wilshire Blvd., Los Angeles 90024. He is director of the firm's business valuation and litigation services group.

Chapter Four

STOP UNCLE SAM FROM STEALING YOUR RETIREMENT DOLLARS

From the moment you make your first deposit in a traditional IRA or 401(k), you're building up a savings account—for the IRS.

Uncle Sam eventually gets a big chunk of your money. All withdrawals are taxable and at ordinary income tax rates of as high as 35%, not at the lower capital gains rate. If your retirement accounts and other assets grow to more than $2 million in 2006, your heirs will owe estate tax on traditional and Roth IRAs upon your death. Five ways to protect your nest egg...

Use Roth IRAs

This is Uncle Sam's greatest gift to retirement savings. Yet seven years after the Roth's debut, relatively few people have taken advantage of it. Roth IRAs give no up-front tax deduction, but your money grows tax-free. Roth IRA beneficiaries do not owe income tax on the distributions. A beneficiary can "stretch" the benefit, leaving the money to continue growing tax-free over his/her life.

What to do...

If you're planning to open a new IRA, make it a Roth. Your adjusted gross income (AGI) must be less than $110,000 (single) or $160,000 (married filing jointly).

Convert a traditional IRA to a Roth. In this case, your AGI must not exceed $100,000, whether you are single or married filing jointly. You will have to pay

14

tax on gains on the traditional IRA. Ask the financial institution that handles your IRA what your tax liability will be. If bear market losses have reduced the value of your IRA, you will owe less tax.

You can't roll over money from a 401(k) directly to a Roth. You must first roll it into a traditional IRA and then convert that to a Roth. Ask your tax adviser for instructions on rollovers and conversions.

Loophole: Your AGI only has to fall below $100,000 for one year to qualify for conversion. If your income is a few thousand dollars more than $100,000, shift some income to next year and/or sell stocks to take capital losses in taxable accounts. Losses also might put you in a lower bracket and reduce tax on the conversion.

Trap: Anyone who is married but files a separate return cannot convert a traditional IRA to a Roth regardless of income.

Help future generations dodge taxes

When 401(k) or IRA assets pass to heirs, they in turn can stretch the tax shelter over their lives. Examples...

Example 1: A husband leaves an IRA to his wife. She names their children as her beneficiaries. After her death, her children can enjoy tax-free compounding on the amount remaining. In this manner, tax deferral could go on for generations.

Example 2: Your daughter is 40 when she inherits your traditional IRA. According to IRS tables, a 40-year-old has a life expectancy of another 43.6 years, but she must begin taking required minimum distributions (RMDs) in the year after the year of the IRA owner's death.

Watch out for withdrawal penalties

Uncle Sam's 10% early withdrawal penalty applies to both Roth and traditional IRA withdrawals made before age 59½.

There is a 50% penalty if you fail to take RMDs on traditional IRAs. If your RMD is $20,000 and you miss the deadline, your penalty is $10,000. What to do...

Traditional IRAs. Start taking RMDs by April 1 of the year after you turn age 70½. The percentage you must withdraw each year is determined by the IRS from life expectancy tables. For more information, call 800-829-1040, or go to *www.irs.gov* or *www.irahelp.com.*

Roth IRAs. There are no required life distributions for Roth IRA owners.

Loophole: You can withdraw money without penalty from any IRA before age 59½ using one of three IRS formulas. But watch out—if you start spending your nest egg early, you might not have enough savings for retirement.

Let life insurance pay your taxes

Employer-sponsored retirement plans, such as 401(k)s, and traditional and Roth IRAs count toward your estate, so purchase insurance to pay the estate tax. Estate tax in 2006 is as high as 46% for estates of more than $2 million. Income tax on distributions from traditional IRAs can be as high as 35%.

While the estate tax is supposed to vanish in 2010, it is scheduled to return in 2011. Base your planning on the tax as it is today, affecting estates that are larger than $2 million. If there is no estate tax, your heirs will get to keep the payout.

What to do: Assume that estate tax will be 50% of the value of assets—cars, homes, retirement plans, other investments, etc. Purchase enough life insurance to cover the potential tax. At your death, insurance proceeds are free from income tax.

Important: Create a life insurance trust to own the policy so that the value is kept out of your estate. You can name beneficiaries—your spouse or children—as trustees. Make annual gifts to beneficiaries, which they should use to pay the insurance premiums. You won't owe gift tax if the payments are no more than $12,000 per recipient per year ($24,000 if given by a couple). For information, consult an experienced trust attorney.

Provide for beneficiaries now

Whether you have a traditional or Roth IRA, you must name your beneficiary on a retirement plan beneficiary form, which takes legal precedence over your will.

If you don't take the right steps, a lengthy, expensive probate court process will determine who inherits your IRA.

Update beneficiary forms when there is a marriage or divorce, new child or grandchild or other change that would affect your beneficiary choice. Keep beneficiary forms filed with other important papers as well as with your attorney and tax adviser. Then they can be located readily by family members and the executor of your will upon your death.

Source: Ed Slott, CPA, editor, *Ed Slott's IRA Advisor,* 100 Merrick Rd., Rockville Centre, NY 11570. He is a nationally recognized IRA distributions expert. *www.irahelp.com.*

Chapter Five
LIMITING YOUR TAX HIT

Limit your tax hit on a big windfall—such as a lump-sum early retirement payment—with a deferral agreement, in which the company pays out the money to you over a period of time. Many companies will agree to this.

Problem: Creditors could take your funds if the firm goes bankrupt. If this concerns you, take half the money this year and the rest next year.

Caution: This arrangement will not cut taxes as much as a long-term agreement would.

Also: Pay next year's state income tax this year, if your state allows this. Those payments then may be deductible on your federal taxes this year.

Important: If your windfall is from a legal settlement (other than from a case arising from discrimination), you may have large legal fees and may have to pay alternative minimum tax (AMT).

Source: Lisa N. Collins, CPA, PFS, former vice president and director of tax services, Harding, Shymanski and Co., PC, Evansville, IN.

Chapter Six

TAX TRAPS TO AVOID IN RETIREMENT PLAN DISTRIBUTIONS

Tax-deferred retirement plans, such as IRAs and 401(k)s, enable you to build up a sizable nest egg. However, you need to be careful when taking distributions and naming beneficiaries. Tax traps to avoid...

Withdrawals

Trap: Withdrawals before age 59½ usually trigger a 10% penalty.

Loophole: There are several exceptions to this penalty, permitting you or your heirs to take some cash from your plan before age 59½.

Examples: Disability, death.

Also, if you retire or change jobs, you can withdraw money from an employer-sponsored plan, penalty free, if the separation occurs during or after the year you turn age 55.

In addition, you can take substantially equal periodic payments (SEPPs), penalty free, for at least five years or until age 59½, whichever comes later.

Caution: The rules for SEPPs are complex, so you need to work with a savvy tax pro.

Trap: If you don't start to take required minimum distributions (RMDs) by April 1 of the year after you reach age 70½, you could face a 50% penalty.

Once you reach that age, you must withdraw the minimum amount each year and pay tax on it. As long as you're alive and there is money left in your account, you will be required to continue to take these minimum distributions.

You can take larger distributions from your retirement account, if you wish, but you must withdraw at least the minimum amounts each year.

Example: Suppose you are 76 years old and have $220,000 in your IRA. According to the IRS's Uniform Lifetime Table—found in IRS Publication 590, *Individual Retirement Arrangements (IRAs)*, 800-829-3676 or *www.irs.gov*—you have a life expectancy of 22 more years. Thus, you must withdraw at least ½₂ of your IRA this year, or $10,000.

If, instead, you withdraw only $2,000, you have an $8,000 shortfall. As a result, you'll owe a $4,000 penalty, which is 50% of the $8,000 shortfall.

Again, calculating the minimum withdrawal can be complicated. Consult your tax adviser (don't rely on bank information).

Loophole: There are no lifetime RMDs for Roth IRAs. And you don't need to take required distributions at age 70½ if you're still working. That's true as long as you don't own more than 5% of your company. If you start working after having started RMDs, you can discontinue RMDs from that company's plan, assuming the plan allows it. You still have to take RMDs from other plans and IRAs.

The exception applies only to withdrawals from employer-sponsored plans. If you roll your account balance to an IRA, the minimum distribution rules apply, even if you're still working.

Loophole: The law permits you to roll IRA money into an employer-sponsored plan if the plan will accept it.

Strategy: If you're working after age 70½ and you don't need to take distributions, roll your IRA into your employer's plan, if possible. You will forgo having to take distributions and avoid the 50% penalty.

Safe, but sorry

In order to avoid the 50% penalty, you might take out more money than you really need.

Example: Before you reach age 79, your required distribution will be less than 5% per year. Thus, if you withdraw 5% of your balance each year, you'll avoid a penalty.

Trap: Taking 5% per year from your retirement plan is fine if you need the money. However, if you currently don't need income and you withdraw more than the minimum, you'll pay more income tax than you need to pay and sooner than you need to pay it. More important, excess withdrawals reduce the amount of tax-deferred wealth-building that you (and possibly your beneficiaries) can enjoy.

If you don't need the money for living expenses, withdraw only the bare minimum.

Naming beneficiaries

Trap: If you don't name a beneficiary, whoever inherits your account will have to withdraw more money sooner and pay more income tax. The same is true if you name your estate as the beneficiary.

Strategy: Name one or more individuals as beneficiaries on the form provided by the custodian or on a custom form you provide.

If you have doubts about your beneficiary's ability to handle a large inheritance, name a trust as the beneficiary, then name your heirs as trust beneficiaries.

Loophole: If handled properly, setting up such a trust can permit your heirs to stretch out required withdrawals. Work with an experienced trust attorney.

Company stock

If you work for a publicly traded company, chances are that your retirement plan account contains some company stock.

Trap: Mishandling the withdrawal of that stock could cost you a prime tax break.

Example: Your 401(k) is $200,000, including $50,000 of company stock. When you retire, you roll over the entire $200,000 to an IRA. All subsequent IRA withdrawals will be subject to ordinary income tax, at rates up to 35%.

Strategy: Before you execute the rollover, ask about your basis in the company stock. That's the amount it was worth when the shares were contributed to your retirement account.

Loophole: You can pull out those shares and pay tax only on your basis, not their current value.

Example: Say your company shares are now worth $50,000 but your basis in those shares is only $10,000. You could withdraw the $50,000 worth of shares but owe tax on only $10,000 worth of income.

The other $40,000 won't be taxed until you sell the shares, which might be right away or many years in the future. In the meantime, you can receive dividends from all the shares and you can borrow against them, if you wish.

Result: Whenever you decide to sell the shares, the $40,000 will be taxed as a long-term capital gain, at a top rate of 15% under current law instead of ordinary income tax rates of up to 35% on regular IRA withdrawals. After more than one year, any additional gains also will qualify for the bargain tax rate.

The remaining assets in your 401(k) can be rolled into an IRA, tax free. You won't pay income tax until you begin making withdrawals.

Source: Ed Slott, CPA, editor, *Ed Slott's IRA Advisor,* 100 Merrick Rd., Rockville Centre, NY 11570. He is a nationally recognized IRA distributions expert. *www.irahelp.com.*

Section 1: Retirement and Estate Planning

Chapter Seven
TAX-WISE RETIREMENT: THE BEST STATES FOR YOU

Where you decide to live after you retire will determine, to a large extent, how much of your income you'll keep, after taxes. While lower taxes may not be the controlling factor in selecting your retirement state, here's a look at the best states for retirement tax-wise—and how to find the best state for you.

First, consider how much retirement income you expect to obtain from sources such as pensions, Social Security and investments. Even "low tax" states have different rules for different kinds of income.

New Hampshire and Tennessee have no general income tax—but do tax interest and dividends. Illinois has a general income tax—but exempts pension income from tax.

Even when a state has low (or no) income tax, it has to get its revenue from property, sales and estate taxes.

What type of lifestyle will you have? Do you plan to own property? Will you make a lot of taxable purchases? Do you have an estate you intend to leave to heirs?

Differences in the taxes on these could be more costly than a difference in income tax rates.

What gets taxed

• General income. Seven states have no income tax—Alaska, Florida, Nevada, South Dakota, Texas, Washington and Wyoming.

Among other states, the top tax bracket rates range from lows of 3% in

Illinois, 3.07% in Pennsylvania and 3.4% in Indiana to highs of 9.5% in Vermont, 9.3% in California and 9% in Oregon.

In addition to income tax rates, you need to consider state-specific income tax rules. Examples...

• Massachusetts does not allow a deduction for charitable contributions.

• New York taxes capital gains and dividends at ordinary income rates, not at reduced rates as on the federal return.

• New York provides a 20% tax credit for the cost of long-term-care insurance—so if a couple pays $10,000 of annual premiums, they would get a $2,000 credit that eliminates state tax on about $33,000 of income.

If one state has a rule that would be costly to you while another has a rule that would be valuable, these rules might more than cancel out any difference in state tax rates. To find such special rules, you must work through a state's tax return and check the instructions for the state tax form.

• Social Security. Most states do not tax Social Security benefits, but 15 states do to some extent—Colorado, Connecticut, Iowa, Kansas, Minnesota, Missouri, Montana, Nebraska, New Mexico, North Dakota, Rhode Island, Utah, Vermont, West Virginia and Wisconsin.

In those states, benefits are usually taxed only if taxable under federal rules. Some states provide additional exemptions. Again, check the details of a state's law.

• Pension income. Pension income is tax favored in most states to some extent. Illinois, Pennsylvania and Mississippi exempt all pension income from tax. Other states offer varying exempt amounts.

New York excludes $20,000 of pension income from tax. Montana excludes $3,600 from tax.

Several states provide different treatment to different kinds of pensions, providing exemptions only to government-paid pensions, or only those paid by state and local governments.

Ten states tax all kinds of pension income—California, Connecticut, Minnesota, Nebraska, New Mexico, Ohio, Rhode Island, Vermont, Virginia and Wisconsin.

Planning: Look at more than income tax rates. If you'll be living on income for which a state provides generous exclusions (such as pension and Social Security income) and the state also has special deductions or credits you can use, it may be a low-tax state to you.

Other key taxes

• Property taxes. These taxes apply to real estate and, in some states, such as Connecticut, to personal property, such as cars.

Property tax rates are set locally so even differences between towns can matter. Be sure to research and compare them if you intend to own taxable property.

• Sales taxes. These, too, are set locally. Not only do rates vary, but specific items may receive exemptions, such as food and medicine, or extra-high tax rates, such as cigarettes and alcohol. Again, check for differences in rates and in taxes that apply to items of importance to you.

• Estate and inheritance taxes. Until recently, state estate taxes generally didn't cost anything extra to taxpayers because they usually were covered by a credit against the federal estate tax.

Now, however, the federal estate tax is scheduled for repeal and the federal credit for state estate tax is being phased out. So now the states must decide whether to "decouple" from the federal system to preserve their revenue or phase out their estate taxes as well.

About 18 states have changed their laws to continue collecting estate tax in spite of the lack of the federal tax credit—meaning the state tax is now a true extra cost.

Also, while the amount exempt from federal estate tax is $2 million in 2006 and rises to $3.5 million in 2009, some states have kept much smaller exemption amounts—it is $675,000 in New Jersey and Wisconsin.

The future status of state estate tax is uncertain in many cases, so check with a local tax expert.

In addition, many states impose inheritance taxes that are collected from heirs rather than from estates and must be planned for apart from estate tax. These include Indiana, Iowa, Kansas, Kentucky, Louisiana, Maryland, Nebraska, New Hampshire, New Jersey, Pennsylvania, Oregon and Tennessee.

Trap for the unwary

A big trap can ensnare those who move from a high-tax to a low-tax state—the high-tax state may continue to tax them! This can happen when the person maintains ties to or interests in the state he/she left.

Example: Many people leave high-tax New York for no-income-tax Florida but continue to own an apartment, or investment properties, or a business, or even a burial plot in New York. New York may continue to tax them—resulting in at least a costly legal fight.

High-tax states, including New York, California and Massachusetts, have become very aggressive about continuing to tax persons who claim to have moved while maintaining contacts in the state.

Exception: Under federal law, a pension can only be taxed in the state where you reside when you collect it.

Best: Break off contacts with the state you leave as completely as possible. Consult with an expert on your state's rules for details.

Source: Mark A. Plostock, a CPA with a practice in Syosset, NY. He lectures for the New York State Society of CPAs on state and local tax issues and is on the accounting advisory board of Quinnipiac University, Hamden, CT.

Section 1: Retirement and Estate Planning

Chapter Seven

THE NEW TAX LAW AND YOUR RETIREMENT—HOW TO MAKE IT WORK BEST FOR YOU

Savvy individuals can use the new tax law to increase both future retirement wealth and current after-tax income. Here's how to make the most of it...

New benefits

• Get more income. Many individuals who live on interest earned from investments, such as bonds and certificates of deposit (CDs), have seen their incomes slashed by current record-low interest rates.

Opportunity: Dividend income is now taxed at no more than 15%, while interest is taxed at ordinary rates up to 35%. This tax break for dividends may let you keep more after-tax income from dividend-paying stock than from interest-paying investments, even if the amount of pretax income is no greater.

Consider boosting after-tax income by moving investment funds from interest-paying assets to a diversified portfolio of high-quality dividend-paying stocks.

• Refinance mortgages. Current historic low interest rates give another way to increase after-tax income—by reducing interest costs through refinancing a home mortgage. There may never be a better time to do this than now. If your interest income has declined, this is one way to offset the loss.

Even better, in a refinancing you may be able to borrow against equity in your home to pay down other much higher-rate borrowing—such as credit card debt that may charge 18% interest or more —to reap major interest savings that boost your cash flow.

Beyond that, such a refinancing may provide funds you can use to invest in stocks to receive tax-favored capital gains and dividend income. This is one of the few instances in which the Tax Code allows tax-favored borrowing to finance tax-favored income.

Caution: Review your entire financial position carefully before increasing borrowing against your home. But for those who are in a "house rich, cash poor" situation, with a largely paid off home but inadequate income, this is a tax-favored way to increase income.

• Time marriage and divorce. The new tax law continues in 2006 two breaks to married couples who file joint returns—the 15% tax bracket covers $61,300 of taxable income (compared with $30,650 for singles) and joint filers receive a standard deduction equal to twice the amount for singles on non-itemized returns.

Impact: This not only reduces the "marriage penalty" faced by two-earner couples but increases tax savings that result for one-earner couples and couples where one spouse has much higher income than the other.

Result: When two people are planning to marry but have only one income, or one person has much more income than the other, they may reduce their total tax bill by marrying before year-end—and get a tax refund.

On the other hand, a couple who fit this description and are planning to divorce may choose to delay doing so until after year-end to avoid increasing their tax bill for the year. Marital status at the end of the year is marital status for the entire year for tax purposes.

• Adjust retirement portfolios. The new law creates a trap in retirement plan investing. Under the new law, capital gains and dividends are taxed at no more than 15% when held in taxable accounts. But when they are realized and distributed from tax-favored retirement accounts—such as 401(k)s and traditional IRAs—they are taxed at ordinary rates up to 35%. Strategies to consider...

• When young and many years from retirement, it may still be best to invest in stocks through tax-favored retirement accounts. That's because you invest using pretax dollars. Doing so lets you invest a larger amount, the extra earnings on which may more than offset the higher tax rate at the end.

Example: If you are in the 33% tax bracket, you can invest $3,000 in a 401(k) or traditional IRA for the after-tax cost of investing $2,000 in a taxable account.

After compounding for decades, the gain on the extra $1,000 may more than offset the higher tax rate that applies to the retirement account when the funds are withdrawn.

This is even more effective when you receive an "employer match" on 401(k) contributions.

• As retirement approaches you will probably want to diversify out of stocks and invest more in safer interest-paying investments.

Best: When you own both stocks and taxable interest-paying investments, try to hold the latter in retirement accounts so interest received on them is tax deferred and compounds on a pretax basis. Try to hold stocks in taxable accounts to benefit from the 15% top tax rate on dividends and long-term gains.

How: On a going-forward basis, shift investments in your retirement accounts from stocks to interest-paying assets. Remain partially invested in stocks by making new investments in them through taxable accounts.

• Review savings for children and grandchildren. The new tax law reduces the need to put money in the name of children and grandchildren years ahead to pay for costs, such as college tuition.

Why: If you intend to pay for a child's costs—such as tuition—by selling appreciated stock, you now can do it by making a gift of the stock to the child at the time and have the child sell it for his/her own account. He will pay only a 5% tax rate—instead of your 15%—on some or all of the gain. The law provides a 5% tax rate on capital gains for persons in the 10% and 15% tax brackets, which in 2006 covers income up to $30,650 on a single return and $61,300 on a joint return.

Result: The tax savings that result from putting the assets in the child's name years before he needs them are reduced or eliminated. And you retain much greater control over the assets by keeping them in your own account.

Planning: Trusts and college savings accounts, such as Section 529 plans, can still offer valuable benefits when providing for children and grandchildren. Consult an expert to review the best way to use them now for your purposes.

- Beware of state taxes. Every state has its own tax rules, and many states do not follow the new changes in the federal tax law. In high-tax states, this can reduce the benefits derived from the law.

Example: New York and California tax both capital gains and dividends at ordinary rates. So people who live in those states and change their investments to earn more dividend and capital gain income may reduce their federal tax bill but increase the state taxes they owe on such income.

Trap: High state tax payments can trigger the federal alternative minimum tax (AMT). So if you take advantage of the new low federal tax rate on capital gains to take large gains that are subject to state tax, a big resulting state tax bill may trigger AMT and cost you federal tax savings as well!

Carefully review the effect of state taxes on any new investment plans you make as a result of the new tax law. If you plan to fund your retirement with income earned as dividends or capital gains, consider the benefits of moving to a no-tax or low-tax state.

- Review withheld and estimated taxes. Don't overpay your taxes this year after the tax cuts. Your employer should automatically adjust your wage withholding for you, but you may want to verify that it is done correctly. And you must adjust your estimated tax payments (such as on investment income) yourself.

Helpful: The IRS has posted new withholding tables on its Web site, *www.irs.gov*. It has also published an updated version of its Publication 505, *Tax Withholding and Estimated Tax*. It is available free on its Web site as well.

Source: Sidney Kess, attorney and CPA, 10 Rockefeller Plaza, New York City 10020. He is coauthor/consulting editor of *Financial and Estate Planning* and coauthor of *1040 Preparation and Planning Guide, 2006 Edition.* (CCH). Over the years, he has taught tax law to more than 710,000 tax professionals.

Section 1: Retirement and Estate Planning

Chapter Eight

SMART BEQUEST TO CHARITY SAVES INCOME TAXES FOR HEIRS

In one IRS ruling, an individual made a gift to charity through his will, funding it with deferred compensation due him from his former employer and with unexercised stock options. IRS ruling: The individual's estate will receive a full charitable deduction for the gifts and will not recognize any income from the deferred compensation or options. Why this was smart planning: If the individual had made his charitable gift with cash and left the deferred compensation and options to his heirs, they would have owed income tax. By instead leaving the taxable assets to charity and cash to his heirs, he cut the IRS out of his will.

Source: IRS Letter Ruling 200002011.

Chapter Nine

THE BEST WAY TO TAKE MONEY OUT OF YOUR RETIREMENT PLAN...EARLY

If you participate in a 401(k) or another type of employer-sponsored retirement plan, when you leave the company, you'll have to decide what to do with your account. Many people roll the balance into an IRA.

Benefits: If handled properly, not only do you maintain tax deferral, you control how your money will be invested.

However, an IRA rollover is not your only choice. Other options...

• Take the cash. If you do this, you'll owe income tax on the full amount right away.

• Keep the money in your former employer's plan. Many companies permit you to do this.

• Transfer money to a new employer's plan. Even if you're not immediately eligible to participate, you can hold cash in the new plan until you can make other investments.

• Crack your nest egg. You can withdraw some of your retirement funds, pay tax on the withdrawal, and roll the balance into a tax-deferred IRA.

Why would you choose one of these alternatives rather than a rollover? Possible reasons...

• You're in a cash crunch. If you need to spend some or all of the money in your plan, you might as well withdraw it from the plan right away. That's especially true if you were born before 1936.

Loophole: People in that age group qualify for a special tax break. They can use tax-favored 10-year averaging if they take all of their money out of the plan. This could cut their taxes to a relatively low rate.

Trap: You don't get this tax break if you do an IRA rollover.

Key: Even if you can't use 10-year averaging, today's lower income tax rates may make withdrawals appealing.

• You need a helping hand. If you don't want to manage your own retirement fund, you may prefer to leave the money with your former employer or transfer it to a new one. Inside an employer's plan, professionals decide who manages the investment options.

• You want to extend tax-free growth. Under the Tax Code, you can defer taking required withdrawals from a company plan, even after you reach age 70½, as long as you're still working. (With an IRA, you must start taking distributions after you reach age 70½.)

Caveat: You can't own more than 5% of the company you work for.

• You need to keep creditors at bay. Money in an employer-sponsored retirement plan is generally protected from creditors, judgments, divorce settlements, etc., under federal law.

Trap: State law may not provide your IRA with the same protection. If you live in a state where IRAs aren't fully sheltered, you may prefer the safe harbor of an employer's plan.

• You need to borrow. Many employer-sponsored plans, including 401(k)s, permit you to borrow half your account balance, up to $50,000.

Advantages: Plan loans may be easier to get than bank loans, with less paperwork. Also, repayments (plus interest) go to your retirement account rather than to a bank.

Trap: You can't borrow from an IRA. And, any outstanding 401(k) loans must be repaid before a rollover, reducing the amount you'll have in your IRA.

Therefore, if you have outstanding loans, or think you might want to borrow in the future, keeping money in an employer's plan may be the best choice.

• You hold appreciated employer stock in your plan. An IRA rollover can cost you a substantial tax break.

Example: Your retirement plan account includes $50,000 worth of your employer's stock, which was worth $10,000 when contributed to your account. If you roll over your entire account, that $50,000 eventually will be taxed at ordinary income rates, now as high as 35%, upon withdrawal.

Strategy: Withdraw the employer shares while rolling the rest of your plan balance into an IRA. You'll owe tax immediately, but only on the value of the shares when contributed to the plan, not on their current value.

In this example, you'll immediately be taxed on $10,000 but the $40,000 in net unrealized appreciation (NUA) remains untaxed until the shares are sold. When you sell those shares, you'll owe tax at a 15% capital gains rate, assuming current law remains in effect.

The penalty box

In between ages 55 and 59½, therefore, you're better off keeping your money in a company plan, if you expect to take distributions.

If you need to tap your retirement plan, withdrawing money from an IRA before age 59½ may expose you to a 10% penalty.

Loophole: You can take money from an employer-sponsored plan, penalty free, if you were at least age 55 in the year you left your job.

Life insurance

If your account in an employer-sponsored plan includes life insurance, you might want to keep your money in that plan in order to keep the policy in force.

Key: You may find it costly to continue your life insurance after you leave the company plan. If you're in poor health, you might not be able to buy needed coverage at a reasonable price.

When IRAs are ideal

If none of the above reasons apply to you, you're probably better off with a rollover IRA. In some situations, IRAs are especially appealing.

Example: You're interested in a Roth IRA conversion. After five years and age 59½, all withdrawals may be tax free.

Required: Only traditional IRAs may be converted to a Roth IRA. Therefore, you must first roll over a company plan distribution to an IRA, in order to subsequently convert to a Roth IRA.

Keep in mind that Roth IRA conversions are permitted only if your adjusted gross income (not counting required minimum distributions from IRAs and the conversion itself) is not over $100,000. You'll owe tax on all the deferred income when you convert an IRA to a Roth IRA.

Key: No matter what your reason, always ask for a "trustee-to-trustee transfer" when you execute an IRA rollover. Keep your hands off the money being rolled over.

Trap: If you handle the funds, you'll face mandatory 20% withholding on the rollover. You'll have to make up the difference from your own pocket to avoid owing income taxes.

Source: Ed Slott, CPA, editor, *Ed Slott's IRA Advisor*, 100 Merrick Rd., Rockville Centre, NY 11570. He is a nationally recognized IRA distributions expert. *www.irahelp.com.*

Chapter Ten
BEST RETIREMENT PLANS FOR SMALL-BUSINESS OWNERS

Tax-deferred retirement plans are among the tax shelters for small-business owners with the explicit blessing of the federal government. Moreover, such plans offer you a prime opportunity to build wealth for the days when you're no longer working.

Challenge: There are many attractive plans from which to choose. These seem to be the cream of the crop...

Solo 401(k) plans

These plans may make sense if you are the only full-time employee of your business. Your spouse can be on the payroll, too.

Simplicity: Participants in solo 401(k) plans merely have to file IRS Form 5500-EZ, Annual Return of One-Participant (Owners and Their Spouses) Retirement Plan, and then only after assets in the plan top $100,000. Administrative costs tend to be modest.

Borrowing power: You can borrow from a solo 401(k) plan that has been properly created. That's not the case with some of the small-business plans described below.

Upper limits: In many situations, solo 401(k) plans permit larger tax-deferred contributions than other retirement plans suitable for one person or one couple. That's because you make contributions as an employer as well as deferring income as an employee.

In 2006, each participant's account may be able to receive as much as

$44,000 altogether. If you're 50 or older, you can add $5,000 this year as a "catch-up" contribution, for a maximum of $49,000.

Trap: These plans are for owners only. They won't work if you have any full-time employees. Then you'll have to have a regular 401(k) plan, which might be subject to antidiscrimination tests and may require contributions to employees' accounts.

Simple IRAs

Savings incentive match plans for employees (SIMPLEs) come in two varieties, SIMPLE IRAs and SIMPLE 401(k)s. SIMPLE 401(k)s are actually not that simple. Most companies prefer SIMPLE IRAs, where participants direct their own investments and the plans require very little maintenance.

Required: Your company can have no more than 100 employees.

The 100% solution: You can contribute 100% of your income, up to $10,000 in 2006.

Example: With a 3%-of-compensation employer match, the maximum amount that can go into your account this year is $18,000.

Catch-up: Participants age 50 and older can defer an additional $2,500 worth of income in 2006.

Starting in 2007, both the basic and catch-up contributions will be adjusted annually for inflation.

When they work best: Because you can contribute 100% of pay, SIMPLE IRAs may be ideal if your income is relatively low, yet you want to make a sizable retirement plan contribution.

SIMPLE IRAs must be offered to all employees but there are no antidiscrimination tests. You and any employed relatives can make maximum contributions to SIMPLE IRAs, if the matching contribution formula is used—even if none of your other employees contributes, in which case no further company match is required.

SEPs

If you're self-employed, a simplified employee pension (SEP) plan may be a good choice.

Easiest: You merely have to fill out a simple form when you set up the plan. There are no further reports and no annual tax filings.

Flexibility: You can reduce or even skip SEP contributions in a year when cash flow is meager.

• Look-back deductions. Contributions to a SEP can be made any time until the due date of your tax return, including extensions.

Example: You can make a contribution to a new or existing SEP by the due date of your 2005 tax return, including extensions, and take a full deduction from your 2005 income.

If you want to make a tax-deductible contribution for the prior year and you have not already established a retirement plan, a SEP is your only choice.

• Contribution limits. The maximum you can contribute to a SEP each year is now $44,000. For the self-employed, about 20% of income can be contributed, so you'll need income of $220,000 to reach the maximum.

Trap: SEPs are usually not appropriate for companies with more than a few employees. If your company contributes to your own account, it has to contribute the same percentage of pay for your eligible employees, too.

401(k) profit-sharing plans

Offering a 401(k) plan may be necessary in order for you to attract and retain exceptional employees. Often, workers expect a 401(k) plan as a perk.

Contributions: In 2006, employees may contribute up to $15,000 worth of income to their 401(k) accounts. Those 50 or older may defer an extra $5,000 catch-up.

Match: You may want to offer a company match to encourage lower-paid workers to participate. If participation among the rank-and-file is scant, prized executives (including yourself) may find their contributions limited.

Trap: If your company sponsors a 401(k), contributions to your own retirement account will be limited to $15,000 or $20,000 in 2006, depending on your age.

Strategy: Adopt a profit-sharing plan that includes a 401(k). Profit-sharing plans are flexible, allowing your company to make a contribution for its employees if it has the required cash.

Payoff: You and other top executives may receive contributions that total $44,000 or $49,000 in 2006 from the 401(k)/profit-sharing combination plan.

Age-weighted profit-sharing plans

Whether or not they include a 401(k) plan, profit-sharing plans can be expensive.

Trap: If your company makes a contribution of, say, 15% of pay to your own account, it will have to contribute 15% of pay for all eligible employees.

Strategy: If you are older than most of your employees, adopt an age-weighted profit-sharing plan.

Rationale: Older employees have fewer years to build up a retirement fund, so larger contributions may be justified.

Example: You're in your 50s so your company might contribute 15% of pay to your profit-sharing account, while your 20-something assistant receives 5% of pay.

Key: Some very sophisticated plan designs may enable your company to skew most of its profit-sharing contributions to you and other older principals. Such plans can be expensive to create and administer but the savings in employee contributions might be worthwhile. Vesting schedules also can apply, making such plans more cost-effective.

Bottom line: If you're 50 or older, with a much younger workforce, contact a CPA or an employee benefits professional to see if your company can have a plan that stacks tax-deductible retirement contributions in your favor.

Source: Roger W. Lusby III, CPA, CMA, AEP, tax partner, Frazier & Deeter, LLC, 600 Peachtree St. NE, Atlanta 30308. Mr. Lusby works with closely held businesses and writes extensively on estate and tax matters.

Chapter Eleven
ESTATE-PLANNING UPDATE FOR YOUR FAMILY BUSINESS

Has talk about increasing the federal estate tax exemption lulled you into a false sense of security about what will happen to your closely held company when you die? Don't let that happen.

Planning is still critical for anyone who wants to preserve his/her business for the next generation, save taxes, and avoid numerous problems.

Tax threats

Taxes continue to pose a substantial threat to the well-being of a family business. Here's why...

• **Insufficient federal exemption.** The federal estate tax exemption amount—$2 million in 2006—may not be large enough to protect all of an owner's estate. The value of the business interest alone may exceed this figure—and a business owner may have other assets (such as a home, retirement plan accounts, personal investments, etc.) that bulk up the size of the estate.

• **Repeal of the special deduction.** Some owners may be under a false impression that there is special estate tax protection for business interests. Prior to 2004, there was a federal estate tax deduction for family-owned businesses. This deduction was repealed for estates of decedents dying after December 31, 2003. As a point of fact, however, eligibility for the deduction was highly complex and did not afford substantial protection in the past. Now, of course, it is nonexistent.

• **Repeal of the credit for state death taxes.** Now, estates can only claim a deduction for state death taxes. A number of states have "decoupled" from the federal estate tax. In the past, the states had relied on the state death tax credit that was claimed against the federal estate tax as their collection mechanism. But with changes in the federal rules, several states have acted to set up distinct (decoupled) death taxes.

Lifetime strategies

Lifetime gifts are the most effective way to accomplish a number of estate-planning goals. Such gifts...

• Ensure that ownership passes to the next generation. Fractional interests in the business are given to children and/or grandchildren. For example, if you own a corporation, you can give shares to family members while you are alive, leaving the balance to them through your will.

• Save transfer taxes. Because such gifts of business interests represent minority ownership, the value of the interests you give away should qualify for significant valuation discounts.

Example: You can give $18,000 worth of stock in a corporation to each child and grandchild tax free if it is reasonable to apply a 33.33% discount for minority interest—each such discounted gift in this case would be under the $12,000 annual gift tax exclusion.

Note: There may be additional discounts for lack of marketability for closely held businesses.

Drawbacks: Business owners may be averse to giving up any control in the business. This issue can be adequately addressed in a number of ways...

• By keeping more than 50%—an ownership interest that can be used to block any adverse transactions, such as the sale of the company.

• By shifting the business into a family limited partnership, with the parent as general partner. In this scenario, the parent controls the day-to-day operations of the company.

Caution: If the parent remains in full control (for example, the parent retains absolute discretion over income distributions), there is the possibility that the IRS may tax the entire business in the parent's estate on the grounds that no real lifetime transfer was made.

Professional practices

For sole practitioners, their practice may lose substantial value upon their death because patient/client lists may be virtually worthless without someone to service them. It is up to sole practitioners to create value during their lifetime by bringing in a younger partner. This person can be groomed to take over the practice one day and can buy into it over time.

Result: The sole practitioner has created a ready market for the practice, fixed its valuation, and ensured that his heirs will obtain the benefit from a lifetime of his working at a profession.

Strategies after death

Even if the parent does not wish to cede any interests during his lifetime, there are estate-planning strategies that can be used to avoid a forced liquidation of the company in order to satisfy death tax payments...

• Marital deduction. If the business owner is married at the time of death, the unlimited marital deduction can be used to protect the business interest from immediate death taxes. This is so even if the owner does not want the business to pass directly to the surviving spouse.

A trust can be used to obtain tax savings while holding the business for the next generation.

• Adequate life insurance. A business owner should anticipate death tax costs and carry life insurance to meet this need. The life insurance can be held in an irrevocable trust so that proceeds are not included in the estate and are available to meet the estate's liquidity needs. The cost of term insurance has declined dramatically, and it is possible to obtain term coverage with premiums locked in for 20 or even 30 years.

Note: In the past, split-dollar life insurance was often used to help the owner obtain necessary coverage—the company paid the premiums and the owner's estate collected the proceeds (minus the company's outlay). Today, however, with new regulations in place, split-dollar coverage is out of favor, at least for those now shopping for life insurance.

- Installment payment of estate taxes. The federal estate tax law provides a payment mechanism when a business interest makes up a sizable portion of the estate. Under Code Section 6166, death taxes can be paid over 14 years (with interest only required in the first five years).

Interest is payable at a special 2% rate on estate tax attributable to the first $1 million in value of a closely held business as adjusted for inflation. For 2006, the dollar amount used to determine the 2% portion for figuring the interest on deferred estate taxes is $1,200,000.

Source: Sanford J. Schlesinger, Esq., a founding partner and head of the wills and estates practice of the law firm Schlesinger Gannon & Lazetera LLP, 499 Park Ave., New York City 10022.

Section 1: Retirement and Estate Planning

Chapter Twelve
TAX-SMART WAY TO HOLD "TIPS" FOR RETIREMENT

Treasury Inflation Protected Securities, or TIPS, can serve as a valuable part of your retirement investment portfolio.

Key: The principal value of TIPS is adjusted every six months for inflation, and the interest paid adjusts accordingly. If inflation increases by 3%, your bond will become 3% more valuable and you will receive 3% more cash interest.

Usefulness: Even today's low inflation rates can greatly reduce the real value of other types of bonds when compounded over 20 or 30 years of retirement. And there's always a risk that inflation will rise.

TIPS can serve in a portfolio to protect part of its value against the long-term inflation risk—with all the security of US bonds.

Snags: The semiannual inflation adjustments to the principal of TIPS are taxed by the IRS as current interest income even though no cash is received from the adjustments until TIPS mature. So, many people keep TIPS in tax-deferred retirement accounts, such as 401(k)s and traditional IRAs.

But that has a tax cost, too. Federal bonds are exempt from state and local taxes, but distributions from retirement plans aren't. Holding TIPS in a 401(k) or traditional IRA will subject them to local taxes—and, the minimum distribution requirements for such accounts will, in time, force the TIPS to be liquidated and taxed.

Better: Hold TIPS in a Roth IRA. That way the periodic TIPS inflation adjustments escape tax by the IRS. After age 59½, cash taken from the Roth IRA will escape federal tax altogether (and perhaps state tax). Also, no minimum

44

distribution requirements apply to Roths, so you can keep TIPS in them as long as you like—and even bequeath them to heirs.

Source: Sue Stevens, CPA, CFP, CFA, director of financial planning, Morningstar Associates, LLC, a financial information provider in Chicago.

TAX BREAK FOR INHERITED IRAs

When an IRA has more than one beneficiary, the general rule is that the life expectancy of the oldest determines the schedule of minimum required annual distributions for all—the IRA balance must be paid out over that person's life expectancy.

If the other, younger beneficiaries wish to use their own longer life expectancies to take smaller minimum annual required distributions, then the IRA must be divided into separate accounts.

Beneficiaries can split an inherited IRA into separate IRAs, but it must be done by the end of the year following the year of the IRA owner's death.

Snag: Under old IRS rules, the split wasn't effective for the purpose of determining separate distribution requirements until the year after the split. So to get separate treatment in the year when distributions are first required—the year after the death of the IRA owner—an IRA had to be split in the same year that the owner died. If the owner died near year-end, that might be impossible.

Saver: The IRS has changed the rules to say that if an IRA is split by September 30 of the year following the year of the owner's death, it is effective for that year. The revised rule is retroactive for purposes of determining minimum required annual distributions on or after January 1, 2003.

Source: Ed Slott, CPA, editor, *Ed Slott's IRA Advisor,* 100 Merrick Rd., Rockville Centre, NY 11570. He is a nationally recognized IRA distributions expert. *www.irahelp.com.*

Chapter Thirteen

HOW NON-SPOUSE BENEFICIARIES CAN STRETCH OUT AN INHERITED RETIREMENT ACCOUNT

In the past, if you inherited an account in an employer-sponsored retirement plan from someone other than your spouse, the tax laws weren't favorable. However, thanks to a private letter ruling issued by the IRS, you may be able to enjoy many years of tax deferral.

Key: The IRS has said that specific types of annuities may be purchased in order to stretch out distributions. Although a private letter ruling isn't binding, it does indicate the thinking of the IRS.

Unfair treatment

If you inherit a retirement account from your spouse, tax deferral won't be a problem. You'll be allowed to take minimum required distributions (MRDs) over your remaining life expectancy, if you wish. Alternatively, you may roll over the account to a spousal IRA and begin distributions when you reach age 70½.

Example: With a 25-year life expectancy, you can take out as little as ⅟₂₅ (4%) of the account balance in the first year.

Strategy: Taking MRDs leaves more money in the plan for continued tax-deferred growth. You are allowed to withdraw more than the minimum, though, if you need the cash.

The IRA advantage: If you inherit an IRA from a non-spouse, you still won't have problems with tax deferral. Any IRA beneficiary is allowed the same life expectancy stretchout, to defer taxable withdrawals.

Trap: The problem arises if you inherit an account in an employer-sponsored plan, such as a 401(k), from a non-spouse. You may have to withdraw all the funds—and pay all the deferred income tax within a short time period.

Technically, an employer-sponsored plan is allowed to stretch out payments to non-spouse beneficiaries, providing decades of tax deferral. However, many small-company plans (and even some large-company plans) don't want the administrative burden of paying out required distributions over many years.

Therefore, many plans make a lump-sum payout of the entire account balance to a non-spouse beneficiary, who will owe all the deferred income tax immediately.

Worst-case scenario: The situation is extremely difficult if you inherit a retirement account from a one-person company, professional practice, or sole proprietorship. The IRS's position has been that the plan dies with that individual, therefore, the assets must be distributed right away.

Outcome: In such circumstances, the plan must be liquidated within one year and all income tax must be paid.

However, if the plan had been rolled over to an IRA before the account owner's death, long-term tax deferral would have been allowed.

The annuity answer

At the IRS, some officials feel it is unfair that an inherited IRA be treated differently from an inherited employer-sponsored plan.

Result: When a taxpayer facing the loss of tax deferral placed a request, the IRS issued a favorable private letter ruling (Letter Ruling 200244023).

Loophole: The IRS said that a retirement plan can buy and distribute a nontransferable annuity without triggering a tax bill.

Definition: A nontransferable annuity is one that can't be sold, given away, assigned, or pledged as collateral for a loan or other obligation.

As mentioned, a private letter ruling applies only to the taxpayer who requested it. However, other taxpayers in this circumstance might feel comfortable taking the IRS at its word and buying a nontransferable annuity for ongoing tax deferral.

From plan to action

Ideally, an annuity used for this purpose will not only be nontransferable, but will also offer certain distribution options.

Such an annuity must pay out at least as much as the MRD each year to avoid a 50% penalty for insufficient distributions.

In addition, the annuity should permit the annuitant to take out a larger amount than the MRD, if that's desired, and pay more income tax. Such an annuity essentially will re-create an inherited IRA.

Flex plan: In the letter ruling, the IRS blessed the use of a variable annuity in this situation. Thus, the beneficiary could invest in any of the separate funds offered by the insurance company.

There is no need to restrict investing to a low-yielding fixed annuity.

Caution: In some cases, a surrender charge may be owed if larger-than-MRD withdrawals are taken in the early years of the annuity contract.

Required: The retirement plan must be authorized to purchase such an annuity with the money in the decedent's account. Some plans must be amended …therefore, the plan administrator must be willing to make an effort to accommodate non-spouse beneficiaries.

When the private letter ruling was first issued, suitable annuities had to be custom-designed at considerable expense. Thus, this strategy was worthwhile only for very large accounts. Now that insurers have a model to work from, non-spouse beneficiaries may be able to buy off-the-shelf annuities with riders to address all the requirements. This technique can work for inherited accounts of virtually any size.

Fine points

There are various situations that may arise in which an annuity purchase can foster tax deferral.

Example: You and your sister are joint beneficiaries of a retirement account after your uncle's death. Your sister wants to withdraw her share to buy a second home, while you want extended tax deferral.

Solution: Separate shares can be created up to September 30 of the year after death. Then, each beneficiary can decide whether or not to purchase an annuity.

In this example, your sister can take her half of the account in cash while the other half can be used to buy a slow-payout annuity for you.

Help on the way? Legislation now before Congress might resolve this issue. The National Employee Savings and Trust Equity Guarantee Act (NESTEG) includes a provision that retirement accounts payable to a non-spouse beneficiary may be transferred directly to an IRA, which would allow extended tax deferral.

However, it's uncertain when—if ever—such a law will pass. In the meantime, if you inherit a retirement account from a generous parent, aunt, or uncle, and you don't need the cash right away, buying an appropriate annuity can help you prolong the pleasure of tax deferral.

Be prepared

Don't assume that Washington will act in time to bail out the beneficiaries of your own retirement account, if you've named someone who's not your spouse.

If you've retired: By rolling your retirement funds into an IRA as soon as possible, you can assure your beneficiary a long, tax-deferred stretchout.

If you're still working: Have your company plan or your Keogh plan amended so that it's clear the plan may buy an annuity for nonspouse beneficiaries.

That will protect your loved ones in case you die before rolling your account balance into an IRA.

Source: Steven G. Lockwood, Esq., president, Lockwood Pension Services, Inc., 1345 Avenue of the Americas, New York City 10105. He is coauthor of *The Individual Retirement Account Answer Book* (Panel).

Chapter Fourteen

GOOD GIFT FOR A CHILD: ROTH IRA

The best gift you can make to a child or grandchild may be the funds to finance annual contributions to a Roth IRA.

Many minors earn income from summer jobs, after-school work, work done for a family business, etc. Such children are eligible to make Roth IRA contributions of up to 100% of their earned income, subject to the limits outlined below. If they don't have the money to do so, you can give it to them.

Big payoff: Distributions from Roth IRAs can be totally tax free, unlike those from traditional IRAs and other kinds of retirement plans. And due to the power of compound earnings over the many future years of a young child's life, the final tax-free payout may be huge.

Example: Roth IRA contribution limits are $4,000 for 2006 and 2007, and $5,000 for later years. Starting this year, a child age 15 makes these maximum contributions for seven years, through age 21. If the average return in the IRA is 7%—the long-term average after inflation for stocks—then at age 21, the child will have about $40,000 in the IRA.

Without investing another dollar, the IRA will grow to more than $700,000 by the time the child reaches 65—all tax free, making it worth much more than the same amount of money in any other kind of retirement account.

At age 21, the child can have attained some future retirement security without having to save any more for retirement during his/her working life.

Even better: Roth contributions can be withdrawn any time tax free. Earnings withdrawals are subject to other restrictions. So during the child's life, he will have access to the funds you provided, tax free.

Source: Seymour Goldberg, Esq., CPA, Goldberg & Goldberg, PC, 1 Huntington Quadrangle, Melville, NY 11747, *www.goldbergira.com*. One of the nation's leading authorities on IRA distributions, Mr. Goldberg is author of *Practical Application of the Retirement Distribution Rules* (IRG Publications, *www.goldbergreports.com*).

THE IMPORTANCE OF IRA TAX BASIS

Tax law allows nondeductible contributions to regular IRAs. Earnings won't be taxed until the money is withdrawn, which generally occurs in retirement when the owner is in a lower tax bracket.

Trap: Nondeductible IRA contributions are made with money that already has been taxed. Unless you keep good records, you'll pay tax again on the money you have contributed, when that money is withdrawn.

Example: You contribute $3,000 to a nondeductible IRA, which grows to $5,000. Only $2,000 should be taxed when that money is withdrawn.

To avoid double taxation on contributions, you must keep thorough records. Be ready to prove your tax cost, or basis, in the non-deductible IRA if you're audited.

Strategy: Report the value of the IRA as well as your basis every year on Form 8606, *Nondeductible IRAs,* and attach that form to your tax return.

This form is not required unless you take an IRA distribution that is partially untaxed. Nevertheless, filing Form 8606 each year will remind you of the basis in your IRA. That basis will reduce the tax you'll owe on future distributions.

Source: Alan S. Zipp, Esq., CPA, 932 Hungerford Dr., Rockville, MD 20850. Mr. Zipp is an instructor of income tax courses for the American Institute of Certified Public Accountants. He specializes in the income tax problems of individuals and small businesses.

Chapter Fifteen
ESTATE TAX LOOPHOLES

With some tax planning, recipients of an inheritance can keep more money for themselves, not give it to the IRS. Consider these strategies...

Loophole: No capital gains tax on inherited assets. Most beneficiaries pay little or no capital gains tax when they sell inherited assets because of a tax break known as stepped-up basis. The recipient's tax cost (basis) for figuring capital gains is the value on the estate tax return, not the property's cost to the decedent.

Example: You inherit a house that cost the decedent $20,000 and is now worth $150,000. You pay no tax when you receive the house and, if you immediately sell it for $150,000, you pay no capital gains tax. Reason: Your basis is equal to the property's value at the date of death (or six months later if the estate chose that date). Since the house was sold for the same price at which you inherited it, you pay no capital gains tax. If you sell the house for more than $150,000, the excess is taxable gain.

Loophole: Deduct capital losses on inherited assets. If you sell inherited property at a loss, you can deduct the loss. If you sell the house in the above example for $120,000, your deductible loss is $30,000, subject to annual deduction limits. Capital losses are deductible dollar for dollar against capital gains and up to $3,000 of ordinary income each year. Excess losses can be carried forward to subsequent tax years.

Loophole: Pay executors' fees to sole beneficiaries. Consider paying executors' fees to beneficiaries, depending on their tax picture. Estates can deduct executors' commissions. So when the executor is the sole beneficiary, it makes sense to pay the fees if the estate is in the 50% bracket (including state taxes) and the executor in the 40% bracket (including state taxes).

Loophole: Disclaim inheritances. In some situations, a great deal of estate tax can be saved when a beneficiary disclaims (gives up) an inheritance.

Example: A wife leaves $500,000 to her husband, who has a $5 million estate. No estate tax is due on the wife's death because of the unlimited marital deduction. But on the husband's death, the extra $500,000 would be taxed to his estate at the top rate (about 50% including state taxes). The tax would be $250,000. That tax could be saved if, on the wife's death, the husband disclaims the $500,000 inheritance and lets it pass to the couple's children or other beneficiaries. The gift would not be taxed in the wife's estate because of her exemption amount—her right to leave up to $2 million in 2006 estate tax free to beneficiaries other than her husband.

Strategy: Use disclaimers with designated beneficiaries of IRAs or pension accounts. When a surviving spouse disclaims an IRA in favor of children and grandchildren as contingent beneficiaries, post-death planning can create dynasty-type extended withdrawals over the life expectancies of the children and/or grandchildren.

Caution: To be valid, disclaimers must be made within nine months of the death and meet other strict criteria—check with an estate tax adviser.

Loophole: Redeem business stock. If the decedent owned stock in a C corporation with high retained earnings, the stock can be redeemed income tax free by the estate. The redemption is treated as a capital gain. There would be no income tax payable because the value of the stock is stepped up to its value on the date of the decedent's death.

Loophole: Don't overlook the income tax deduction for estate tax paid. Federal estate tax paid on income in respect of a decedent is deductible as an itemized deduction on your personal tax return when you report the income. Generally, when you inherit assets, your tax cost is stepped up to the asset's date-of-death value. However, this does not apply to income earned by the decedent but paid after death, including distributions from pension, 401(k),

403(b), and IRA funds.

Note: Post-death income may be subject to both estate tax and income tax. The income tax deduction mitigates some of this double tax.

Caution: The deduction is only for the federal estate tax and not state estate or inheritance tax.

Opportunity: A surviving spouse can elect to roll over a pension distribution into an IRA and defer the payment of income tax.

Loophole: Delay the payment of the estate tax. Estate tax can be paid in installments, with interest, over 14 years. The decision to pay estate tax on the due date or to elect installment payments is made after the death, although it is usually considered and planned for—or against—during the estate-planning process.

Caution: When you elect installment payments, the IRS files a lien on the estate's assets.

Source: Edward Mendlowitz, CPA, shareholder in the CPA firm WithumSmith+Brown, 120 Albany St., New Brunswick, NJ 08901. He is author of *Estate Planning* (Practical Programs).

Section 1: Retirement and Estate Planning

Chapter Sixteen

SIMPLE RETIREMENT PLANS: ACT NOW TO CATCH THE OCTOBER DEADLINE

One of the best retirement plans for small companies and the self-employed has a fast-approaching deadline...you need to act soon to cash in on this tax shelter this year.

Required: A Savings Incentive Match Plan for Employees (SIMPLE plan) must be in place before October 1 if you want to make contributions for 2006. New employers who come into existence after October 1 may establish a plan as soon as administratively possible.

Most banks, brokerage firms, insurers, and mutual fund companies will help you handle the paperwork. These plans are easy to create and maintain.

Loophole: There is a tax credit for new retirement plans and SIMPLE plans qualify for it. The credit can provide your company with up to $500 in annual tax savings for three years.

Required: To claim the credit, an employer generally cannot have sponsored a qualified retirement plan within the previous three years and must cover at least one employee who is not the owner or the owner's spouse.

How they work

Self-employed individuals can have SIMPLE plans, as can employers with no more than 100 employees who have earned $5,000 or more during the preceding calendar year.

Neither employers nor those who are self-employed can maintain a SIMPLE plan if they have another employer-sponsored qualified retirement plan.

Who can be in them: To qualify for participation in a SIMPLE, an employee must have earned at least $5,000 during any two preceding years and be expected to earn at least $5,000 during the current year. Therefore, you can cut costs by excluding some part-time employees.

SIMPLEs come in two varieties: SIMPLE IRAs and SIMPLE 401(k)s.

Trap: SIMPLE 401(k)s are not particularly simple. Such plans must set up a trust with a financial institution and may require the annual filing of Form 5500, Annual Return/Report of Employee Benefit Plan, thus further increasing costs.

Certain compensation limits apply to SIMPLE 401(k)s, and required employer contributions may be significantly higher than for SIMPLE IRAs.

Result: Most employers prefer SIMPLE IRAs.

SIMPLE IRAs truly live up to their name, requiring very little administration. Moreover, with a SIMPLE IRA you won't have fiduciary responsibility or liability for employees' investments. (Employers have an obligation to invest prudently with other types of plans, such as profit-sharing plans. If you invest your employees' money, as you do with a profit-sharing plan, you may have liability for poor results.)

Benefit: With a SIMPLE IRA, each employee self-directs his/her account, with many investment alternatives.

You'll have more freedom investing your own funds, too, compared with the limited menu of a SIMPLE 401(k).

The 100% solution

For SIMPLE 401(k)s and SIMPLE IRAs, participants can contribute 100% of their self-employment income or employee compensation, up to $10,000 in 2005. Other plans, such as profit-sharing plans, generally limit contributions to no more than 25% of compensation.

Maximum: With a 3%-of-compensation employer match (see below), the maximum amount that can go into your SIMPLE IRA this year, based on compensation of $300,000, is $19,000. (A compensation cap of $220,000 in 2006 doesn't apply when the 3% match is used for SIMPLE IRAs.)

Catch-up: Participants age 50 and older can contribute an additional $2,500 of income in 2006, raising the ceiling to $20,500. After that, the basic and catch-up amounts will be adjusted annually for inflation.

Sharing the wealth

There are no antidiscrimination tests with SIMPLE IRAs.

Benefit: You and any relatives employed at the same business can push the upper limits of SIMPLE IRAs even if no other employee contributes.

Simple, not perfect

While considering the above advantages, you should be aware of the disadvantages of SIMPLE IRAS, too...

•Other types of retirement plans, such as profit-sharing and defined-benefit plans, may permit you to contribute (and deduct) $49,000 or even more to your own account this year, versus the $20,500 limit for SIMPLE plans.

•SIMPLE plans can be expensive because of mandatory contributions on behalf of those employees who choose to defer some taxable income. There are two ways to comply with the mandatory contribution rules...

1. Employers may contribute a flat 2% of compensation to the account of each eligible employee. With this option, you must contribute for all employees, including those who choose not to contribute on their own behalf.

2. Or employers may provide a dollar-for-dollar match of the amount each eligible employee contributes, up to 3% of that employee's salary.

Example: Your assistant, who earns $40,000 per year, decides to participate in your SIMPLE plan and contributes $2,000. Your company must kick in a matching $1,200 (3% of $40,000).

Better choice: You might prefer choice No. 2, the 3% match, because it will result in (a) a larger contribution for you and (b) a smaller match for other employees, if only a few participate. If most of your employees participate to the maximum allowed, No. 1 (2% match) might be less expensive than No. 2 (3% match).

• With either matching formula, all contributions are fully vested, therefore, employees who leave will take your SIMPLE matches with them.

There also are some specific drawbacks to SIMPLE IRAs, as compared with SIMPLE 401(k)s. In the first two years you participate, a 25% penalty applies for withdrawals before age 59½. After that, the regular 10% early withdrawal penalty takes effect.

Similarly, rollovers from a SIMPLE IRA to a regular IRA are not allowed in the first two years.

Trap: Loans aren't permitted from any IRA, including a SIMPLE IRA.

Thus, if you think that you might want to borrow from your retirement account, or do a rollover within two years, a SIMPLE 401(k) might be a better choice.

Bottom line

Given the pros and cons, SIMPLE IRAs make sense when you have...

• Low income. Because you can contribute 100% of your pay, SIMPLE IRAs may be ideal if your income is relatively low yet you want to make a sizable retirement plan contribution.

A SIMPLE might help you shelter income from a part-time or sideline business while you make other retirement plan arrangements for the company you run full-time.

Trap: If you have a SIMPLE plan for a sideline business while you're in a 401(k) or 403(b) plan at another job, the total amount you can put into both plans can't exceed $15,000 in 2006, or $20,000 if you're age 50 or over. (This amount does not include any employer matches.)

Example: You're 44 years old and you put $8,000 into your 401(k) or 403(b) account this year. Your SIMPLE plan contribution will be capped at $6,000.

• Few, mainly low-paid employees. SIMPLE plans may be good if you're an employer with a small workforce and most of your workers don't earn much.

Low-income employees aren't likely to contribute heavily to the plan. The smaller the amount of employee deferrals, the smaller your company's match will have to be if using the 3% formula.

• Start-up companies. SIMPLE plans provide an easy, relatively inexpensive way to provide retirement benefits to interested employees.

• Modest means. If a $10,000–$20,000 contribution this year is all you need or can afford, there's no reason to adopt another type of retirement plan until you grow.

Source: John Battaglia, CPA, tax director, private client advisers practice, Deloitte & Touche LLP, Two World Financial Center, New York City 10281.

Section 1: Retirement and Estate Planning

Chapter Seventeen
USE AN IRA TO BE CHARITABLE...AND STILL LEAVE MORE TO YOUR HEIRS

A little-known way to include charitable intentions in your estate planning is to make bequests from your IRA or another tax-deferred retirement account. For tax purposes, this technique will probably yield the best overall result.

Payoff: Deferred income tax can be entirely avoided. Moreover, you may be able to pass appreciated assets to other heirs, who will inherit with a tax-saving step-up in basis.

Split shift

Suppose, for example, that Joan Wilson is a widow with a total estate of $4 million, half in an IRA and half in highly appreciated securities and real estate. Joan wants to leave $2 million to her children and $2 million to various charities. If the appreciated assets are left to charity while the IRA goes to the children, no federal estate tax will be due, under current law.

Trap: With this plan, the children eventually will have to pay income tax on the IRA money as it is withdrawn. At a 35% rate, the ultimate federal income tax bill could be up to $700,000.

Better approach: Leave the IRA to charity and the appreciated assets to the children. Again, there will be no estate tax, but the children will inherit the appreciated assets with a step-up in basis, under current law.

The children would never owe any capital gains tax on the appreciation that occurred during Joan's lifetime.

Bottom line: The latter approach passes on the estate completely tax free, saving hundreds of thousands of dollars in taxes.

Caution: Planning for charitable bequests is the opposite of planning for lifetime donations. While you are alive, it often makes sense to give away appreciated assets and let your tax-deferred retirement plans continue to compound.

Sooner or later

There are four methods you can use to make charitable bequests from your retirement plan...

- Leave your IRA directly to charity.

- Leave your IRA to your spouse, who will leave it to charity at his/her death.

- Leave your IRA to a marital trust with all distributions going to your surviving spouse. At his death, whatever remains goes to charity.

- Leave your IRA to a charitable remainder trust (CRT), which can pay income to any individual you want to name, with the charity as the recipient of the remainder interest. (Ask the charity or your tax adviser to explain how a CRT works.)

Outright bequests are most suitable if you are not married or if the bequest is relatively small in relation to your entire estate. If you're married, your spouse may not want to give up the IRA to charity.

What about the other methods? If you are confident that your spouse always will be able to handle the IRA wisely, and make the appropriate charitable bequest, simply leave the IRA to your spouse.

Reality check: In many situations, you'll be better off using a trust, which can provide control and protection.

Trust tactics

The Tax Code permits you to create a trust where the surviving spouse gets all the income while the first spouse to die gets to name the ultimate beneficiary, which can be a charity.

Benefits: No federal estate tax will be due at the first death. In case of need, the trustee can distribute more funds to the surviving spouse.

At the survivor's death, whatever remains in the IRA goes to the charity you've named, tax free.

Alternative: If you want to limit the survivor's income to provide more to charity, a CRT may be appropriate. With a CRT, the spouse's income will be a fixed amount or a fixed percentage of CRT assets.

If you want to name children or grandchildren to also receive income from the trust, a CRT would be more suitable.

Caution: A present value will be placed on the projected future income to younger generations, and that amount may be subject to estate tax.

Trap: A CRT also may result in speedier distributions from an inherited IRA, so some tax deferral may be lost.

Work with a knowledgeable tax pro who can crunch the numbers and suggest the type of trust most suitable for your family and charitable goals. This is especially important whenever an IRA is left to a trust and the trust ultimately goes to charity.

Reason: It becomes more complicated to obtain an income tax deduction and extend tax deferral.

Divide and conquer

The above strategies may make sense if you have $2 million in an IRA and want to leave $2 million to charity. But what if you want to leave only $100,000 to charity? Or $50,000?

You can make a specific charitable bequest from an IRA or qualified plan, but the tax treatment is unclear.

Danger: If you specify, say, an $80,000 bequest, the IRS might treat that as an $80,000 withdrawal from the IRA and assess income tax on the amount. Strategies...

• Name co-beneficiaries.

Example: You might say that 4% of the IRA goes to charity while 96% goes to a family member. With a $2 million IRA, that would mean an $80,000 charitable bequest. Note: Satisfying a fractional bequest with the right to receive an IRA is not a taxable event.

• Split your IRA. Break off a smaller IRA, destined for charity. Example: From a $2 million IRA, you could roll over $80,000 to a new IRA, tax free. The charity could be named as beneficiary of the new IRA while a family member remains beneficiary of the old IRA, now worth $1,920,000.

Subsequent withdrawals from the new IRA could keep the balance at $80,000, if that's the amount you intend to bequeath to charity.

Tactic: When minimum required distributions (MRD) begin after age 70½, take some of the amount from your charitable IRA, leaving more in your family IRA.

Example: You split your IRA, as above. After some years of growth, you have $1.8 million in your family IRA (going to your spouse) and $100,000 in the IRA that will go to charity.

Say your MRD for the year is $75,000. Distributions need not be pro rata, so you can take $20,000 from the charitable IRA.

Result: This reduces the charitable IRA to $80,000, the amount you intend to donate. Only $55,000 (the $75,000 MRD minus the $20,000 withdrawn from the charitable IRA) need be taken from your family IRA, increasing the amount that can compound, tax deferred, for yourself and your beneficiary.

The same process can continue, year after year.

By remaining vigilant, you can fulfill philanthropic goals while providing for your loved ones, too.

Source: Jere Doyle, senior director of estate planning, Mellon Private Wealth Management, one of the nation's leading private wealth managers, One Boston Place, Boston 02108.

Chapter Eighteen
REVISED IRA TRUST RULES CAN HURT CLIENTS AND PROS

Individuals often leave their IRA accounts to heirs through trusts.

Why: To protect against creditor claims (or divorce claims)...provide professional management for IRA funds...leave funds to a minor...ensure that funds won't be squandered...and provide for "secondary beneficiaries" of the trust.

Danger: The Uniform Principal And Income Act (UPAIA), adopted in more than 40 states, creates planning traps for IRA trusts—and legal dangers for attorneys, accountants, and trustees who deal with them. Yet, most of these professionals may not understand the act and its implications.

Planning problem

The UPAIA sets accounting rules for the "principal" and "income" of trusts.

The first big trap in the law is that it uses definitions for these terms that may be very different from those in the minds of IRA owners—and that they use when setting up IRA trusts.

Example: An IRA holding $1 million has as its beneficiary a trust for a child with a 50-year life expectancy. The IRA must be distributed over that period, so 1/50th of its assets ($20,000) must be paid to the trust this year. The trust's creator wanted these funds from the IRA to be paid by the trust to the child. Therefore, the trust's terms unfortunately state "trust income will be paid to the beneficiary annually."

Trap: The UPAIA defines "trust income" as including only 10% of a required distribution from an IRA—so the beneficiary can receive $2,000 from the trust, not $20,000. The remaining $18,000 is trust "principal."

Source of confusion: All IRA distributions are taxable income to recipients, so people naturally think of all of them as being "income." But if an IRA is left to a trust, its assets at the date of the owner's death are principal.

The new UPAIA codifies a new rule to settle this—but the rule contradicts how most people think, and the intention behind many existing trusts.

Even most accountants, lawyers, and trustees don't yet appreciate the impact of the law—and in many states the law applies retroactively. Dangers...

- Improper distributions are being made from many trusts right now.

- Intended distributions to beneficiaries may be slashed by 90%.

- When undistributed funds "pile up" in a trust, they are subject to income tax at rates much higher than personal rates.

What do to: Review any trust that is set up to be a beneficiary of an IRA. Remove from it any instruction to distribute trust "income"—unless it is a qualified terminable interest property (QTIP) trust (see below). Instead, have the trust state that "required distributions received from the IRA shall be paid to the beneficiary each year." Then, add a provision stating that the UPAIA shall not apply to the trust (if your state hasn't adopted it yet, although it may in the future).

Note: A QTIP trust that is left for a spouse should not elect out of the UPAIA.

Professionals' problems

That's only the start of potential legal problems posed by the UPAIA.

For attorneys, accountants, and estate planners who deal with trusts, the UPAIA creates new risk of malpractice lawsuits and ethics violations.

A beneficiary of an IRA trust who sees expected distributions cut by 90%—with the funds piling up in the trust subject to needless excess taxes—may become angry at the professionals who put the trust together and sue. But there are more dangers as well.

Many states that have adopted the UPAIA may have other provisions that pose dangers for professionals—"power of adjustment" and "unitrust" rules.

Details vary by state. The basics...

• Power of adjustment (POA) gives the trustee the power to adjust the size of distributions to beneficiaries according to what seems "reasonable" in the trustee's judgment.

Example: An IRA trust was expected to pay $20,000 annually to a non-spouse beneficiary, but UPAIA rules cut that to $2,000. A trustee who thinks that's unfair might use POA to increase the payout to $4,000.

• Unitrust provisions. These allow a trustee to choose to pay from a trust a percentage of its total value, instead of its income to the beneficiary.

The idea: Since income may vary greatly year to year with investment returns, it may be best to fix distributions to trust value.

In New York, for example, when unitrust rules are elected, they require a beneficiary to receive 4% of a trust's total value annually.

Both provisions seem reasonable—but create big litigation traps. Here's how...

• When POA rules apply, a beneficiary may sue the trustee for not using POA rules to increase distributions.

• Unitrust rules can be even more dangerous. For instance, in New York, they could be used by a beneficiary to take 4% of the value of the entire IRA in the trust—or $40,000 annually from a $1 million IRA trust, even if that is double what the trust's creator expected.

Moreover, in New York, the law creates a "rebuttable presumption" in favor of unitrust rules if a beneficiary sues a trustee over them—so if the beneficiary sues to boost payouts to more than the trust creator expected, the trustee will have an uphill legal fight in defending the suit.

But there's even worse legal danger. Conflict of interest can create legal liability for those managing a trust no matter what decision is made regarding trust distributions.

Important: The primary beneficiary is not the only person with an interest in a trust. Any residuary beneficiary (such as a child of the primary beneficiary, third party, or charity) has a legal interest, too. And the law requires that the trustee represent these beneficiaries "fairly"—protecting their interest in the trust.

Conflict: Acting to increase payouts to the primary beneficiary by POA or unitrust rules will reduce the amount left to the residuary beneficiary—who can sue. But not doing so may cause the primary beneficiary to sue.

Common mistake: Very often a person who sets up an IRA trust will name a primary beneficiary and residuary beneficiary, then leave the family lawyer to handle its affairs. But which beneficiary does the lawyer represent?

The problem is that the one lawyer is representing both sides of a conflict of interest. The solution is that every party to the trust—each beneficiary and the trustee—needs to be represented by his/her own lawyer. But this greatly increases the cost as well as difficulty.

The same argument, and legal liability, may arise with accountants and estate planners who deal with the trust.

Strategy: The professional can seek a waiver from both sides regarding the conflict—and if they don't give it, quit the case.

Self-defense strategies

Don't leave an IRA to a trust without a specific reason, such as a need to protect minor children, or the advice of an expert. And if you do...

• Set up a separate IRA trust. Rules for IRA trusts are very different from trusts set up by will.

• Have trust language specifically opt out of the UPAIA and any POA or unitrust laws (unless it is a QTIP trust).

• Consider conflict of interest issues in advance—and make sure your expert advisers consider them.

If you are a trustee, lawyer, or accountant dealing with trusts, be aware of the new rules—and of potential malpractice, conflict of interest, and other litigation claims that may arise.

Source: Seymour Goldberg, Esq., CPA, Goldberg & Goldberg, PC, 1 Huntington Quadrangle, Melville, NY 11747, *www.goldbergira.com*. One of the nation's leading authorities on IRA distributions, Mr. Goldberg is author of *Practical Application of the Retirement Distribution Rules* (IRG Publications, *www.goldbergreports.com*).

Chapter Nineteen

RETIREMENT PLAN TAX TRAPS THAT BUSINESS OWNERS MUST AVOID

Sponsoring a retirement plan can help cut current taxes, build your wealth, and attract desirable employees. Nevertheless, the rules are complex and the IRS pays close attention to small-company plans.

To derive maximum benefit from your company's plan, you must comply with a host of laws and regulations. An error can result in costly fines or, in the worst case, disqualification of your plan, which would trigger all the deferred taxes. Traps to avoid...

Eligibility

Trap: Excluding eligible employees. Some business owners make the mistake of contributing to their own account within a retirement plan, but not to their employees' accounts. If your company makes contributions to any employee's retirement account, you are required to make contributions for all eligible employees each year. Different types of plans, however, permit you to exclude certain employees, based on age or length of service.

Examples: With a 401(k) plan, employees over age 21 who have worked for your company at least one year must be included. With profit-sharing plans, you may make employees wait for two years if the plan provides for immediate 100% vesting.

Generally, contributions must be made for all eligible participants in accordance with the plan document. Some sophisticated plans, though, permit skewing of contributions to older employees, including the company's owners.

Keeping current

Trap: Failing to update your plan. If you sponsor a qualified retirement plan, you probably have a prototype plan offered by a bank, brokerage firm, mutual fund company, insurer, or some other financial institution. If so, new tax laws often require technical amendments.

Example: You have until the last day of the plan year beginning in 2005 to amend your plan to comply with the Economic Growth and Tax Relief Reconciliation Act of 2001 (EGTRRA).

Your custodian should have sent the documents for you to complete. If not, ask for them and have your tax adviser begin working on them.

Beware: Your plan may not have been amended to comply with tax laws. If your plan isn't up to date, your tax adviser may be able to negotiate a modest fine with the IRS. That would be much better than paying the larger penalty likely if your noncompliance is detected during an audit.

Trap: Overfunding your pension. Defined-benefit plans are designed to build up a certain amount to pay participants a pension in retirement. Excess accumulations are not permitted.

Example: A plan may be designed to pay out $150,000 per year, which might require $1.8 million in capital. If such a plan has $2.2 million, it's overfunded by $400,000—no further contributions are permitted.

Key: When stock prices rise sharply, as they did in 2003, some defined-benefit plans become overfunded. Some sponsors continue to make contributions, although they're not permitted.

Strategy: Monitor any defined-benefit plan carefully. Seek advice from an actuary regarding funding. If your plan is overfunded, check with a professional about starting a new one, qualified or nonqualified.

Jumping the gun

Trap: Taking impermissible withdrawals. The 10% tax penalty for early withdrawals does not apply to distributions after age 59½. Therefore, you might assume that you can withdraw money from your plan once you reach that age.

But such withdrawals may be illegal unless they're permitted by the plan's language. Some plans, for example, don't allow distributions until retirement.

Strategy: Amend your plan to permit distributions to employees after age 59½. This will allow you to take penalty-free withdrawals, yet still benefit from further contributions.

Trap: Undervaluing life insurance held inside a plan. The IRS recently published a series of rules describing transactions that are considered abusive.

Example: You are the 100% owner of a closely held company. You buy a $1 million policy on your own life through your company's retirement plan. The company pays $100,000 in premiums each year, for five years.

After five years, the policy has a cash value of $450,000 but an enormous surrender charge is in place, reducing the supposed surrender value to $100,000. Thus, when an irrevocable trust you have created buys the policy, only $100,000 is paid to the retirement plan. The insurance contract is sold to the employee when the cash surrender value is temporarily depressed—significantly below the premiums paid. However, the cash surrender value increases significantly after it is transferred to the employee.

The IRS considers this transaction abusive because it results in tax deductions to the employer for amounts far in excess of the amount paid to the plan by the employee to purchase the policy. Additionally, the IRS considers this transaction a tax shelter, which requires disclosure.

Self-dealing

Trap: Moving money between your own pockets. Transactions between retirement plans and "disqualified persons" are prohibited. If you sponsor a qualified plan, don't permit your plan to enter into transactions with yourself, your family, or your company. Even if you sell property to your plan at a bargain price and the plan makes money, that would be a prohibited transaction.

Trap: Neglecting spousal consent. For married participants in defined-benefit plans, distributions generally need to have the spouse's written consent. This may apply to some other types of plans, too, depending on the plan language.

Often, a spouse has the right to be named as account beneficiary.

If you sponsor a plan for which such rules apply and you don't enforce them, you may be vulnerable to a lawsuit from an employee's spouse as well as IRS penalties.

Trap: Relying on a prenuptial agreement. Chances are that part of any prenuptial agreement will cover your retirement plan, if that's a valuable asset for you.

But, before a marriage, your future spouse can't sign away any rights to your retirement plan. Only a spouse can legally do that.

Strategies: One approach is to have your spouse-to-be promise to sign a postnuptial agreement, in which rights to your retirement plan will be waived.

A better solution might be to terminate the retirement plan before the marriage and roll your balance into an IRA, where spousal rights don't apply.

Outcome: You can start a new plan after the marriage, at which time your spouse can waive his/her rights, if that's desirable. Make sure such a waiver is included in the plan administration documents.

Trap: Missing deadlines. Different types of plans are on different schedules.

Example: A Keogh plan must be in place by December 31, 2006, to permit deductible contributions for this year.

If you are late by even a day or two, you may lose a full year of tax-deferred retirement investing.

Source: Sandy Soltis, CPA, tax partner, Blackman Kallick Bartelstein LLP, 10 S. Riverside Plaza, Chicago 60606. Ms. Soltis provides tax-consulting services to middle market businesses and their owners.

Chapter Twenty

IRA WITHDRAWAL OPPORTUNITY FOR BUSINESS OWNERS

Owners of small businesses may have the opportunity to take distributions from their IRAs at low tax rates before year-end.

Key: Most small businesses today are organized as pass-through entities (S corporations, partnerships, limited liability companies) or proprietorships. These have their income and losses taxed on the personal tax returns of their owners.

When such a business has a low-income or loss year, it may put its owner in a low tax bracket —and thereby create a "window" in which the owner can take IRA distributions at a lower tax rate than will be possible in profitable years to come.

Extra benefit: Long-term capital gains and dividends are taxed at no more than 15%—but IRA distributions are taxed at ordinary rates even when they come from capital gains and dividends earned in the IRA.

Thus, taking funds from an IRA when temporarily in a low tax bracket can provide a double benefit—reducing the tax on the distribution itself, as well as the tax on future investment returns earned on the same funds.

Planning: Business owners may be able to reduce their tax brackets by acting to reduce taxable business income before year-end.

Example: Acquiring and deducting up to $108,000 of equipment placed in service by December 31, 2006, will reduce income accordingly.

IRA distributions must be taken by year-end to be taxable this year, so now is the time to project the business's tax results for the year and plan year-end steps to take.

If you aren't yet age 59½, remember to consider the cost of the 10% early distribution penalty.

Source: Steven Hurok, CPA, director, BDO Seidman, LLP, 90 Woodbridge Center Dr., Woodbridge, NJ 07095.

IRA PROTECTION

IRAs get new protection from creditors under the new bankruptcy law that went into effect on October 17, 2005. When an IRA owner declares bankruptcy under the new law, contributions to IRAs and Roth IRAs as well as the earnings on them—up to a total of $1 million—are protected from creditors. In addition, all funds rolled over into an IRA from an employer's retirement plan are protected. In practice, this should mean that virtually all IRA funds are protected in bankruptcy.

Safety: If you think that you may ever have a total of more than $1 million in your IRAs, place any rollover from an employer plan in a segregated "conduit IRA" to identify the source of the funds.

Source: Ed Slott, CPA, editor, *Ed Slott's IRA Advisor,* 100 Merrick Rd., Rockville Centre, NY 11570. He is a nationally recognized IRA distributions expert. *www.irahelp.com.*

Chapter Twenty-One

FOR THE SELF-EMPLOYED— GREAT FLEXIBILITY WITH ONE-PERSON 401(k)s

If you're self-employed, or if you have some self-employment income from freelancing or consulting, there are several retirement plans you can use to shelter that income from tax. In some situations, your best choice will be a one-person 401(k) plan.

The advantages

If you have no employees, there are several retirement plans from which you can choose. Reasons why a one-person 401(k) is a good choice...

• Borrowing power. You can borrow from a one-person 401(k) without paying tax or an early withdrawal penalty. As long as your plan documents include the required language, you can borrow half the balance, up to $50,000. Just be certain that you are ready and able to repay the loan.

Why this helps: Such loans can be obtained without the paperwork hassles you run into when you deal with a bank.

Key: When you pay back principal and interest, they go into your retirement account, not into the pockets of a third-party lender.

Other retirement plans for the self-employed, such as simplified employee pension (SEP) plans and savings incentive match plans for employee (SIMPLE) IRAs, don't permit borrowing.

• Low administration costs. Compared with some other retirement plans, there's little paperwork with a one-person 401(k).

Required: Until you have more than $100,000 in your one-person 401(k), there are no IRS filings required. After that, the only form you must file is IRS Form 5500-EZ, Annual Return of One-Participant (Owners and Their Spouses) Retirement Plan. This annual form is brief and straightforward.

Some custodians of one-person 401(k) plans will offer to file Form 5500-EZ for you, at a modest fee, or give you thorough filing instructions at no charge.

Numbers game

The main reason you might want to adopt a one-person 401(k), though, is that in many situations such a plan can maximize your deductible contributions.

How it works: With a one-person 401(k), you can make both employer and employee contributions as well as additional "catch-up" contributions if you're at least age 50.

As an employer: You can make deductible contributions up to 25% of compensation.

Example: With $50,000 of covered income, your contribution may be as much as $12,500.

(If your self-employment income comes from an unincorporated business, the maximum employer contribution is about 20%.)

As an employee: You can defer compensation up to $15,000 in 2006.

The same compensation can be used to calculate both employer and employee contributions.

Catch-up contributions: If eligible, you can contribute another $5,000 in 2006.

Example: If you're 50 years old, with $50,000 of covered income from a corporation, total contributions in 2006 amount to $32,500, or an impressive 65% of compensation.

If your $50,000 came from an unincorporated business, the maximum contribution would be $10,000 as an employer (20% of $50,000) plus $15,000 as an employee plus $5,000 catch-up, for a total of $30,000.

Comparison: At that level of income, you could contribute no more than

$14,000 to a SEP, SIMPLE IRA, Keogh, or profit-sharing plan in 2006.

Up the income ladder: Suppose you have $150,000 in income from an owner-only business in 2006. You can contribute—and deduct—as much as $49,000 (the absolute limit) to a one-person 401(k) plan, regardless of whether your business is incorporated or unincorporated.

With that income, you could contribute no more than $37,500 to a SEP, profit-sharing plan, or Keogh in 2006. With a SIMPLE IRA, the maximum contribution would be only $17,000.

Bottom line: For most owner-only enterprises, you can maximize retirement plan contributions with a one-person 401(k) plan.

Flex plan: While you may contribute the maximum to a one-person 401(k), you can contribute less, or nothing at all, from year to year. You're not locked in to any level of contribution.

Spouses, too

A one-person 401(k) plan can cover you if your only employee is your spouse.

Moreover, these plans can include multiple business owners as long as there are no employees beyond owners and their spouses.

Required: Each owner and spouse must receive the same percentage-of-pay employer contribution.

Example: If you give yourself a 25%-of-pay employer contribution, your spouse must get the same, as must your co-owner and his/her spouse, if they're both on the payroll.

Exception: The above rule does not apply to salary deferral contributions. You might elect to defer $16,000 worth of your pay in 2006 while your spouse defers only $5,000 of pay.

Exclusions: What if you pay a neighbor's teenager to do some filing occasionally? No problem—you can exclude from the whole plan any employees who work fewer than 1,000 hours per year.

Caution: For your spouse to participate in your one-person 401(k), he must be on the payroll. This means that the government will collect payroll (Social

Security and Medicare) taxes and your state will collect any applicable state payroll taxes.

You must decide whether putting your spouse on the company payroll is worthwhile even considering payroll taxes. The greater your spouse's compensation, the larger the net financial benefit to your family.

Sidelines

As mentioned, you can have a one-person 401(k) plan, even if you are an employee somewhere, as long as you have self-employment income from a sideline business.

Trap: If you participate in a 401(k) from another job, your total salary deferral can't exceed the $15,000 ceiling in 2006 ($20,000 once you reach age 50).

Example I: Ann Brown, age 44, has a full-time job with no 401(k) plan. As a freelance graphic designer (a business she has incorporated), she also earns $20,000.

With a one-person 401(k), Ann can make a $5,000 employer contribution (25% of $20,000) plus a $15,000 salary-deferral contribution, thus sheltering most of her freelance income from tax.

Example II: Larry Williams, 44, also has a full-time job and $20,000 in income from an incorporated sideline business. However, he has elected to defer $7,000 worth of salary into the 401(k) at his full-time job.

Therefore, with a one-person 401(k), Larry can defer only $7,000 this year, bringing his total deferral to $14,000. He also can make a $5,000 employer contribution from his sideline business, bringing his total 2006 contribution to his one-person 401(k) to $12,000.

Combination plan

If you're interested in a one-person 401(k) plan, it must be established no later than the last day of the business's tax year. Many brokers, mutual fund companies, and other financial firms will help you get started.

Strategy: After you set up a one-person 401(k), consider rolling your other retirement accounts, including IRAs, into this 401(k). Having all of your tax-deferred accounts in one place may be a big help with portfolio management.

Source: Richard K. Newman, CPA, director and founder of Newman + Cohen Financial Management, 2500 N. Military Tr., Boca Raton, FL 33431. He is founder of The Institute for Retirement and Estate Planning, also in Boca Raton.

Chapter Twenty-Two
YOU CAN BUY REAL ESTATE WITH YOUR IRA

Something your stockbroker won't tell you—you can buy the retirement home of your dreams with your IRA.

Traditional and Roth IRAs can purchase all kinds of property, from homes to apartment buildings.

By owning real estate, you diversify away from stocks and bonds and keep ahead of inflation. Returns for real estate average 14% a year, versus the 12% 30-year average for stocks.*

Although banks and brokerage firms typically don't offer this alternative—it is costly to administer and doesn't generate trading commissions—it's easy to add a real estate strategy to your retirement plan.

Reasonable allocation now: 25% or more of your retirement assets.

Beware: If you buy a home for retirement, you can't live in it until you take its entire value as a distribution from your IRA after age 59½. Until then, rent it out to a permissible third party. Profits are reinvested in your IRA.

Case studies

• Residential property...

Harry dreamed of retiring to Galveston, Texas, near his brother. He bought a house there using money in his IRA.

Purchase price: $120,000.

Expenses: $4,500/year for taxes, insurance, utilities, etc.

*According to Ibbotson Associates, which used real estate investment trusts as a proxy for real estate.

Net operating income: $7,500/year (annual rent of $12,000 less annual expenses of $4,500).

Annual income: 6.25% (net operating income divided by the purchase price). Assuming that the home appreciates in value by 6% a year, Harry ends up with a 12.25% annual return.

Harry achieved his goal by renting out the house until retirement and then taking the house as a distribution from his IRA. His tenants moved out. He moved in and became the new owner instead of his IRA.

• Commercial property...

Steve's IRA purchased a building that housed a Pizza Hut restaurant in Malta, Montana. The tenant was three years into a 10-year lease with options to extend the lease for five years.

Purchase price: $325,000.

Expenses: Nominal. Utilities, taxes and insurance were paid by the tenant.

Net operating income: $30,000/year.

Annual income: 9.23%.

While Steve's income is at the low end of the average for commercial property (the range is 8% to 14% a year), Steve liked the security of the long-term lease. Costs also were contained because the tenant was responsible for most expenses. Steve got the building for less than the $350,000 asking price because he agreed to pay cash and was able to close quickly. He still owns this building.

Set up your program

Transfer your existing IRA or roll over money from a qualified plan—a 401(k) or a pension—to a special account called a self-directed IRA. It should be overseen by a custodian, such as a bank, which receives an annual fee of 0.5% to 1.5% of assets. Fees decline as assets increase.

My favorite custodians: Fiserv, 800-825-2501, *www.fiserviss-iaservices.com* ...PENSCO Trust Co., 800-969-4472, *www.pensco.com*.

You also will need a property manager to maintain and rent out the property to tenants. You are not legally permitted to manage it yourself because the

IRS considers you a "disqualified party."

Finance your purchases

Banks generally won't provide mortgages to IRAs because they can't seize IRA assets other than the property in the event of a default. If you can't afford to buy a property outright...

Ask the seller to finance the purchase.

Invest your money with others in a limited liability company (LLC). The LLC invests in the property. There are no restrictions on eligible investors. For instance, the LLC can buy the property with your IRA and/or your spouse's IRA as well as with non-retirement accounts belonging to you and your spouse.

Watch out for tax traps

If you want to rent to family members, consult a tax attorney. If you violate IRS rules, you will pay tax on the entire investment. IRS rules are tricky...

You cannot lease the property to parties that have been disqualified by the IRS, such as yourself, parents, children, spouse, grandchildren or their spouses. The law does allow you to lease the property to siblings, cousins, uncles and aunts. You also can name a sibling, etc., to manage the property. You pay that person a salary.

You cannot use IRA-owned property as collateral for a home-equity loan or line of credit.

You cannot use non-IRA funds to pay for expenses, such as insurance, taxes and repairs.

Exception: Legal fees. Make sure the property generates enough income to cover these costs. If necessary, you could transfer money from other IRAs to your self-directed IRA in order to cover expenses.

To keep legal fees down, only use an attorney to draw up and review documents, not to negotiate deals. It is best to pay legal fees with non-IRA money so that you can deduct the cost from your taxes.

If you move into the property after age 59½, you must take it as a distribution from your IRA and pay tax based on the current value of the property. Plan for the tax—it could be sizable. If the property is in a Roth IRA, you pay no taxes.

Choose your investments

Base real estate decisions on the amount of time you're willing to commit, your risk tolerance and the size of your IRA.

• Residential property...

Who it is good for: Conservative investors who want to secure their dream home now or purchase a home for an investment.

How it works: Since you will have to hire a property manager to take care of the property anyway, there is no reason to limit your search to your own neighborhood. Consider homes around the US.

• Commercial property...

Who it is good for: Investors who are willing to take more risk for higher capital appreciation.

How it works: You will need a commercial broker to help you select the potential investments—such as stores, office buildings, hotels and land.

For referrals to real estate agents, contact the National Council of Exchangors, a nonprofit organization, 800-324-1031, *www.infoville.com*.

Hire a firm that handles a well-maintained property in the area to manage your commercial property.

Cost: 4% to 10% of the annual rent collected.

There are good buys on commercial properties all over the US now. I recently purchased properties in California, Kentucky, Missouri, New York and Washington.

Source: Patrick W. Rice, licensed real estate broker and investment manager for more than 25 years. His firm, IRA Resource Associates, in Camas, WA, purchases properties for its clients' IRAs, *www.iraresources.com*. He is coauthor of *IRA Wealth: Revolutionary IRA Strategies for Real Estate Investment* (Square One).

Section 1: Retirement and Estate Planning

Chapter Twenty-Three
SURPRISINGLY HIGH TAXES ON SOCIAL SECURITY BENEFITS

Social Security recipients now can incur the highest tax rates of anybody. While the normal top tax bracket rate has been reduced to 35%, Social Security recipients may face effective marginal tax rates of 50% or more.

Why: Up to 50% of Social Security benefits become subject to income tax when adjusted gross income (AGI) exceeds $25,000 on a single return or $32,000 on other returns—and up to 85% of benefits are taxed when AGI exceeds $34,000 on a single return or $44,000 on other returns.

Example: A single individual with AGI over $34,000 will have an income range where every extra dollar of regular income causes $0.85 of Social Security benefits to be taxed as well—so tax becomes due on $1.85. If the individual is in the 28% tax bracket at that range, the extra dollar of income will generate 52 cents of tax (1.85 x 0.28 = 0.518)—an effective marginal tax rate of 52%. The rate may be higher when state taxes are counted. Also, check for state tax exemptions for Social Security benefits (visit *www.retirementliving.com*).

Twist: Interest on tax-exempt bonds is counted in AGI for this purpose—so even tax-free interest can cause Social Security benefits to be taxed.

What do to: Before you retire, learn the amount of your expected Social Security benefit and project your other income. Next, project your tax bracket situation with the help of IRS Publication 915, *Social Security and Equivalent Railroad Retirement Benefits*, available at *www.irs.gov*.

Then you can plan steps to reduce your future tax rate as your situation dictates. Possibilities...

• If you will keep working after your full retirement age, defer receiving your Social Security benefit to take a proportionately increased benefit later.

• Reduce AGI by taking capital losses and incurring business expenses.

• Defer cashing in investments and taking distributions from IRAs and retirement accounts until you need the money, or are required to take minimum distributions.

• Invest in appreciating assets rather than income-producing assets, and in tax-efficient mutual funds that pay minimal taxable distributions.

Source: Bob Carlson, editor, *Bob Carlson's Retirement Watch,* 3700 Annandale Rd., Annandale, VA 22003.

Section 1: Retirement and Estate Planning

Chapter Twenty-Four

A CASCADING BENEFICIARY PLAN FOR MAXIMUM IRA TAX DEFERRAL

For many people, an IRA is one of their largest (if not the largest) financial assets. A sizable IRA can help to finance a comfortable retirement.

Some people, though, will take only minimum required distributions from their IRA, relying on other sources of retirement income. Some IRA owners will die prematurely, before significant withdrawals are taken.

Result: In many cases, an ample IRA will be left to a beneficiary or beneficiaries. With proper planning, ongoing tax deferral can enrich your heirs.

A poor plan, though, may rob your beneficiaries of a prime wealth-building opportunity.

To set the stage for maximum tax deferral after your death, a cascading beneficiary plan may be ideal.

Ground rules: Your IRA will go to a designated beneficiary or beneficiaries at your death. No matter what you put in your will, that won't govern the disposition of your IRA. Therefore, it is vital that the proper paperwork is in place, outside of your will.

How it works: You probably keep your IRA with a bank, brokerage firm, mutual fund family, or insurance company that acts as the IRA custodian. This firm will have provided a beneficiary designation form when you opened the account, but you probably had to work with a small card that left no room for special provisions.

Trap: These standard forms are designed for the convenience of the IRA custodian. At many firms, thousands of IRA beneficiary forms are handled by relatively unsophisticated personnel.

Therefore, IRA custodians want to make things simple for their own people. Such simplicity, though, may not serve the interests of your loved ones after your death.

Strategy: To make the most of this extremely valuable asset, you must take an active role in selecting IRA beneficiaries. A cascading beneficiary designation can give your survivors more flexibility as well as a chance to build extraordinary amounts of wealth.

Required: You probably need to draw up your own beneficiary form, drafted by an attorney. On this form you can spell out your instructions in some detail.

Send this customized form to the IRA custodian and ask for a receipt acknowledging your instructions. Keep a copy of this paperwork with your will and let your IRA beneficiary know where it's located.

Exit strategy: If your IRA custodian refuses to accept your instructions, find a more cooperative custodian.

Dealing with disclaimers

Here's how a cascading beneficiary plan might flow...

1. Name your spouse as the primary beneficiary of the IRA. At your death, your spouse can claim the inherited IRA as his/her own and designate your children as the beneficiaries.

2. Name your children as secondary beneficiaries. This provides your surviving spouse with flexibility.

Example: At your death, your spouse has sufficient wealth from other assets, aside from your IRA. She decides that she won't need your IRA to live comfortably. In these circumstances, if you have named your children as contingent beneficiaries, your spouse can disclaim, that is, give up her interest in the IRA. Then your children will inherit your IRA.

3. Name your grandchildren as tertiary beneficiaries, in case your children as well as your spouse disclaim.

4. If you have great-grandchildren, you can add them to the list, in case your grandchildren disclaim.

Key: The person who disclaims can't direct the inheritance. He merely steps aside and the IRA goes to the next person in line, as specified on the beneficiary designation document.

Double play

The plan described above may have two advantages...

• Income tax deferral. Your children and grandchildren will have longer life expectancies than your surviving spouse. If your spouse decides that she can disclaim, the younger heirs can stretch out minimum required withdrawals over a longer period and get more benefit from the IRA's tax deferral.

• Potential estate tax reduction. Disclaiming the IRA will keep that account from being in your surviving spouse's estate. If your surviving spouse has ample assets, estate tax might be due at her death. Disclaiming the IRA will put the account into your taxable estate, but the overall estate tax bill may be lower.

Action plan

For this plan to work, each grandchild or great-grandchild must be individually named as a beneficiary. Ideally, you should revise your beneficiary form right after each birth, adding the newcomers by name.

Trap: You can't designate "grandchildren" or "great-grandchildren" as a class of beneficiaries. Individuals must be named, or you can designate a trust for certain individuals.

Strategy: The younger the beneficiaries, the greater the tax-deferred buildup. However, as long as some of the beneficiaries or contingent beneficiaries are minors, you should designate a trust as the IRA beneficiary and name the youngsters as beneficiaries of that trust.

Powerful payoff

Multigenerational IRA planning may allow you to leave a large legacy.

Example: Assume that Mark Rogers waits until age 70½ to begin to take IRA distributions and limits himself to the required minimum distribution.

Over the next 20 years, Mark and his wife, Nancy, who survives him, would take out only the required minimum distributions calculated under the current IRS tables.

Key: If the IRA earned more than the required distributions, they could leave the balance in the IRA to their two children, and it would continue to grow.

Loophole: For her 50% share of this inherited IRA, their daughter, Emily, can disclaim. Her own daughter, Ashley, as the contingent beneficiary, would immediately succeed her. Ashley would withdraw from the IRA over her lifetime.

Their son, Kevin, has health problems and elects to take only the minimum distributions from his 50% share over his life expectancy. With a subsequent beneficiary designation, Kevin's heirs can take distributions over Kevin's expected lifetime. Make sure your IRA custodian allows subsequent beneficiaries to an inherited IRA.

Bottom line: Thanks to the power of tax deferral and compound earnings, an IRA may provide to Mark, his spouse, and their descendants.

It's true that an IRA might earn less than the required distribution, which would reduce the amount passing to heirs.

Also keep in mind that all withdrawals will be subject to income tax at ordinary rates.

Nevertheless, this type of tax deferral plan can generate wealth and a stream of income for your heirs.

Generation-skipping tax

Leaving an IRA to grandchildren, outright or in trust, may trigger the generation-skipping transfer (GST) tax.

Trap: If a grandparent-to-grandchild IRA bequest is subject to estate tax and GST tax, most of the IRA's value may be lost to the tax collectors. The GST will apply if the IRA exceeds the GST exemption amount, which is $2 million in 2006.

Outcome: Even counting the effects of the GST tax, leaving your IRA to a grandchild still makes sense. That's especially true if the taxes can be paid from other sources, keeping the inherited IRA intact for tax-deferred future growth.

In essence, your family might be better off paying the GST now, on a relatively small amount. If you try to avoid the GST tax by leaving the IRA to a child rather than a grandchild, more estate tax may be paid later (at the child's death), on a larger amount.

Source: David S. Rhine, regional director, family wealth planning, Sagemark Consulting, a division of Lincoln Financial Advisors Corp., a registered investment adviser, 395 W. Passaic St., Rochelle Park, NJ 07662.

Section 1: Retirement and Estate Planning

Chapter Twenty-Five

401(k) ALERT—THE RULES HAVE CHANGED

With attention focused on possible changes in the Social Security system that might include scaling back benefits, especially for financially comfortable individuals, the need to increase personal savings is more important than ever.

401(k) plans, which are already used by more than 40 million employees, can achieve this.

New rules: Company owners should be aware of new regulations from the IRS and the Department of Labor that will impact decision making on 401(k) plans this year and for years to come.

Regulation update

At the end of 2004, the Treasury issued final regulations governing a number of rules for 401(k) plans. The new regulations are largely an endorsement of proposed rules issued in July 2003, which were intended to provide guidance on legislative changes that occurred over the decade.

The regulations are intended to simplify the rules, largely to encourage more employers to sponsor 401(k) plans—and to strengthen protection for rank-and-file employees.

The final regulations cover nondiscrimination rules. Plans must follow these rules to ensure that they do not favor highly compensated employees (those earning more than $100,000 in 2006). The regulations also cover matching and employee contribution requirements and the rules for SIMPLE 401(k) plans. Here are details on some of the key provisions...

- Automatic enrollment. The final regulations adopt the rules for automatic enrollment, a move that is helpful in avoiding discrimination. Automatic enrollment of employees in a plan is allowed as long as there is a reasonable time in which they can opt out if they desire.

The IRS has recognized that up to a 3% automatic contribution via an elective deferral from employee compensation is a "safe harbor." Employers can increase this percentage.

As a practical matter, automatic enrollment not only is a means to help ensure plan compliance, it's also a mechanism to increase the savings rate for employees, some of whom might otherwise fail to enroll because of a lack of understanding or simply inertia. This is a desirable result in view of the uncertainty of Social Security.

- Undoing high contributions. If highly compensated employees contribute too much, thus making a plan discriminatory, these employees—typically management—must take back excess amounts. The correction method is now changed to distribute first to those highly compensated with the largest deferral amount. Prior regulations were based on the highest percentage. Alternatively, to the extent that a highly compensated employee is eligible to make catch-up contributions, the deferrals may be characterized as such.

Disappointing: The final regulations do not include some provisions favored by employers.

Employers also had (prior to 2006) the opportunity to contribute separately to the lowest paid employees' accounts as a way to meet nondiscrimination tests— a practice called "bottom-up" or leveling technique. The new regulations have now greatly limited the ability to use this technique by limiting the contribution to 5% of pay.

Effective date: The final regulations apply for plan years beginning on or after January 1, 2006. However, plans can apply the regulations to any plan year ending after December 29, 2004, provided the plan applies all (and not just some) of the rules of the final regulations. A decision to implement the final regulations mid-year can be made only if the plan has already been operating in compliance with the regulations throughout the year.

Bottom line: The new regulations generally will not require comprehensive plan amendments, since many plans have already been operating in conformity with the rules. However, plan language should be reviewed with a pension expert to see where changes may be needed.

Savings opportunities

For 2006, the elective deferral limit for employees is $15,000. Those who will be at least 50 years old by December 31, 2006, can contribute an additional $5,000. While the contribution limits are generous, in most cases only highly compensated employees take full advantage of them. Lesser-paid participants typically wind up contributing only 3% to 6% of their compensation, despite the opportunity to save more.

Suggestion: Employers not using automatic enrollment can encourage employee savings with little or no downside to the company by permitting new employees immediate participation in the plan rather than having a waiting period of three months, six months, or more. This allows new hires to complete the necessary paperwork for plan participation at the same time they fill in other employment forms.

If an employer has a matching formula for company contributions, then immediate participation will entail some cost to the company—but this will generally be worthwhile because it improves the chances that a plan will pass nondiscrimination testing. Also, the employer may subject the matching contribution to a vesting schedule—meaning shorter-term employees may receive none or only a small portion of any employer contribution when they leave.

Employers can also allow employees to contribute salary raises and/or bonuses to the plan as long as employees have the right to receive these payments in cash.

Hardship withdrawals

While 401(k) plans are intended to provide retirement income, they can be written so that they can be tapped by employees facing financial hardship.

The final regulations expand the list of hardship situations. They had already included such events as buying a home and paying for medical expenses. Now they include paying for funeral expenses and home repairs. (The latter is welcome relief to employees with uninsured home damage due to a hurricane, mud slide, or other natural disaster.) Plan rules determine the requirements for hardship withdrawals.

Caution: A change in work status from employee to leased employee (someone who continues to perform work for the same company but is an employee of a leasing company) does not constitute a permissible hardship.

Matching contributions

Companies may contribute on behalf of employees up to a set amount or percentage of elective deferrals based on a percentage of compensation. Matching contributions are often used to encourage employee contributions in order for plans to avoid discrimination.

Many companies, particularly small employers, do not provide any matching contributions. They may, however, use profit-sharing contributions to share a company's good fortune in profitable years.

Fiduciary actions

The Department of Labor and the IRS are focusing more heavily on fiduciary activity (or lack thereof)—the actions that the plan administrator does or does not take. In small companies, the fiduciary is often the business owner. At larger firms, the fiduciary typically is an outside benefits firm.

Example: The government has begun to scrutinize obligations with respect to the selection of mutual funds into which employees can direct their contributions.

Fiduciaries are supposed to prudently select and monitor investment options within the plan. But just how much monitoring is required? For example, if a mutual fund is under federal investigation, should a fiduciary remove the fund from the investment menu? The Department of Labor says a fiduciary should look at the nature of the allegations, the potential impact on investments, and whether the fund has taken steps to avoid future abuses—and then decide on retaining or removing the fund.

Looking ahead: There are proposals to help employers provide investment information to employees without running afoul of the rule that bans fiduciaries from giving investment advice. For instance, one proposal would require employers to provide a summary of each investment option, detailing the characteristics of the investment, so that employees could make informed investment decisions.

The final regulations discussed earlier allow employers to use electronic notices to employees of their rights and obligations under the plan. In the future, similar notification may be extended to investment information.

Source: Peter Alwardt, CPA, president, Eisner LLC, 750 Third Ave., New York City 10017. His specialty is employee benefit plans and ERISA.

Section 1: Retirement and Estate Planning

Chapter Twenty-Six

RETIREMENT PLAN LOOPHOLES FOR BUSINESS OWNERS

Remember that retirement plans offer some of the best opportunities for tax savings, so plan ahead to make the most of them. Consider these strategies...

Loophole: Shelter business income with tax-deferred retirement plans. You can contribute up to $44,000 in 2006 to a defined-contribution plan using a formula of 25% of compensation. If you are self-employed, you can contribute the maximum to Keogh and simplified employee pension (SEP) plans using a formula of 20% of net business income.

Strategy: People who are older than age 45 should consider setting up defined-benefit plans. Because you fund a specific amount, and you have fewer years in which to do so, defined-benefit plans may permit larger contributions than those available in defined-contribution plans. In some instances, contributions can exceed $100,000 per person.

Loophole: Maximize your overall contributions by setting up a 401(k) plan. The maximum deduction for a 401(k) plan in 2006 is $15,000, and no percentage limitations apply to the contributions. For example, if you earn $20,000 from a sideline business, you can contribute all of it—$20,000—to retirement plans (25% of $20,000, or $5,000, to a defined-contribution plan for a corporation and another $15,000 to a 401(k) plan).

Loophole: Consider a SIMPLE retirement plan if your business earns about $40,000 or less. When your net income from a part-time or a start-up business is $40,000 or less, set up a savings incentive match plan for employees (SIMPLE).

Reason: You can put away the lesser of earned income or $10,000 and also make a matching contribution of 3% of net income. For example, with net income of $40,000, the match is $1,200 (3% of net income).

Loophole: A SEP plan is a good solution for people who will miss the deadlines for setting up retirement plans by the end of 2006. You can open a SEP by the extended due date of your 2005 tax return, retroactive to December 31, 2006. The maximum contribution to a SEP is $44,000 (for 2006), calculated at up to 25% of employee compensation. If you use percentages under 25%, the maximum compensation base is $220,000 in 2006.

Loophole: Catch-up contributions can be made for people age 50 and older. When you are age 50 or older, you can make catch-up contributions of $5,000 for 2006 to a SEP or 401(k), regardless of the plan's overall limits.

Loophole: Business owners can set up employee stock ownership plans (ESOPs), which are similar to qualified employee profit-sharing plans.

How they work: ESOPs allow you to take cash out of the company without paying tax and enable you to diversify your assets by investing in other domestic companies. Here are some of the basic rules...

• The employer makes annual contributions to the ESOP, usually with company stock.

• The contributions of stock are fully deductible by the corporation.

• Employees will be 100% vested in their accounts after three to seven years, depending on the plan's vesting schedule and whether the plan is top-heavy.

Loophole: An ESOP trust must be set up for the benefit of the company's employees, including the owners of the business and any family members who work for them. However, the main stockholders of the company can also be the trustees, so they control the voting of the stock in the plans.

Loophole: Business owners can sell their business to an ESOP without having to pay immediate tax on any profit.

How to do it: The ESOP borrows money from a bank to purchase stock from the controlling stockholders. As long as the controlling stockholders sell at least 30% of the stock of the company to the ESOP, they are permitted to make a tax-free rollover of the funds to purchase other companies' common stock. The rollover has to take place within one year of the transaction.

Key: No taxes have to be paid until the stockholder sells the replacement shares.

Bonus: If you die without selling any of the replacement shares, your estate gets a "stepped-up basis," meaning that no capital gains taxes are owed on the sale of the company stock.

Note: ESOPs are eligible stockholders of S corporations. Special rules apply to S-ESOPs, so check with your adviser.

Source: Edward Mendlowitz, CPA, shareholder in the CPA firm WithumSmith+Brown, 120 Albany St., New Brunswick, NJ 08901. He is author of *Estate Planning* (Practical Programs).

Section 1: Retirement and Estate Planning

Chapter Twenty-Seven
THE THREE KINDS OF JOINT OWNERSHIP

There are three forms that joint ownership can take...

1. Joint tenants with right of survivorship (JTWROS). Here, property automatically passes to the surviving co-owner/co-owners at the death of one owner. No other succession is possible.

Example: Nick Parker, age 93, names his nephew Andrew as joint owner of his bank and brokerage accounts, with right of survivorship. At Nick's death, those accounts will belong to Andrew, if he survives Nick. That's true even if Nick makes a will specifying a different outcome. JTWROS trumps a will.

2. Tenancy in common (TIC). With this form of title, each owner holds a share in the property. That share may be sold, bequeathed, or given away.

Example: Bill Smith and Carol Jones are not married. They live in a house that they own as TIC, with each owning one-half. In her will, Carol is entitled to leave her half of the house to Nancy, her aunt.

3. Tenancy by the entirety. This form of ownership is recognized by 27 states, sometimes only in regard to real estate held by a married couple. It's similar to JTWROS (one spouse can't pass his/her share to someone else), but in addition, it protects the property from creditors of either spouse while both are alive. While laws vary among states, creditors usually can't force the split of the property to get at one spouse's half.

Source: Sanford J. Schlesinger, Esq., a founding partner and head of the wills and estates department of the law firm Schlesinger Gannon & Lazetera LLP, 499 Park Ave., New York City 10022.

Section 2: Tax Strategies and Savings

Don't Miss These Tax Savers 101

Key Midyear Tax-Planning Moves for Your Business... 106

Like-Kind Exchange Loopholes 109

Tax Traps and Tax Savers for Gamblers 112

No Records? No Problem—You Can Still Rescue Big Deductions 116

For Richer or Poorer—Tax Planning with Marriage in Mind 120

Bankruptcy Rules 124

Best Strategies for Joint Ownership of Real Estate...
    Bank Accounts...Cars...Other Assets 125

How to Shelter Your Income from the IRS 129

How to Reduce Gain When Selling an Investment Property 133

Money-Saving Tax Moves to Make Now 134

Shrewd Ways to Use Your Home as a Tax Shelter 138

Very Valuable Tax Deductions Even If You Don't Itemize 141

Converting an IRA to a Roth IRA 144

Enjoy the Tax Rewards of Charity, Club and Union Memberships 145

Estimated Taxes...The Very Costly Trap for Those with Nonwage Income . . .149

How to Squeeze the Most Tax-Free Profit from Selling Your Home 154

Use Voluntary Withholding to Beat Penalties .157

Don't Let Your Corporation Own Real Estate .158

Section 2: Tax Strategies and Savings

Chapter One
DON'T MISS THESE TAX SAVERS

What's hot in every season? Tax breaks. While you make your vacation plans, do some tax planning as well.

For business travelers

Transportation costs are tax deductible if the primary purpose of your trip is business related.

Strategy: Say you would like to travel to New Orleans this summer. You can make plans to see customers, prospects, suppliers, etc., in that area. Or, if you travel to a convention in San Francisco, you might tack on a couple of vacation days before or after the program.

Tactic: Investigate where conventions for your industry or profession are being held. Then plan a trip to an attractive destination.

Key: The trip must be primarily for business for your travel expenses (such as airfare) to be fully deductible along with most, if not all, of your hotel bills.

Example: You take a four-day business trip. After four days of work-related appointments, you spend two days at the same hotel, swimming and sightseeing. Because you devoted more time to business than to pleasure, your airfare will be deductible. Other outlays (hotels, meals) may be written off for the business related portion of the trip.

Important: Keep a log to show that the first four days were focused on business. Retain copies of pre-trip correspondence arranging meetings, agendas for the conference, and post-trip follow-ups.

Loophole: If you have business meetings on, say, Friday and Monday, there's no need to go home for the weekend. You can spend Saturday and Sunday at the ballpark and still take the travel write-off, plus a portion of your other costs.

If you travel outside the US, you can write off 100% of your transportation costs if your trip was primarily for business and you were outside the US for a week or less. On longer foreign trips, a business-pleasure allocation may be necessary.

For you to deduct a second airfare for a spouse or significant other, your companion must be an employee of your company, with a business purpose for going along. However, even if your companion has no business purpose, any of the expenses incurred by him/her, such as lodging, cab fares, and car rentals, will effectively be deductible because you incur them for yourself.

For property owners

You can rent out your home (including a vacation home) for up to 14 days a year without having to report any rental income.

This may be a lucrative opportunity if you own a place near a major sports event. Residents of Boston and New York might command hefty rentals during the political conventions this summer.

Strategy: If you have a business or professional practice, rent your primary home or a second home to your own company for managers' or employees' meetings or retreats. Charge a rent comparable to what similar meeting space commands for short-term stays.

Add to that amount the price participants would have to pay for lodging and you have the total amount your company can pay you for the rental.

Payoff: Your company can take a deduction for a business expense, while the money you receive for this up-to-14-day rental need not be reported on your personal tax return.

If you have a vacation home that you rent out for more than 14 days a year, all the income must be reported (you can't exclude the 14 days).

Loophole: If the home is considered rental property, business expenses may offset rental income.

Required: For a vacation home to be rental property, either...

• Your personal use of the home is no more than 14 days and you rent your vacation home more than 14 days, or...

• Your personal use is more than 14 days, yet this personal use is no more than 10% of rental days.

Loophole: If you have a tax loss from rental property, it may be deducted immediately, depending on the amount and sources of your income, or carried forward and deducted when you sell the property.

For parents

When school is out, you may have to pay for child care so that a parent can go to work or be a full-time student.

Loophole: Such outlays can qualify for a dependent care credit.

Limits: As much as $3,000 that you spend on one child under age 13 will qualify. For two or more children that age, the maximum is $6,000.

Covered: Home care, day care, day camp tuition. Not covered: Overnight camp.

What it's worth: If your family's adjusted gross income (AGI) is more than $43,000, the credit rate is 20% (lower incomes get a credit rate as high as 35%).

Example: You and your spouse both work. Your joint AGI is $100,000. This summer, you send your two young children to day camp. The first $6,000 is eligible for a 20% credit, which cuts your tax bill by $1,200 (20% of $6,000).

Loophole: Extra savings might be available if you or your spouse can participate in an employer's flexible savings account (FSA) that covers dependent care. Up to $5,000 can be contributed to the FSA and used for dependent care expenses tax free.

Doing the math: If your tax bracket is at least 25% (over $61,300 in taxable income on a joint return in 2006), you're better off using an FSA to pay for child care.

Example: You spend $10,000 on day camp. The first $5,000 can be paid from an FSA. In a top 35% bracket, you'll save $1,750 (35% of $5,000).

Using $5,000 from the FSA reduces the amount you can use for the dependent care credit from $6,000 to $1,000. Then, your dependent care credit would save you another $200 (20% of $1,000).

For employers

Loophole: Hire your children or grandchildren while they're out of school. You'll get a deduction for wages at rates up to 35%, while your children pick up untaxed income.

Key: Your child or grandchild can earn up to $5,000 in 2005 without owing any federal income tax. That number, equal to the standard deduction for single taxpayers, rises each year, with inflation.

Example: You hire your teenage daughter to help with your sole proprietorship this summer, and she earns $3,000. If you're in a 35% tax bracket, you cut your federal income tax by $1,050 (35% of $3,000), while your daughter won't owe any tax.

Required: You must pay your children a reasonable wage for work they actually perform. Keep records to support your tax deductions if they're questioned.

Even very young children may do simple tasks, such as running errands and helping with office paperwork. Plus, they'll gain valuable insights into what it takes to earn spending money.

Continuing education

If you take courses, some tax breaks may be available. As long as the education maintains or improves skills related to your trade/business, costs incurred are deductible, just as they are if the education is required by law or by your employer to keep your current position.

Key: This tax break had been heavily used by teachers, who would claim that travel itself is educational. Now, the educational travel must be work-related.

Example: Bob Smith, who teaches English literature at the local high school, goes to London on his summer vacation to study at the British Museum and take a course on Dickens that's offered nowhere else.

Bob can deduct his airfare, lodging costs, direct educational expenses, and 50% of his away-from-home meal costs.

Floor: All those costs fall into the category of miscellaneous itemized deductions, which are deductible only to the extent that they exceed 2% of AGI.

Source: Sidney Kess, attorney and CPA, 10 Rockefeller Plaza, New York City 10020. Mr. Kess is coauthor/consulting editor of *Financial and Estate Planning* and coauthor of *1040 Preparation and Planning Guide, 2006 Edition* (CCH). Over the years, he has taught tax law to more than 710,000 tax professionals.

Chapter Two
KEY MIDYEAR TAX-PLANNING MOVES FOR YOUR BUSINESS

Business owners devote most of their time to handling day-to-day problems, leaving little time for long-range planning. But planning as early in the year as possible is the key to tax savings—this year and in the future. Midyear is a great time to get started for year-end.

Meet with advisers

Tax advisers are swamped at the end of the year dealing with clients' problems and providing last-minute advice. To avoid the rush, schedule an appointment with your adviser now. You'll have plenty of time to mull over the strategies he/she recommends to improve your business and save taxes.

Cash-flow planning

Sales, more than anything, drive your taxes. The more you sell, the more you'll owe in taxes. Calculate your projected sales for the year now. It may be desirable to book some sales into 2006, rather than 2007.

Example: Assuming you sell your goods or services on 30- to 90-day terms, your accounts receivable on sales made now will be collected in the last quarter of 2006. Use this information to project your cash flow needs for the remainder of the year to...

• Calculate year-end bonuses, if bonuses are a goal. Don't wait until the last minute to decide what you'll pay—you may not have the cash to meet your goal.

• Pay estimated taxes. If you're a self-employed individual or an owner of a pass-through entity, such as an S corporation, the third installment of estimated tax on your share of business profits is due on September 15, 2006. (The fourth installment is due on January 16, 2007.)

For calendar-year C corporations, the third installment of estimated tax is also due on September 15, but the fourth and final installment is due on December 15, 2006.

Equipment purchases

If your business is showing signs of recovery, now may be a great time to upgrade your equipment. Two key tax breaks can help you offset the cost...

• First-year expensing. This gives you an immediate deduction of up to $108,000 in 2006 on equipment purchases (subject to limitations).

While equipment purchased at the end of the year can still qualify for these tax breaks, you may need lead time.

Reason: These breaks depend on when equipment is "placed in service," not the date it is purchased. Special-order equipment may take months to be delivered, so consider placing these orders now.

Expensing and bonus depreciation don't depend on when you pay for the equipment. You can finance their cost and receive a full tax break this year even though you pay for the items over several years (subject to at-risk limitations).

Retirement plans

You still have time to set up a qualified retirement plan to cover yourself and your employees for 2006. But the earlier you select which plan is best for your situation, the more options you'll have.

For example, small businesses that want to use savings incentive match plans for employees (SIMPLEs) for 2006 must set them up no later than October 1, 2006. This early setup date applies because you must give notice to your employees of their right to participate.

For profit-sharing, 401(k), and other qualified retirement plans, the setup deadline for 2006 is December 31, 2006. If you opt for a defined-benefit pension plan, setup isn't so simple and may require some time, so give yourself leeway.

Note: Setting up a plan before the end of the year does not obligate you to fund the plan at that time. You generally have until the extended due date of your return to make contributions for the year.

Bonus: If you don't yet have a qualified plan and set one up for 2006, you may qualify for a tax credit of up to $500 per year for three years for qualified start-up costs or administrating the plan and educating employees about participation rules. You can even opt to apply the credit to the prior year (2005) and obtain a tax refund by filing an amended return if the original return has already been filed.

Source: Jeff Chazen, CPA, partner, financial services group, Eisner LLP, 750 Third Ave., New York City 10017.

Section 2: Tax Strategies and Savings

Chapter Three
LIKE-KIND EXCHANGE LOOPHOLES

You can defer tax on real estate transactions under Tax Code Section 1031, which permits tax-free rollovers when investment or business properties are exchanged for "like-kind" property.

Examples: You pay no tax when you swap a motel in Virginia for an apartment building in Sacramento because this is considered a "like-kind" exchange. You can also exchange a warehouse or a piece of vacant land for an office building tax free.

Here are some of the smartest ways to use real estate swaps...

Loophole: Vacation homes may be eligible for tax-free rollover treatment. While personal residences and other noncommercial real estate cannot be swapped tax free under Section 1031, you may be able to do a tax-free rollover of a vacation home.

To qualify, you must hold the property for investment. You must prove that your personal use of the vacation home was only nominal. Under Tax Code Section 280A, "nominal use" means that you can't have used the property yourself for more than 10% of the days that the property was rented out to others in one year, or more than 14 days in a year. If you meet these criteria, the vacation home is not considered a "personal residence," and is thus eligible for 1031 treatment.

Loophole: Vacation homes that have been used too frequently by the owner to qualify for tax-free rollover treatment can be converted to eligibility. To achieve this, you must rent out the property for a minimum of one year before the tax-free exchange. During that year, you may use the property yourself only nominally. (See Tax Code Section 280A definition above.)

The vacation home (or other investment realty) that you receive in an exchange can be converted to personal use, typically after three years, based on IRS decisions in audits of these types of transactions. Once you do that, the property can become eligible for the home-sale exclusion for personal residences under Code Section 121.

Loophole: A portion of "mixed-use" property can be swapped tax free. For example, you occupy one apartment in a building that you own, and you rent out the rest. The portion of the value of the entire building that is allocated to commercial use is eligible for a tax-free rollover (the part allocated to personal use is ineligible).

Loophole: When you swap like-kind property, you can defer the entire gain if you properly structure the transaction. To do so...

• You must reinvest into the new property the entire equity received from the sale, and...

• Your debt on the new property must be equal to or greater than that on the old property.

Note: If the values of the properties are unequal, any extra cash you receive may be taxable, and any amount you pay can be added to the basis of the replacement property.

Loophole: You can "identify" more than one replacement property for purposes of the tax-free exchange. When you structure a Section 1031 transaction, you can "identify" on the legal forms a maximum of three properties of any fair market value as replacement property for the tax-free swap. Because exchanged property must be identified within 45 days, this gives you flexibility and time to decide which specific property will be swapped.

Alternative: To give yourself even more flexibility, you can identify an unlimited number of properties, if they have an aggregate fair market value of no more than 200% of the aggregate fair market value of the properties that you are giving up.

Loophole: Consider a "Reverse Starker" exchange to facilitate the tax-free swap. Say the property you want becomes available but you can't immediately exchange your own property. You can do the tax-free swap anyway by using a "Reverse Starker" exchange under IRS Revenue Procedure 2000-37. The guidelines call for a "qualified intermediary" (like an escrow agent) to acquire title to the replacement property.

Benefits: The "Reverse Starker" exchange gives you more time to complete your transaction. It can also let you acquire replacement property before you give up your own property.

Loophole: You can increase (or create) depreciation deductions on property you receive in a tax-free exchange.

Examples: You exchange a fully-depreciated building for one that is not fully depreciated, or you exchange nondepreciable land for a building that can be depreciated.

Source: Edward Mendlowitz, CPA, shareholder in the CPA firm WithumSmith+Brown, 120 Albany St., New Brunswick, NJ 08901. He is author of *Estate Planning* (Practical Programs).

Section 2: Tax Strategies and Savings

Chapter Four
TAX TRAPS AND TAX SAVERS FOR GAMBLERS

Recreational gambling is more popular than ever in venues ranging from casinos to state lotteries and charity raffles. But winning wagers can be more costly tax-wise than most people realize. Learn the tax rules in advance to avoid paying more than you need to...

Tax traps

The basic tax rule of gambling is that winnings are taxable income while losses are deductible on an itemized tax return only up to the amount of winnings reported.

Income tax trap: Large winnings are reported by the payer to the IRS on Form W-2G, Certain Gambling Winnings. Included...

• Winnings of $600 or more that are at least 300 times the size of the bet (such as a $600 payoff on a $2 racetrack ticket).

• $1,200 or more from slot machines or bingo.

• $1,500 or more from keno.

But losing wagers aren't reported and many casual gamblers don't keep track of them.

They thus risk owing a big tax bill on a lucky win in spite of having net losses from gambling for the year—due to not having proof of the losses.

Worse: Winnings also increase adjusted gross income (AGI) and so can affect other items on your return. Examples...

• Social Security benefits may become subject to higher taxes due to increased AGI.

- Deductions that are allowed to the extent that they exceed AGI "floors" will be reduced.

Included: Miscellaneous itemized deductions (for such items as investment expenses and employee business expenses) are deductible only to the extent that they exceed 2% of AGI...medical expenses, 7.5% of AGI...and casualty losses, 10% of AGI.

- Total itemized deductions generally are reduced by 3% of the amount by which AGI exceeds $150,150 in 2006—so gambling winnings may push you over the AGI threshold (though gambling losses are not subject to reduction).

State tax trap: In addition, wagering outside the state you live in can result in multistate tax liability. Tax is incurred where income is earned, so you must file a return there.

Example: Residents of New York who win money in Atlantic City must file a New Jersey state tax return. Those who wager in several different states may have tax filing and payment obligations in each.

Snags: Generally, one's home state will provide a tax credit for taxes paid to another. But rules vary by state—and credits aren't always provided for out-of-state taxes paid on all kinds of income—so check the rules in your home state.

Also, if the state where your winnings are earned has a higher tax rate than your home state, you won't get a full credit for the tax paid there.

Example: A person from Florida who has winnings in Atlantic City and pays tax to New Jersey on them can't get an income tax credit in Florida for them, since Florida has no income tax.

Self-defense

The high tax cost of gambling winnings makes it vital to document all losses, small and large, from the start of a year if you expect to have any chance of winning a payoff large enough to be reported to the IRS.

Most regular gamblers have net losses, of course, so with adequate records, they can legitimately take all their winnings tax free.

And if you are lucky enough to hit a jackpot that makes you a real net winner for the year, your record of offsetting losses may substantially reduce the tax on it.

What to do: Keep a contemporaneous record, such as a diary, of your gambling expenditures. Record all losing wagers no matter how small—everything from money spent on school raffles and lottery tickets on up. Keep documentation to support your entries.

Trap: A record of losses pulled together only after hitting a big winning wager will likely be unpersuasive to the IRS. Moreover, losing tickets are not proof of losing wagers because anyone can collect losing lottery tickets, raffle tickets, or racetrack betting slips.

Instead, keep proof of expenditures by paying for wagers by check or credit card, noting on the checks and charge receipts exactly what they are for and keeping them in your files.

In addition, use the gambling house's own record-keeping system when possible.

Examples: Some casinos now provide cards that record your wagering for use with slot machines. Some racetracks now sell "cash cards" for making racing wagers. Resulting records will be more persuasive to the IRS than claiming you spent cash out of your pocket.

Also, casinos keep track of the spending of their regular customers to determine how much to provide them in "comps" (such as free rooms and meals) to encourage their continued patronage. If a casino has such a record for you, you can obtain it. Concentrating your gaming in one casino instead of spreading it around several may help you ease your record-keeping burden—as well as receive more comps.

Important: Keep your diary honest and comprehensive. If it includes a large number of losing wagers but no winning wagers other than the ones big enough to be reported to the IRS, the IRS and Tax Court are likely to find it unbelievable. All winning wagers must be reported as taxable income, including the small ones.

114

Tax payment

• **Paying and withholding.** Large winning bets are subject to income tax withholding of 25%. These include payoffs of more than $5,000 from any sweepstakes, wagering pool, or lottery, as well as payoffs 300 times or more the amount of a bet.

Winnings from bingo, keno, and slots are not generally subject to withholding. But when you win a large amount, you must provide the payer (casino, etc.) with your Social Security number so it can report your winnings to the IRS. If you do not, the payer will withhold tax from the amount it gives you.

• **Noncash prizes.** If you win a non-cash prize—such as a car, boat, or vacation—of $5,000 or more in value, it is subject to withholding even though there is no cash involved to be withheld. Moreover, the payer of the prize may require you to provide the cash needed to cover withholding.

Saver: If your diary shows you have offsetting wagering losses so you won't owe any tax on your winnings or prize, you can safely reduce your wage withholding or estimated tax payments to offset the withholding on the winnings or prize, and not be out-of-pocket any tax on net.

Source: Laurence I. Foster, CPA/PFS, consultant, and former partner at Eisner LLP, 750 Third Ave., New York City 10017. Mr. Foster was chairman of The Personal Financial Specialist Credential Committee at the American Institute of Certified Public Accountants.

Chapter Five

NO RECORDS? NO PROBLEM— YOU CAN STILL RESCUE BIG DEDUCTIONS

A lack of records proving your business expenses when an IRS auditor asks for them need not be fatal to those deductions.

If you can show that the expenses must have been incurred, they may remain deductible under the "Cohan rule"—named after the famous Broadway producer George M. Cohan and the case in which he was able to deduct his expenses although he had not kept records to prove them.

How to make the "Cohan rule" work for you...

Famous deductions

The Cohan rule arose in 1930 when—as the court that heard the case related—"...Cohan was obliged to be free-handed in entertaining actors, employees, and, as he naively adds, dramatic critics...These expenses amounted to substantial sums, but he kept no account."

When the IRS questioned Cohan's deduction for these expenses, he admitted he hadn't kept records of them, but also said it was obvious that he had incurred them and that his estimate of their cost was fair.

The IRS in turn admitted that Cohan had incurred a large amount of such expenses but said that because he hadn't kept records of them he could not deduct any of them. Cohan went to court.

Court's ruling: "Absolute certainty in such matters is usually impossible and is not necessary...to allow nothing at all appears to us inconsistent with saying that something was spent...there was basis for some allowance, and it was wrong to refuse any." So Mr. Cohan got his deductions. [Cohan, 39 F.2d 540.]

Since then, Congress has changed the law to require that specific records be kept to deduct meals and entertainment, business use of autos, and the use of "listed properties"—personal computers located in places other than an office, and similar electronic items that are readily put to personal use. So, the Cohan rule no longer applies to these.

Apart from these few exceptions, the Cohan rule is still in effect to hold that expenses that must have been incurred by a business remain deductible in spite of a lack of records documenting them.

Modern times

Today's deduction-saving power of the Cohan rule was shown in the recent case of Carroll Furnish, who ran a contracting business as a self-employed individual.

Furnish's accountant died and the accountant's wife threw out all the business's records—and then the IRS auditor called. The IRS disallowed $500,000 —virtually all—of Furnish's deductions because he couldn't document them. Furnish was reduced to selling his car to pay another lawyer to handle his case, and when that money ran out, he represented himself before the Tax Court.

Court: Furnish was able to obtain records from third parties—contracts, invoices, and so on—to prove he ran a real business as he claimed, one which must have incurred expenses. The deductions he had claimed were reasonable in amount for such a business. The loss of his records had not been his fault. And his testimony was "honest, forthright, and credible." So more than 98% of the $500,000 of deductions that the IRS had disallowed were restored. [Carroll R. Furnish, TC Memo 2001-286.]

Guidelines to using the Cohan rule...

While the rule holds that undocumented expenses that must have been incurred are deductible, the amount of such expenses has to be estimated—and the IRS and courts have a great deal of leeway in estimating how much "must" have been incurred. They may allow many claimed expenses or only a few. The Furnish case shows the keys to getting the best result...

• The Cohan rule is not a blanket substitute for record keeping. Furnish had kept full records but lost them due to a factor not under his control. In such a case, the courts are much more sympathetic than when a taxpayer is negligent about keeping records.

If records simply haven't been kept, expect a much smaller deduction through the Cohan rule than if records were kept but lost.

• Third-party records save deductions. If your own records are lost, records from third parties may document expenses that your business incurred. Examples...

☐ Payroll tax records obtained from the IRS prove wages paid.

☐ Leases can show amounts paid for real estate and equipment rentals.

☐ Phone bills show how much was paid for phone service if the phones weren't cut off.

☐ Invoices can indicate how much was paid for inventory and other items.

Example from my practice: A retail store located near the World Trade Center on 9/11/01 was forced to relocate after the disaster, in which it lost most of its records.

By using third-party records, we reconstructed its expenses, and by prorating limited surviving checking records over the entire year, we showed corresponding expenditures. The IRS has had no problem with this.

• Personal credibility is vital. The fact that the Tax Court found Furnish's testimony to be "honest, forthright, and credible" was key to its allowing almost all his $500,000 of claimed deductions.

Even when a lack of records is your own fault, if you present the best records you can in as good order as possible, and are honest, cooperative, and believable, the IRS may allow you more than your records support.

Example from my practice: An individual sold coins for $250,000 while reporting he had paid $150,000 for them, resulting in a gain of $100,000—but in an IRS audit, his records supported a total cost of only $75,000 for the coins.

Still, he was able to provide the auditor with records for numerous individual purchases of coins dating back more than 20 years, and did so in a very organized manner.

On this evidence, the IRS concluded it was reasonable to believe paper records of other purchases had been innocently lost over the long period. Thus, while the lack of records was the individual's own fault, he had acted in good faith and the coins probably had cost more than was proven.

So the IRS increased his cost basis in the coins by one-third to $100,000 —less than he had claimed, but $25,000 more than he had records to show.

Limits

Remember that the Cohan rule today does not apply to meals and entertainment, or to auto driving deductions—major expenses for many businesses, and for which diary-type records are necessary.

If you lack records for these, to have any hope of saving deductions for them, you must show that proper records were kept and lost due to factors beyond your control. In that case, the IRS may allow deductions for items it believes you incurred—but only at its discretion. You cannot invoke the Cohan rule to require it to do so.

But generally for other deductions that lack documentation, whether due to accident or carelessness, the Cohan rule remains a valuable deduction saver.

Source: Martin S. Kaplan, CPA, 11 Penn Plaza, New York City 10001, *www.irsmaven. com.* He is a frequent guest speaker at insurance, banking, and financial-planning seminars and author of *What the IRS Doesn't Want You to Know* (Wiley).

Section 2: Tax Strategies and Savings

Chapter Six

FOR RICHER OR FOR POORER— TAX PLANNING WITH MARRIAGE IN MIND

Marrying creates a tax situation that can either increase or decrease taxes significantly.

Marital status on the last day of the year applies for tax purposes for the entire year. This means that late-in-the-year marriage can have a retroactive effect—changing tax bracket rates and available deductions for the entire year.

It also creates a timing opportunity—if marriage will reduce taxes, then getting married by December 31 can cut the full year's tax bill. But, if marriage will increase taxes, delaying marriage until next year will avert a tax increase this year. Key tax effects of marriage...

• The marriage penalty. The so-called "marriage penalty" increases the tax owed by two individuals who have approximately the same amount of taxable income when they marry each other.

This is due to tax bracket rates being higher on a joint return at income levels lower than twice the levels on a single return. So when individuals with similar incomes add them together on a joint return, they are likely to be subject to a higher top bracket rate than on a single return.

The marriage penalty has been reduced, but not eliminated, by the *Jobs and Growth Tax Relief Reconciliation Act of 2003*. It expanded the 15% tax bracket and the standard deduction on a joint return to cover twice the amounts they do on a single return.

This eliminates the penalty for moderate-income taxpayers (up to $61,300 on a joint return in 2006) who don't itemize deductions. But the penalty continues to exist at higher tax brackets, which still apply on joint returns at less than twice the level on single returns. Examples...

☐ The 28% tax bracket begins at $74,200 on a single return but at $123,700 on a joint return.

☐ The 33% tax bracket begins at $154,800 on a single return but at $188,450 on a joint return.

☐ The 35% tax bracket begins at $336,550 on both single and joint returns.

The marriage penalty can also have an effect through itemized deductions. Some deductions are allowed only to the extent that they exceed a percentage of adjusted gross income (AGI).

And, itemized deductions generally are reduced by 3% of the extent to which AGI exceeds $150,150 on either a joint or single return in 2006.

So increasing AGI can reduce these deductions as well.

• IRAs and retirement accounts. If only one spouse has earned income, marriage increases allowable deductible IRA contributions by permitting the spouse with earned income to make a contribution of up to $4,000 in 2006 for the nonworking spouse.

However, converting a regular IRA to a Roth IRA is allowed only when AGI does not exceed $100,000 on a single or joint return—so combining two incomes to total more than that amount will make a conversion impossible.

Beneficiary traps: Deduction limits for employer-sponsored plans such as 401(k)s aren't affected by marriage—but beneficiary designations may be. Federal law generally requires a spouse to be a plan participant's beneficiary unless the spouse waives his/her rights—so marriage may have the unexpected effect of changing beneficiaries. Examine your plan beneficiary designations with an expert.

• Social Security benefits. These are subject to marriage penalty–type taxation. Up to 50% of benefits are taxable if "provisional income" (basically AGI, tax-exempt income, and half of Social Security benefits) exceeds $25,000 on a single return or $32,000 on a joint return—less than twice the single-return amount. Up to 85% of benefits are taxed if income exceeds $34,000 on a single return or $44,000 joint.

So combining incomes on a joint return may increase the tax on Social Security benefits.

• Personal residences. Marriage may save tax on the sale of a highly appreciated home. A single person can take up to $250,000 of gain tax free on a home if he owned it and lived in it as a principal residence during at least two of the prior five years.

But for a married couple, the maximum tax-free gain is $500,000—and only one spouse need be owner of the home, though both must meet the two-year residency requirement. If you married someone who has used the exclusion within the previous two years, that person's exclusion would not be allowed and the couple would be limited to $250,000. Tactics...

☐ If one spouse owns a home that has appreciated in value by more than $250,000, sell it after marrying and after both spouses have lived in it for two years. You can even do this sequentially with two homes, selling the second at least two years after the first.

☐ When an unmarried couple has lived together for two years in a home owned by one of them, they can marry and then sell the home immediately for up to $500,000 of tax-free gain. In fact, they can even sell the home before they marry, so long as they marry by December 31. They meet the requirements because they filed a joint return for the year, one of them owned the house, and they both used it as their residence for the two years—even if they weren't married while they did.

• Estate tax. When one spouse owns significant assets and the other doesn't, marriage can increase the amount of their total wealth that will escape estate tax, by permitting use of two personal "exempt amounts."

An individual can leave $2 million in assets free of estate tax in 2006. So if one single person has $3.9 million of assets and another has $100,000, the wealthier person faces estate tax on $2.4 million. But if the two marry, they can equalize their estates (such as by using tax-free marital gifts) at $2 million to eliminate all estate tax.

After marrying, they can also use tax-free joint gifts (up to $24,000 per recipient annually) to make larger estate-reducing transfers to the younger generation than one could while single ($12,000 per gift).

Adjusting

The retroactive effect of a marriage that occurs well into the year can produce either a surprise big tax bill or a tax overpayment that you may have to wait months to have refunded.

Best: Calculate the tax effects of marriage beforehand. Then, if you are sure you will marry, modify your estimated and withheld tax payments before you marry, to make the smoothest possible adjustment for year-end liabilities.

Source: Laurence I. Foster, CPA/PFS, consultant, and former partner at Eisner LLP, 750 Third Ave., New York City 10017. Mr. Foster was chairman of The Personal Financial Specialist Credential Committee at the American Institute of Certified Public Accountants.

Section 2: Tax Strategies and Savings

Chapter Seven
BANKRUPTCY RULES

The new bankruptcy act, signed into law by President Bush on April 20, changes the treatment of tax obligations in personal bankruptcy.

Old law: Bankrupt individuals filing under Chapter 13—the old "wage earner" repayment plan—could obtain a discharge of tax obligations in certain situations.

Example: Under the old law, if you did not file a return, you might qualify for discharge.

New law: Taxes are not dischargeable in bankruptcy.

The new bankruptcy act does, however, contain some protection for most funds in Section 529 college savings plans and Coverdell education savings accounts, something completely missing under prior law.

Source: Barbara Weltman, Esq., small-business expert and author of *J.K. Lasser's Small Business Taxes* (Wiley). One of her books is *The Complete Idiot's Guide to Starting an eBay Business* (Penguin). *www.barbaraweltman.com.*

Chapter Eight

BEST STRATEGIES FOR JOINT OWNERSHIP OF REAL ESTATE ...BANK ACCOUNTS...CARS... OTHER ASSETS

Holding assets—such as bank accounts, securities, or real estate—jointly is common, especially among married couples. Joint ownership also may be used by cohabitants and elderly individuals who want a younger person to be able to pay bills, handle investments, etc.

There probably will be income, gift, and estate tax consequences of joint ownership. Here are the rules...

Income tax

If income-producing property is held jointly by a married couple filing a joint tax return, the income tax consequences are straightforward—the couple owes tax on the income.

But what if the married couple files separate returns? Or if the co-owners aren't married and thus can't file a joint return?

Typically, the income will be taxed 50-50 between the joint owners.

If the funds in a joint account belong to one person, that person's name is listed first on the account, along with his/her Social Security number. If the joint account contains combined funds, each person's share of any income from the property is determined by state law.

Example: Sam Miner has put his niece Sarah's name as joint owner with right of survivorship on his bank and brokerage accounts so that she can help manage his affairs if it should become necessary.

Sam and Sarah should make sure that Sam's Social Security number is the one on the account, so that each annual Form 1099 reports income taxable to Sam, not to Sarah.

Gift tax

Putting a spouse's name on property as joint owner won't trigger gift tax because spousal gifts are untaxed. The situation is different for nonspouses and non-US-citizen spouses, though.

Generally, putting someone's name on an account won't trigger a gift if assets aren't withdrawn by the noncontributing joint tenant. (There may be exceptions under some state laws.)

Adding a joint tenant to real estate becomes a taxable gift if the new joint tenant has the right under state law to sever his interest in the joint tenancy and receive half of the property.

Example: As above, Sam puts Sarah's name on his accounts. As long as Sarah leaves those accounts alone, no gift is incurred.

Trap: Say that Sarah takes $20,000 from Sam's bank account. A gift tax return may have to be filed and gift tax might be owed.

Strategy: Sarah should keep careful track of her use of Sam's assets. If she writes a $20,000 check to an assisted-living facility, for example, to provide care for Sam, no gift will have occurred.

On the other hand, if Sarah writes that $20,000 check to buy a car for herself, that will be a gift from Sam unless she can show that the car was used solely for Sam's care.

Caution: Joint accounts owned by unmarried couples are potentially troublesome. Suppose, as above, Bill Smith and Carol Jones are unmarried but living together. Bill earns the income, which goes into a joint account.

Trap: Every check that Carol writes might be considered a gift if she uses the funds to pay for her personal expenses. That's true even if Bill writes checks to pay for personal items Carol has charged on a credit card.

This problem isn't easy to resolve if Carol spends more than $11,000 from the account on herself—that's the annual gift tax exclusion for 2005.

Strategy: Keep careful records of all expenses from joint accounts. Money that is used for common expenses generally won't be considered a taxable gift.

Estate taxes

Property held as "joint tenants with right of survivorship" (JTWROS) must go to the survivor. This might create estate tax problems.

Example: Dan and Ellen Collins are married and have $4 million in assets. Everything is owned as JTWROS. They are also the beneficiaries of each other's retirement accounts.

If Dan dies in 2006, everything will pass to Ellen, who will now have a $4 million estate.

Trap: This arrangement prohibits them from leaving anything to other heirs, including their children, upon Dan's death. Thus, they won't be able to use the federal estate tax exemption, set at $2 million for 2006 to 2008.

Suppose, in our example, Ellen dies in 2007 with the $4 million estate. That would be $2 million over the exemption amount, taxed at 45%, so the federal estate tax bill would be $900,000.

That tax could have been avoided with a $2 million bequest at Dan's death in 2006. That bequest might have gone to their children, for example, or to a trust structured to benefit Ellen but be out of her estate.

Strategy: Families with estate tax concerns should modify their use of joint ownership between spouses. Each spouse should have some assets in his own name that can be left to other parties or to a trust at the first death, sheltered by the estate tax exemption.

Capital gains tax

When assets pass from a decedent to heirs, estate tax is not the only concern. Under current law, appreciated assets get a step-up in basis as of the date of death. (An alternative valuation date, six months later, also may be used for all estate assets, if this produces a lower estate tax.)

This step-up can eliminate capital gains tax.

Example: Ed Russell owns $1 million in stocks and stock funds, held outside of retirement plans. His basis in those securities is $200,000.

A sale during Ed's life would result in an $800,000 capital gain and a $120,000 tax bill, assuming all the securities qualify for the 15% rate on long-term gains.

Assuming no predeath sale, if Ed owns those securities by himself and leaves them to his wife, Phyllis, she'll have a stepped-up basis of $1 million. She could sell them after his death for $1 million and owe no capital gains tax.

Trap: If Ed holds these stocks as JTWROS with Phyllis, they will all pass to her at death but only half (Ed's half of the joint account) will get a basis step-up, giving her a $600,000 basis ($500,000 in his half and $100,000, or half the original cost basis, in her half).

As a result, a sale for $1 million would produce a $400,000 capital gain ($1 million minus her new $600,000 basis) and a $60,000 tax bill, at 15%.

Strategy: Highly appreciated assets might be held in sole name rather than jointly, to get a full basis step-up.

The rules are a bit different in the states with community property laws (Arizona, California, Idaho, Louisiana, Nevada, New Mexico, Texas, Washington, and Wisconsin). A spouse can leave his half of community property to a nonspouse. But, if community property is left to a spouse, the spouse who inherits might be able to get a full basis step-up.

In the above example, if they live in a community property state, Phyllis may get a $1 million basis on the securities she holds, after inheriting Ed's half.

If so, she can sell the shares after Ed's death for $1 million and owe no capital gains tax. Check with a professional adviser to see if specific actions (such as putting community property in writing) are necessary in your state to qualify for a full basis step-up.

Source: Sanford J. Schlesinger, Esq., a founding partner and head of the wills and estates department of the law firm Schlesinger Gannon & Lazetera LLP, 499 Park Ave., New York City 10022.

Section 2: Tax Strategies and Savings

Chapter Nine
HOW TO SHELTER YOUR INCOME FROM THE IRS

In tax planning, even just a few dollars in the wrong place can cost you thousands.

How to preserve tax breaks, including those made more generous by recent tax legislation...

Shelter personal income

Ways to reduce AGI if you don't own your own business...

• Defined-contribution plans. If your employer sponsors a 401(k) or similar salary-deferral plan, contribute the maximum—$15,000 in 2006...$20,000 if you're age 50 or older.

Even if your employer doesn't match your contributions, putting the maximum allowable amount in a 401(k) reduces your AGI and expands your eligibility for other tax benefits.

• Deductible IRAs. If your employer does not sponsor a retirement plan, you can deduct a $4,000 contribution to a traditional IRA in 2006—$5,000 if you're age 50 or older.

If you participate in your employer's retirement plan, you can make a fully deductible IRA contribution if your 2006 AGI is $75,000 or less on a joint return ($50,000 single). Smaller deductible contributions are allowed for AGIs of up to $85,000 ($60,000 single).

• Capital losses. Up to $3,000 of net capital losses can be deducted each year. Additional losses can be carried forward indefinitely.

Example: Near year-end, you tally your investment trades for the year and discover a $2,700 gain. Sell enough holdings to generate $5,700 worth of losses for a deductible $3,000 net loss.

• Tax-free income. If you are in a high tax bracket, choose municipal bonds, tax-managed mutual funds and growth stocks—which don't pay dividends—instead of investments that raise your AGI with large amounts of interest and dividends.

Helpful: Keep only emergency funds in bank accounts and money market funds to reduce taxable income and monthly interest payments. Use any surplus to pay down credit card balances.

Shelter social security income

Even moderate-income seniors may find some or all of their Social Security subject to income tax—but there are ways to reduce it.

Whether benefits are taxable depends on your "provisional income." To calculate it, total...

• Your AGI.

• Tax-exempt interest income from municipal bonds and bond funds.

• One-half of annual Social Security benefits.

Example: With AGI of $20,000, tax-exempt income of $5,000 and annual Social Security benefits of $12,000, provisional income is $31,000 ($20,000 + $5,000 + $6,000).

No Social Security benefits are counted as taxable income if provisional income is up to $32,000 married, filing jointly ($25,000 single).

Up to 50% of benefits are included if provisional income is more than $32,000 ($25,000 single).

Up to 85% of benefits are included if provisional income is greater than $44,000 ($34,000 single).

Use these tools to safeguard Social Security benefits from Uncle Sam...

• Tax-deferred annuities. Even with the recent tax-law change, these provide a shelter that is not subject to income limits. They make sense for people who have maxed out retirement plan contributions and want to build more savings for retirement.

Two types of annuities...

• Fixed. An insurance company provides a guaranteed rate of return for a certain period. You might invest $50,000 and get a 5% guarantee for one year. After a year, your account balance will be $52,500 and a new—usually lower—interest rate will be set.

• Variable. These don't offer a guaranteed return. Instead, they allow you to invest in mutual fund–like accounts with higher potential returns and risks. Look for low commissions and no surrender fees (payments to the annuity issuer if you sell before a certain period).

• Loans. Borrowing allows you to generate cash flow without boosting taxable income. Consider these options...

☐ Tap a home-equity line of credit or a margin account.

☐ Take out a reverse mortgage.

☐ Refinance your home or investment property.

☐ Borrow against your home or cash-value life insurance, such as whole life or variable universal life. Make sure tax savings offset your interest payments.

Shelter business in me (even a sideline business!)

Opportunities to trim your AGI are greatest if you or your spouse is a business owner. Deductions...

• Health insurance. All of premiums paid by self-employed individuals (as well as by owners of S corporations and limited liability companies) became deductible.

• Retirement plans. Many plans offer rich writeoffs for those with business income.

Simplified employee pension (SEP-IRA) plans. You can deposit up to $44,000 in 2006, pretax, with these small-business IRAs. To set one up, fill out a simple form at a mutual fund firm or other institution.

Defined-benefit pension plans. These types of plans can provide even higher deductions than a SEP if you're in your late 40s or older. Rules are complex.

Consult a professional adviser.

• Children on the payroll. You can deduct the salaries of your children and grandchildren on your Schedule C, and they will owe no tax on up to $5,150 in earned income in 2006.

• Equipment. Up to $108,000 worth of expenses for business equipment may be written off in 2006, subject to income limitations.

Tax breaks for everyone

These strategies provide generous tax breaks regardless of income...

• Tax-deferred annuities. Again, you are taxed when you withdraw the money—but at that point, you are likely to be retired and in a lower income tax bracket. There is a 10% penalty on withdrawals made before age 59 ½.

• Permanent life insurance. These policies have high premiums, so they make sense only if you need life insurance for many years—for instance, if you are the sole breadwinner in a family with a disabled child. Cash value grows tax-free. After a buildup period, you or your beneficiaries can tap it via tax-free withdrawals and loans against the cash value of your policy.

• College savings plans. Consider these options...

Section 529 college savings plans. In most states, you can set up plans for yourself, your child, grandchild, other relatives and friends. Some states, including New York and Missouri, allow you to deduct contributions from state taxes. There's no federal income tax deduction for contributions, but investment income is tax-free if used for education expenses.

If the money is withdrawn to pay higher-education expenses, no tax will be due.

More information: Visit *Savingforcollege.com*, or check with your state's department of education.

Coverdell education savings accounts (ESAs). Officially, married couples with AGIs of more than $190,000 ($95,000 single) can't make a full contribution.

Loophole: If you're over the limit, give money to relatives in a lower bracket or even to your children, who then can use it to contribute up to $2,000 per year to Coverdell ESAs. There are no deductions, but the investment grows tax-free.

Source: Sidney Kess, attorney and CPA, 10 Rockefeller Plaza, New York City 10020. Mr. Kess is coauthor/consulting editor of *Financial and Estate Planning* and coauthor of *1040 Preparation and Planning Guide, 2006* (CCH). Over the years, he has taught tax law to more than 710,000 tax professionals.

HOW TO REDUCE GAIN WHEN SELLING AN INVESTMENT PROPERTY

When you sell a real property, you may realize a capital gain—the amount by which the proceeds you receive exceed your cost basis in the investment.

Don't just take the sale price and subtract your original purchase price to figure your gain. Adjustments that reduce gain...

•Basis can be increased by expenses incurred when you bought the investment —such as commissions, appraisals, legal fees, closing costs, recording fees, and similar purchase-related expenses. And note that for an inherited property, the basis is the fair market value at time of death.

You can also add the cost of any improvements made to an investment property while you owned it.

So record all purchase-related expenses when you buy an investment and keep a record of all improvements you make to it while you own it.

• From the sale price you receive you can subtract the cost of advertising and other expenses incurred to attract a buyer, as well as sale-related expenses such as fees, commissions, and legal expenses.

Remembering to adjust both basis and sale price by these items will boost the amount you keep after taxes.

Source: Peter Weitsen, CPA/PFS, shareholder in the CPA firm WithumSmith+Brown, 120 Albany St., New Brunswick, NJ 08901.

Chapter Ten

MONEY-SAVING TAX MOVES TO MAKE NOW

Don't wait until year-end to start planning your taxes. By taking these steps now, you can cut your tax bill for 2006 and future years...

• Max out your retirement plan. Contribute the maximum to your 401(k) or other employer-sponsored retirement plan this year. You can defer tax on up to $15,000 in contributions to a 401(k), 403(b), 457 or similar defined-contribution plan. If you'll be at least 50 years old by year-end, you can contribute another $5,000. Over a period of 10 years, that extra $5,000 could grow, tax-free, to almost $7,400, assuming an annual return of 7%.

While 2006 contributions to IRAs can be made until April 16, 2007, and contributions to SEP, up to the extended due date of the return, 401(k) contributions must be made by the end of this year for a 2006 tax benefit.

• Create a Savings Incentive Match Plan for Employees (SIMPLE) account if you're self-employed or run a sideline business. You can make SIMPLE as well as 401(k) contributions. SIMPLE plans are desirable if you'll have a small amount of self-employment income this year. You can contribute (and deduct) up to 100% to a maximum of $10,000. People age 50 or older can contribute an additional $2,000. Other small-business retirement plans usually permit no more than a 25% contribution. To get SIMPLE write-offs for 2006, you must set up a plan by September 30. They can be established at most financial institutions.

• Evaluate estimated tax payments. If you file estimated taxes, your third payment is due September 15. By then, you should know your total 2006 income.

Safe harbor: If your payments through the third quarter are at least 100%

of your 2005 tax liability, you are protected from a penalty by a "safe harbor" rule, even if you end up owing more tax because your income increases. If your adjusted gross income (AGI) was more than $150,000 in 2005, the requirement rises to 110%.

Example: Filing jointly, you and your spouse had a total AGI of $180,000 in 2005 and owed $30,000 in taxes. To reach the safe harbor, your estimated tax payments through the third quarter must be at least $33,000—110% of $30,000.

If you don't have enough withheld from your paychecks, you must send the balance to the IRS in quarterly estimated payments to qualify for the safe harbor.

Trap: If you make larger payments in the year's last two quarters, you could owe a penalty for underpayments in earlier quarters. To avoid this, have more tax withheld from paychecks near year-end. Income tax withholding is treated as if it were paid evenly throughout the year.

Loophole: If tax owed for 2006 will be lower than it was in 2005, you can pay less withholding and estimated tax this year and avoid a penalty if total payments are at least 90% of your 2006 obligation.

• Profit from losses. Stocks are struggling, and with interest rates rising, bonds sold before maturity may have lost value. If you have losses, consider selling securities or funds to take tax deductions.

Loophole: You can deduct up to $3,000 of capital losses in excess of capital gains from wages, pension, interest and other higher-taxed income in 2005. Additional losses then can be carried forward to future years.

Example: You end the year with $20,000 in losses in excess of capital gains (not paper losses). You can take a $3,000 deduction in 2006 and carry forward the other $17,000. The excess losses can offset future gains—up to $3,000 per year—effectively making those gains tax-free.

Trap: If you sell a security and buy it back within 30 days, the loss won't count. This is known as the "wash-sale rule." To avoid it, wait at least 31 days to buy back the same security. If you want to remain invested throughout the process...

• Purchase a similar but not identical security. For example, take a loss on a large-cap growth fund, and immediately buy another large-cap growth fund.

- Buy new shares of the stock you wish to sell. Then wait more than 30 days, and sell the original lot. To use this strategy this year, you must purchase the duplicate lot before November 30.

- Be smart about school bills. If you plan to sell appreciated securities to pay a child's college tuition this fall, give the securities to the student, who then can make the sale.

Advantage: Your child will have to report the capital gain, but he/she will be in a low bracket and owe tax at a 5% rate, not your 15% rate. In 2006, a married couple can give up to $24,000 in assets to each of any number of recipients, without owing gift tax.

- Fund an Education Savings Account (ESA). While 529 savings plans are worthwhile for funding higher education, unless your state provides a tax deduction, it's better to first fund a Coverdell Education Savings Account (ESA). The limit is $2,000 per year per student. There are income limits for ESAs. Married couples with incomes over $190,000 can't make a full contribution. If you're over the limit, you can give money to children, grandchildren, etc., who can contribute to their own ESAs.

Benefits: Like 529s, ESAs permit income to accumulate tax-free. Withdrawals are tax-free if the money is used for certain education-related expenses. But ESAs have advantages over 529s...

- Withdrawals may be used for a range of education expenses, such as tuition, room and board, uniforms and computer equipment, beginning in kindergarten. 529s must be used for college costs.

- You have complete control over how the money is invested. 529 investment options are selected by their sponsors.

- There is no time limit for tax-free withdrawals. Tax-free withdrawals from 529 plans are scheduled to expire after 2010, though Congress may extend them.

- Pay a parent's expenses. If you support a parent—even if he/she lives elsewhere—you might be able to claim him as a dependent. In 2006, you can deduct $3,300 for each dependent, whether or not you itemize. In the 25%

federal tax bracket ($61,300 to $123,700 in taxable income on a joint return), a $3,300 deduction saves you $825. There may be state tax savings as well.

To claim a dependency exemption for a parent, several tests must be met but these are the two toughest...

• You must provide more than half of your parent's support, and...

• Your parent's gross income must be less than $3,300. Gross income does not include untaxed Social Security benefits or interest on tax-exempt investments.

Strategy: Track your parent's expenses carefully—food, medical care, etc.—and make sure that you pay more than 50% of them during the year. If your parent lives in your home, put a value on the housing you supply.

• Ward off the AMT.* Increasingly, middle-income taxpayers are encountering the alternative minimum tax (AMT). If you are subject to the AMT this year, you will lose federal deductions on state and local taxes as well as miscellaneous itemized deductions.

Strategy: Postpone AMT income. For example, defer the exercise of certain types of stock options or don't make early payments of real estate and state income tax around year-end, since they are not deductible for AMT purposes. AMT planning is complex. Arrange a midyear meeting with your tax preparer to discuss strategies.

Source: Bob D. Scharin, JD, editor of *Warren, Gorham & Lamont/RIA's Practical Tax Strategies*, a monthly journal for tax professionals, New York City. He has edited leading tax publications for more than 20 years.

*AMT is a tax that an increasing number of Americans must pay instead of regular tax. You must calculate your tax with and without AMT and pay the higher amount. Especially vulnerable: People with many dependents, high state income tax or high miscellaneous deductions.

Section 2: Tax Strategies and Savings

Chapter Eleven
SHREWD WAYS TO USE YOUR HOME AS A TAX SHELTER

From a tax perspective, there's never been a better time to own a home. Here are four loopholes to take advantage of...

Short-term ownership

The home-sale exclusion is one of the most generous tax breaks in the Internal Revenue Code. Married couples can avoid tax on up to $500,000 in capital gains ($250,000 for a single person). This break can be used over and over.

To get it, you have to have owned the home and used it as your principal residence for at least two of the five years before the sale. Most people, however, don't realize how easy it is to use the exclusion even if you don't meet this two-year test.

Loophole: If you had to move out of a house before the two years were up because of an "unforeseen circumstance," you still can get a partial tax break. Unforeseen circumstances are defined liberally. They include, for example, natural disasters, a change in employment or becoming self-employed, divorce or legal separation, and multiple births from the same pregnancy.

How it works: Say you are promoted—or even demoted—at work. This is considered a change in employment, so you can sell your house and take a partial tax break even if you don't satisfy the two-year test. The same is true if you start, change or discontinue a business.

Example: You want to move from an appreciated property in which you have lived for less than two years. Before selling, you start a simple home-based

138

business. Assuming that you sell the house after living in it for one year, you would get half of the maximum tax break because one year is half of two. You and your spouse could exclude up to $250,000 (half of $500,000) of any gain on the sale. A single filer could exclude up to $125,000 (half of $250,000).

Home-office deduction

Some people don't deduct depreciation for a home office because they think it will cause them to owe tax on the gain allocated to the office when they sell the home. This is not the case.

Loophole: As long as the home office is part of your house—and not a separate structure—you will get the full principal-residence capital gains exclusion.

How it works: If you have taken a depreciation deduction for the office portion of your residence, you need to "recapture" the depreciation when you sell the home.

Example: If you have taken $10,000 of depreciation and are in the 25% bracket, you would owe $2,500 in tax—25% of $10,000—when you sell the home. You can keep whatever is left of the $500,000 or $250,000 exclusion on gains.

Paying less tax now (by depreciating) is worth more than the cost of recapturing depreciation later. For rules on depreciation, see IRS Publication 946, *How to Depreciate Property*, available by contacting 800-829-1040, *www. irs.gov.*

Asset protection

In these litigious times, it's easy to imagine someone tripping on your driveway and suing you, putting your home and other assets at risk.

Strategy: To protect your home from creditors, transfer it to a single-member limited liability company (LLC). This isn't necessary if you live in states with "unlimited homestead protection"—where equity is protected—such as Texas and Florida as long as you don't file for bankruptcy within 40 months of establishing residence.

Loophole: Under new regulations, home owners who make such transfers still will be entitled to the mortgage interest deduction and capital gains exclusion. There can be only one owner, perhaps you and your spouse holding the title as joint tenants. You don't need to file an additional business tax return for the LLC.

Divide and conquer

You may be able to sell part of your property at a profit and still get the benefit of the capital gains exclusion.

Example: Your home sits on 40 acres. A developer buys 39 acres, from which you make a $300,000 profit. A year later, you sell the house and the remaining acre for an additional $150,000 profit.

Loophole: According to the Treasury Department, you can take the full $500,000 or $250,000 capital gains exclusion on the combined gain if you complete the "split sale" within two years.

In this example, the total $450,000 gain ($300,000 plus $150,000) would be tax-free, provided the house was sold within two years of the prior sale of the land and all other conditions were met.

Source: Diane Kennedy, CPA, a tax strategist for more than 20 years, D. Kennedy & Associates, certified public accountants, Phoenix. She is coauthor of several books, including *Real Estate Loopholes: Secrets of Successful Real Estate Investing* (Warner Business).

Chapter Twelve

VERY VALUABLE TAX DEDUCTIONS EVEN IF YOU DON'T ITEMIZE

Many taxpayers don't take common deductions—for mortgage interest, charitable donations and medical expenses. The reason? They don't "itemize" by claiming these or any other expenses on Schedule A of Form 1040.

It's easy to see why. For many people, the standard deduction—$10,300 for couples filing jointly...$5,150 for single taxpayers in 2006—is higher than the total of their itemized deductions, so they're better off taking the standard deduction.

There are several smart ways to boost your tax savings even if you don't itemize and instead take the standard deduction. A number of so-called above-the-line write-offs are available. Common examples...

Individual retirement accounts (IRAs)

In 2006, you can contribute up to $4,000 to an IRA ($5,000 for those age 50 and older). Roth IRA contributions are never tax-deductible, but there are situations in which you can deduct contributions to a traditional IRA...

• If you are not covered by an employer-sponsored retirement plan.

• If your income is under certain thresholds, even if you are covered by an employer-sponsored retirement plan. Single filers must have incomes of less than $50,000 in 2006 to be eligible for a full IRA write-off. Lesser deductions are available for those with incomes up to $60,000. For joint filers, the limits are $75,000 and $85,000, respectively.

• If your joint income is under $150,000 and only one spouse works. The nonworking spouse can take this deduction even if the working spouse is covered by an employer-sponsored retirement plan.

Health savings accounts (HSAs)

HSAs, created under the 2003 Medicare drug law, became effective in 2004 and continue to grow in popularity.

How HSAs work: They are IRA-like accounts that can be used to pay health-care expenses.

Contributions: To deduct your contributions to an HSA, you must be covered by a high-deductible health plan and not covered by Medicare. The annual deductible on health insurance in 2006 must be at least $1,050 ($2,100 for joint filers).

You can contribute up to the amount of your policy's deductible, to a maximum set by the IRS.

Example: With a $1,050 deductible, you can put as much as $1,050 per year into an HSA.

If you are age 55 or older by year-end, you can contribute $700 more than the policy deductible. The maximum HSA contribution for 2006 is $2,700...or $5,450 for those with family coverage. If you have an HSA, you still can contribute to an IRA, a 401(k) and a flexible spending account at work.

Withdrawals: Withdrawals can be made tax-free from the HSA to pay medical bills. Unused HSA money can be carried over to subsequent years to grow tax-deferred, through investments in mutual funds, stocks, bonds, etc.—potentially for decades. Money withdrawn before age 65 that is not used for health-related purposes is subject to income tax and a 10% penalty. After age 65, you pay only income tax. (For more information on HSAs, see IRS Publication 969, *Health Savings Accounts and Other Tax-Favored Health Plans* at *www.irs.gov*.)

Student-loan interest

You can deduct up to $2,500 worth of interest paid on student loans this year, regardless of how many students there are in the family and whether the loan financed higher education for you, your spouse and/or a dependent.

Alimony

Alimony is 100% deductible for the payer and is considered taxable income for the recipient. If you're the payer, you'll have to provide your former spouse's Social Security number on your return so that the IRS can check on the resulting tax collection.

Moving expenses

If you move because of a new job or for other business reasons, certain expenses are deductible—costs to transport household goods and personal effects as well as your travel to the new residence. This includes lodging but not meals. To qualify, your new workplace must be more than 50 miles farther from your old home than your former workplace was from your old home.

Early withdrawal penalties

If you cash in a bank CD, any resulting penalty can be deducted.

Special write-offs for the self-employed

Self-employment retirement plans. If you have self-employment income, even from a sideline business, several types of retirement plans are available, among them SEP, SIMPLE, individual 401(k) and Keogh plans. Contributions to these plans are deductible regardless of whether you itemize. For rules on deducting these contributions, see IRS Publication 560, *Retirement Plans for Small Business*, available by calling 800-TAX-FORM or visiting *www.irs.gov*.

Self-employment tax. The bad news is that self-employed individuals must pay both the employer's and the employee's share of Medicare and Social Security taxes. The good news is that you can deduct half of those payments even if you don't itemize.

Self-employment health insurance. You can deduct 100% of health insurance premiums that you pay for yourself, your spouse and your dependents. The amount you deduct can't exceed your self-employment income.

Source: Mary Wilson, CPA, JD, senior tax manager, Rothstein Kass, an international accounting and consulting firm in Roseland, NJ. *www.rkco.com*.

CONVERTING AN IRA TO A ROTH IRA

Converting a traditional IRA to a Roth IRA by year-end is a can't-lose strategy.

Key: The value of the traditional IRA (minus the amount of nondeductible contributions to it) is taxed in income on the conversion. If you expect the value of the IRA to rise, it's better to make the conversion now rather than later.

But if the value of the IRA falls after the conversion due to poor investment returns, you can revoke the conversion as late as October 15 of the following year—and make another conversion at lower tax cost.

This is a unique situation since the IRS lets you make an election with hindsight—effectively giving a choice of times to make it on the best terms.

Source: Ed Slott, CPA, editor, *Ed Slott's IRA Advisor*, 100 Merrick Rd., Rockville Centre, NY 11570.

Chapter Thirteen

ENJOY THE TAX REWARDS OF CHARITY, CLUB AND UNION MEMBERSHIPS

American Express's slogan, "Membership has its privileges," applies to taxes, too. Membership fees and ancillary costs for organizations and associations are often fully deductible.

Charitable organizations

Belonging to a charitable organization and working for your favorite cause may entitle you to a write-off if you itemize deductions. Make sure the organization is IRS-approved. Tax-exempt organizations are listed in IRS Publication 78, *Cumulative List of Organizations*, available by calling 800-829-3676 or visiting *www.irs.gov/charities* (click on "Search for Charities"). Expenses not to overlook...

• Dues. Fees paid to be a member of a charitable organization usually are fully deductible. This includes dues to churches and synagogues.

Exception: The portion of dues that entitle you to goods or services (other than token amounts) is not deductible. For instance, if you pay dues to your public broadcasting station and receive a DVD of a special program (valued at $20), the amount deductible is the dues minus the value of the DVD. The organization is required to provide donors with an estimate of the value of goods and services received if the dues exceed $75.

If the dues are $75 or less, you can deduct the entire amount and disregard any membership benefits, as long as they are restricted to privileges that can be exercised frequently, or are items worth only token amounts.

145

Examples: Free parking, discounts on gift shop merchandise, admission to members-only events if the cost of attendance is treated as a "low-cost article" ($8.60 or less in 2006), a mug or totebag.

- Mileage. If you use your car to do volunteer work or attend meetings, you can deduct 14 cents per mile, plus tolls and parking.

- Unreimbursed expenses. If you do volunteer work for a charity, you can deduct out-of-pocket expenses. Examples...

☐ Convention expenses to represent your charitable organization. If you are not an official delegate to the convention, but merely an attendee, you may not deduct travel costs, meals, or lodging. However, you can deduct related expenses incurred for the benefit of the organization.

☐ Fund-raising costs you incur to host an event, such as invitations, food, and beverages.

☐ Long-distance phone calls on behalf of the charity.

☐ Travel expenses to do volunteer work. For instance, Red Cross volunteers who travel to a disaster site...or Habitat for Humanity volunteers who travel to work sites.

Caution: No deduction can be claimed if the trip involves a significant amount of pleasure, recreation, or vacation—before, during, or after the volunteer work.

☐ Uniforms, supplies, and equipment used to do volunteer work, such as a hospital volunteer's uniform.

Exceptions: Not every expense you incur for charity is deductible. You may not write off...

☐ The value of your time. For example, an attorney who bills at $250 per hour who does some legal work for his church may not deduct what he would normally charge for this activity.

☐ The rental value of your home when you allow an organization to use it in its fund-raising activities. For instance, if your organization auctions off a week's stay at your beach condo, you cannot deduct what you could have charged in rent.

☐ Baby-sitting costs you incur in order to perform your charitable works.

Business clubs and associations

You may deduct dues to business and professional organizations that further your business. These include...

• Business organizations. Business leagues, trade associations, chambers of commerce, boards of trade and real estate boards, and business luncheon clubs.

• Professional organizations. Bar associations, medical associations, and state CPA societies.

• Civic organizations. Kiwanis, Lions, Rotary, and Civitan.

• Union dues. These include initiation fees and assessments for unemployment benefits if payment is required as a condition of remaining in the union. No deduction is allowed for voluntary payments to union unemployment or strike funds, mandatory contributions to a union pension fund applied to buy an annuity, or assessments for a construction fund to build a union recreation center.

Caution: If you are an employee, the dues are miscellaneous itemized expenses deductible only to the extent total itemized expenses exceed 2% of your adjusted gross income. If you are the sole proprietor, use Schedule C to deduct dues. If your company is an S corporation, use Form 1120S, US Income Tax Return for an S Corporation.

Tax law prevents you from deducting certain dues and fees, even though there is a business element to the cost. These include...

☐ Airline clubs.

☐ Athletic clubs.

☐ Country clubs.

☐ Hotel clubs.

☐ Social clubs.

Special rules for country club dues: While country club dues are not deductible, the cost of business entertainment at the club can be deducted.

Example: Greens fees and cart rentals for a round of golf with a client may be deductible.

If a business pays club dues for an employee, the business can turn what would otherwise be a nondeductible expense into a deductible one by treating the payment as additional compensation to the employee. This deduction option applies only if the club is used for business so that the cost of membership would have been deductible but for the ban on deducting the dues.

If the employee uses the club solely for personal recreation, the business cannot treat the dues as compensation.

Note: The employee cannot claim a personal deduction by treating the costs deemed to be compensation as unreimbursed employee business expenses.

Source: Lisa N. Collins, CPA/PFS, former vice president and director of tax services, Harding, Shymanski & Co., PSC, Evansville, IN. She is author of *The Complete Idiot's Guide to Tax Deductions* (Alpha).

Chapter Fourteen

ESTIMATED TAXES...THE VERY COSTLY TRAP FOR THOSE WITH NONWAGE INCOME

If you have nonwage income, you'll probably owe tax over what you'll pay through wage withholding. If so, you are required to pay this tax through quarterly estimated tax payments or additional withholding—or face underpayment penalties.

Here's how to avoid estimated tax underpayment penalties at the end of this year and minimize the burden of quarterly taxes throughout 2006...

Equal in size

Nonwage income includes...

- Investment income.
- Business income.
- Rents from real estate holdings.
- Gambling winnings.
- Distributions from an IRA or pension plan.
- Taxable Social Security benefits.
- Income from any other non-salary source.

When your total tax bill for the year exceeds the amount of tax paid through withholding by $1,000 or more, you must pay estimated taxes.

To avoid underpayment penalties, estimated tax payments must be large enough so that when combined with wage withholding they total at least...

- 90% of the final tax bill shown on the year's tax return, or

• 100% of the tax that was owed for the prior year (110% if the prior year's adjusted gross income exceeded $150,000 on a single or joint return, $75,000 if married filing separately).

The four quarterly estimated tax payments generally also must be equal in size—if you make three small payments followed by a big, final "catch-up" payment, the early payments will be subject to underpayment penalties, though an exception to the "equal size" rule is noted below.

Payments are due on April 15, June 15, September 15, and January 15 following year-end.

The penalty for underpayment is the IRS interest rate, which changes quarterly and is 7% for the fourth quarter of 2005. Payments are made by filing the IRS Form 1040-ES voucher, *Estimated Tax for Individuals*, or electronically through the IRS's Electronic Federal Tax Payment System (EFTPS).

Note: Electronic tax payment offers several advantages—less paperwork, far fewer misdirected payments and paperwork mistakes, fast proof of payment, ability to make payment 24 hours a day, seven days a week, and ability to program payments to be made up to a year in advance.

Helpful: To learn about managing your taxes electronically, visit *www.irs.gov* and click on the EFTPS logo.

Year-end complications

While the basic rules for estimated taxes are simple, applying them can be difficult if, for example, you aren't supplied the information you need. So review your situation before year-end to be sure you won't incur underpayment penalties or make an interest-free loan to the IRS by overpaying tax. Traps to beware of...

• Lack of information. This can be a serious problem, especially for investors in pass-through entities (partnerships, S corporations, and limited liability companies).

The income of such entities is taxed directly on the tax returns of their owners—they must provide for tax on the income through their own personal estimated tax payments.

Snags: Investors in a pass-through entity may not know the amount or nature of the income that will be passed through to them, even near year-end. If management doesn't inform them of the entity's tax situation, they'll be unable to manage their estimated taxes correctly.

This problem is becoming more common as pass-through entities become the most popular form of organization for real estate investments, family investment partnerships, and private businesses.

Important: It's not just the amount of income that passes through to investors that matters, but the kind. The income may be in the form of tax-favored capital gains and dividends, for example. Even the kinds of deductions that are passed through can matter. For instance, large deductions for state and local taxes or accelerated depreciation may result in an investor incurring the alternative minimum tax and unexpected liabilities.

Safety: The managing partners of pass-through entities should estimate the final tax situation well before year-end, providing time for investors to make year-end moves accordingly. If you are a passive investor in such an entity and haven't received such information, ask for it now. If you manage and control your own business as a proprietorship or pass-through entity, be aware of its tax situation to date.

• Year-end income. If you unexpectedly receive a substantial amount of income—such as from an investment gain or lottery win—late in the year, it may be too late to adjust earlier quarter estimated payments accordingly.

In this situation, you can avoid the penalty that would result from the equal-payments requirement by using the *annualizing method* exception to the general rule.

The annualizing method lets quarterly payments be made in amounts that generally correspond to the amount of income received in each quarter. If most income is received in the last quarter of the year, the last quarter's payment can be larger than the earlier quarters without penalty.

To use the annualizing method, see the instructions to Form 2210,

Underpayment of Estimated Tax by Individuals, Estates, and Trusts.

• Faulty projections. If you simply guessed wrong about your 2005 income and so have paid the wrong amount of tax, you can still minimize the cost of the mistake with your final payment for 2005, due January 17, 2006. If you've paid too little tax to date, increase the payment—if you've paid too much, reduce or eliminate it.

Either way, you'll do better than if you wait to correct things on your tax return, when penalties will have piled up—but to do so, you must learn of your situation now, while there is still time to act.

Withholding loophole: Wage withholding is treated as if it takes place at an even rate through the year, even if it is increased at year-end. So increasing withholding from the last paychecks can retroactively eliminate estimated tax underpayment penalties from earlier quarters.

Caution: Do not intentionally underpay estimated and withheld taxes in early quarters intending to make them up with a late withholding increase —the IRS considers that an abuse.

Smart planning

When planning estimated taxes for the coming year, anticipate changes in your situation that may occur during the year that can affect your tax situation for the entire year.

Examples: Marriage, divorce (and payment or receipt of alimony), planned investment gains or losses, sales of properties, retirement, etc. Plan out your use of withholding and estimated tax payments accordingly.

Tactic: If you will receive a large one-shot amount of income early in the year, such as from the sale of an asset, you can pay tax on it at an equal rate through the year, effectively deferring the tax beyond the quarter in which you received the income.

Strategy: Use withholding to cover taxes on nonwage income to the extent possible. Wage withholding can be increased to cover tax on investment gains and other forms of nonwage income by filing a new Form W-4 with your employer.

Similarly, tax can be withheld from Social Security payments by filing Form W-4V, *Voluntary Withholding Request*, with the Social Security Administration, and from pension payments by filing a new Form W-4P, *Withholding Certificate for Pension or Annuity Payments*, with the pension plan administrator.

Withholding is easiest, smooths payments over the year, and can be reduced later in the year if taxes are overpaid.

Quarterly estimated payments, which require more calculation and filing effort, then can be used to supplement withholding if needed.

Source: Martin S. Kaplan, CPA, 11 Penn Plaza, New York City 10001, *www.irsmaven.com*. He is a frequent guest speaker at insurance, banking, and financial-planning seminars and author of *What the IRS Doesn't Want You to Know* (Wiley).

Chapter Fifteen

HOW TO SQUEEZE THE MOST TAX-FREE PROFIT FROM SELLING YOUR HOME

Like-kind exchanges are a way to defer tax on a home's appreciation.

Even better: Avoiding tax altogether by using the home-sale exclusion.

Key: You can avoid tax on gains up to $500,000 ($250,000 if you're a single taxpayer). If you know how to work the rules, you can use this tax break much more frequently—and flexibly—than you might think.

Beyond the basics

The basic rule for qualifying for the home-sale exclusion is that you must have owned the home and used it as your principal residence for at least two out of the five years before the sale.

Proving the dates of ownership generally will not be hard to do if you have records of buying and selling the house. Showing how long you lived there might be difficult, though, if you are challenged by the IRS.

What to do: Keep a moving-company receipt to show when you moved into your home. Keep copies of some early bills (from the phone company, for example) and payroll check stubs showing your address.

What if you owned and/or lived in the home for less than two years before a sale?

Loophole: If you moved out because of "unforeseen circumstances," you can get a partial exclusion.

Unforeseen circumstances, as defined by the Treasury Department, could be a natural disaster, change in employment or self-employment, divorce or legal separation, or multiple births from the same pregnancy, among other events.

Example: You decide to start a part-time business, so you sell your house and buy another with a room you can use as a home office. You lived in the former house for one year and made a $50,000 profit on the sale.

Result: Because one year is 50% of the required two years, you would get 50% of the maximum tax exclusion—up to $250,000 on any gain on the house's sale, or up to $125,000 if you're a single filer.

Thus, your $50,000 gain would be completely sheltered by the allowable exclusion.

Multiple choice

If you own two or more homes, you may be able to take advantage of the exclusion for each place.

Example: John and Mary Smith have lived in a house in suburban Chicago for many years. A few years ago, they bought a condo in a Colorado ski resort area.

The Smiths would like to sell their Colorado condo and use the proceeds to buy a condo in Florida. However, their Colorado vacation home has appreciated so much that they would owe tax on a $400,000 gain.

Strategy: The Smiths can take actions that would establish that their Colorado condo is their principal residence.

"Principal residence" is not defined precisely in the tax law. The most important factor is where you spend a majority of your time. But additional factors are considered, including, but not limited to, your place of employment... residence of immediate family members...address for tax filing, motor vehicle and voter registration...mailing address for bills...location of banks, clubs, and religious organizations.

Steps the Smiths might take: Spend a majority of each year in Colorado ...change voters' registrations and drivers' licenses to Colorado...file Form 8822, *Change of Address,* to give the IRS official notice of a change of residence...file state resident tax returns in Colorado rather than Illinois.

The more evidence they can show that Colorado is their principal residence, the weaker the case that the IRS—and Illinois—will have to say otherwise. Illinois may fight it, though, to retain tax revenues.

Result: Two years after the Smiths have taken the necessary steps to show that their home in Colorado is their principal residence, they can sell the Colorado condo and exclude gain up to $500,000.

Trap: Failure to follow such guidelines could cost a taxpayer the exclusion. In one case (James M. Guinan, DC AZ, 4/9/03), a couple had spent more time in their Wisconsin home than in any other single home, during the overall five-year period before they sold their house there.

However, within those five years there was only one year in which they spent more time in the Wisconsin home than in their other two homes...their voters' registrations and drivers' licenses were not from Wisconsin...they filed tax returns in states where they had other homes.

Outcome: They received no exclusion on the sale of the Wisconsin home.

Just because you've changed your principal residence, don't give up on using the capital gains exclusion for your former principal residence. After you make the change, you still have three years to sell the former primary residence and claim the exclusion.

Source: Diane Kennedy, CPA, tax strategist, founder, D. Kennedy & Associates, 821 N. Fifth Ave., Phoenix 89003. She is author of *Loopholes of the Rich* (Wiley) and runs the *www.taxloopholes.com* Web site.

Chapter Sixteen
USE VOLUNTARY WITHHOLDING TO BEAT PENALTIES

Seniors who were used to having taxes withheld from their pay often make mistakes when called upon to manage for themselves the estimated taxes due on Social Security benefits, annuity payments, IRA distributions, and other amounts they receive.

But failing to make timely payments or miscalculating amounts due can result in costly penalties.

Easier: Use voluntary withholding so that taxes are withheld just as from salary. To have tax withheld from Social Security benefits, visit *www.ssa.gov/taxwithhold.html* or request a Form W-4V, *Voluntary Withholding Request*, from the IRS at 800-829-3676. To have tax withheld from IRA distributions, contact the IRA's trustee. In fact, you can have tax withheld in many other cases as well, so check with whomever sends you a 1099.

Saver: Withholding is treated as if it occurs at an even rate all year long even if it actually increases later in the year. So, if you mistakenly underpaid estimated taxes for the first half of this year, by making "makeup" withholding payments for the rest of the year, you can retroactively avoid penalty.

Caution: Don't intentionally underpay taxes all year long and then make a big year-end "makeup" withholding payment, or the IRS may impose a penalty.

Source: James Glass, tax attorney based in New York City and a contributing writer to *Tax Hotline*.

Chapter Seventeen
DON'T LET YOUR CORPORATION OWN REAL ESTATE

Real estate should never be owned by a regular (C) corporation. Here's why—If you want to get the value of the real estate out of the corporation, you'll be taxed twice. If the corporation sells the property, it will have taxable gain—and there is no favorable capital gains rate for corporate income, and so the tax will be at ordinary rates. Next, the corporation's payment of the sale proceeds to you will be a distribution taxable to you.

Much better: Own the real estate personally, or through a pass-through entity such as a family limited partnership or a limited liability company. Then lease it to the business. Advantages...

• The lease payments provide you with income from the business that is not subject to employment tax.

• You take depreciation deductions for the property on your personal return.

• You can borrow against the property personally to raise cash.

• If you sell it, gain will be subject to low capital gain rates.

• If heirs inherit the property, they receive stepped-up basis in it—so appreciation in its value becomes income tax free to them.

• Ownership through the family partnership creates opportunities to reduce income and estate taxes.

Source: Barbara Weltman, Esq., small-business authority and author of *J.K. Lasser's Small Business Taxes* (Wiley). Her newest book is *The Complete Idiot's Guide to Starting an eBay Business* (Penguin). *www.barbaraweltman.com.*

Section 3: Charitable Contributions And Helping the IRS

Charitable Contribution Loopholes 161

Charitable Contribution Loopholes Part 2 164

How to Protect Your Charity Deductions 167

Make Charity Sweeter with Innovative Donation Techniques 168

Year-End Charitable Strategies 173

New Auto Donation Rules and Exceptions 177

Selling Your Company? Use a Charity to Sweeten the Deal 178

A Boost for Your Heirs 183

Charitable-Gift Annuity 184

How to Turn in a Tax Cheat (And Maybe Even Get a Reward) 185

Section 3: Charitable Contributions and Helping the IRS

Chapter One

CHARITABLE CONTRIBUTION LOOPHOLES

Making charitable contributions is a good thing to do but how you make the contributions is important, too. The Tax Code gives taxpayers bigger breaks for certain kinds of donations than for others.

Here are some smart ways to maximize the tax benefits of charitable giving...

Loophole: Donate appreciated securities instead of cash. Giving cash is an expensive way to make a donation because you're giving money that has already been taxed.

Better: Give securities that have gone up in value since you bought them. You get a tax deduction for the full market value of the securities and you avoid capital gains tax on the securities' appreciation.

Example: To fulfill your annual $500 pledge to the March of Dimes, you donate $500 worth of shares in a stock you bought several years ago for $200. If you cashed in these shares you would owe $45 in tax (15% rate on a $300 capital gain) for a net of $455. As a result, when you donate the shares, you get a $500 tax benefit for an asset worth only $455 to you.

Caution: You must have owned the appreciated assets for more than 12 months to get the full write-off. Otherwise, your deduction will be limited to your basis (tax cost) in the securities.

Limits: Annual deductions for gifts of appreciated property are limited to

30% of your adjusted gross income. (The excess can be carried forward up to five years.)

Loophole: Donate appreciated securities equivalent to your next three to five years' contributions to a local charitable trust. You can deduct the securities' entire market value in the year you make the contribution and you can designate how and when the funds are disbursed by the charitable trust.

Break: The charity doesn't pay capital gains tax on the sale. The March of Dimes (or any IRS-approved charity) can sell the shares tax free and keep the full $500.

Loophole: Deduct membership dues paid to a charity to the extent you receive nothing in return. If you do receive something in return, its value must be subtracted from the gift.

Example: If you receive a magazine subscription, the value of that subscription is subtracted from the dues to calculate your charitable deduction. The same is also true when you receive items of nominal value, such as jackets or shirts.

Loophole: Get tax breaks for doing volunteer work. You can't deduct the value of your time or the services you provide as a volunteer, but you can deduct many expenses. Examples...

• You can deduct actual out-of-pocket costs, including any supplies you buy.

• When you host a fund-raiser, the cost of invitations, food, drink, and other expenses is deductible.

• You can deduct any driving you do for a charitable organization (14 cents a mile) plus tolls and parking fees.

• When you attend a convention of a qualified charity as a chosen representative, you can deduct unreimbursed expenses including reasonable amounts for meals and lodging.

• Travel costs are deductible if you take an active role in leading a trip for a tax-exempt group, such as the Boy Scouts.

Loophole: Deduct contributions to a religious organization for after-school educational programs. The supplementary schooling is not in lieu of a secular education nor is it parochial school education. Rather, it is religious training for a young child. The only benefit is an "intangible religious benefit," which has no financial value in terms of reducing charitable donations.

Caution: The IRS has not ruled on this issue, and tax practitioners differ on whether to take the deduction.

Loophole: Set up your own charitable foundation. Contributions of appreciated securities are tax deductible. You control the timing and method of distribution, and to whom, as long as the recipient is a fully recognized charity (see IRS Publication 78, *Cumulative List of Organizations*, at *www.irs.gov*, or call 877-829-5500). You can even pay yourself (or family members) a reasonable salary for operating the foundation.

Caution: Contributions to charities must equal a minimum of 5% of foundation assets each year. Also, contributions, once made, cannot be used for any other purpose.

Strategy: Set up a bequest for your private charitable foundation in your will. The payments to the foundation will completely escape estate tax, and your family members can administer the foundation for years thereafter. They can use payments from the foundation to make charitable donations they would have made from their own funds, thus preserving their cash.

Source: Edward Mendlowitz, CPA, shareholder in the CPA firm WithumSmith+Brown, 120 Albany St., New Brunswick, NJ 08901. He is author of *Estate Planning* (Practical Programs).

Section 3: Charitable Contributions and Helping the IRS

Chapter Two
CHARITABLE CONTRIBUTION LOOPHOLES PART 2

The Tax Code gives taxpayers bigger breaks for certain kinds of charitable contributions than for others. Here are even more smart ways to maximize the tax benefits of your charitable giving...

Loophole: Charitable remainder trusts (CRTs) can provide you with income and tax deductions when you fund the trusts with appreciated assets. A CRT can sell the assets tax free and pay you—or you and your spouse—income for life. You get an up-front charitable deduction for the charity's interest based on the full value of the assets you donate.

Note: Your tax deduction is reduced by the present value of the lifetime income that you and your spouse will receive. Also, the trust pays no tax on the capital gains resulting from the sale of appreciated stocks.

Loophole: Consider setting up a unitrust CRT. This format lets you revalue the CRT's assets each year. As value increases, you can adjust the distribution accordingly. Another option is a CRT annuity trust, in which the annual withdrawal amount is fixed.

Loophole: When you donate art and collectibles to meet your charitable commitments, you can deduct the full value of the gifts when the items are used in the charity's main activity or purpose.

Examples: You give a painting to a university for use in an art appreciation course. Or you give a collection of 19th-century magazines to a research library.

Caution: This deduction does not apply to self-created work, for which the deduction is limited to your basis.

Trap: If, at the time of the donation, it is reasonably anticipated that the charity will sell the property you donate to it, your deduction is limited to your basis in the property—usually, what you paid for it—rather than the full appreciated value.

Self-defense: Shop around for a charity that will use your gift in its main activity. Protect your deduction by getting a letter from the charity saying how it intends to use your gift.

Loophole: Use a charitable lead trust to make annual distributions to a charity while reserving the assets for your children (or grandchildren or other beneficiaries). This creates a current tax deduction for the present value of the charitable distributions. It also lets you transfer the assets later at a reduced gift tax value. If the assets appreciate, the growth is transferred to your beneficiaries free of gift and estate taxes. However, these trusts are not intended to provide significant income tax benefits to the grantor.

Loophole: Make a charitable bequest in your will that reduces your taxable estate (it's taxable if it exceeds $2 million in 2006, when assets are not left to a spouse). The charitable bequest directly reduces the amount subject to the estate tax.

Caution: If the bequest is a share in a business or real estate, the estate's charitable deduction might be lower than the asset value in the gross estate. Check with your tax adviser.

Loophole: Bequeath IRAs and pension funds to charities. Generally, the value of an IRA or pension is included in the gross estate and the recipient is taxed on the IRA or pension withdrawals. Leaving the funds to a charity avoids income tax (as well as the estate tax). If you can choose which funds to leave to charity, select an IRA or pension over assets that are not double taxed.

Loophole: Give assets to charity during your lifetime, not after death. A lifetime charity contribution reduces your taxable estate and can provide a lifetime income tax deduction, reducing the cost of the contribution.

Loophole: Gifts valued at $5,000 or less do not need formal appraisals.

Contributions over $5,000 do need written appraisals, and the appraiser must sign IRS Form 8283, *Noncash Charitable Contributions*. Use an experienced, qualified appraiser who is familiar with the strict appraisal requirements of the IRS.

Special rule: You can request a special IRS statement of value for gifts of property worth $50,000 or more.

Caution: Special rates apply to car donations.

Note: Appraisals are not necessary for donations of publicly traded securities, regardless of their value.

Loophole: Contribute a qualified "conservation easement" and receive a full tax deduction for the current fair market value of the easement. A conservation easement is a permanent restriction on the use of real property.

Examples: Empty lots or open space used for soil drainage or wildlife preservation, or an historic building facade.

Source: Edward Mendlowitz, CPA, shareholder in the CPA firm WithumSmith+Brown, 120 Albany St., New Brunswick, NJ 08901. He is author of *Estate Planning* (Practical Programs).

Section 3: Charitable Contributions and Helping the IRS

Chapter Three

HOW TO PROTECT YOUR CHARITY DEDUCTIONS

You may lose your deductions for genuine gifts to charity if you fail to meet IRS documentation requirements. Key rules...

• For every single gift of $250 or more, you must obtain a written acknowledgment from the charity documenting the gift. This is true even if you have a canceled check as proof of the gift.

Deadline: You must obtain an acknowledgment by the date you actually file your return or the filing deadline, including extensions, whichever is earlier.

Get all the acknowledgments you need now. If you wait until after filing your return, when an auditor calls, it will be too late.

• If you donate property valued at more than $5,000, you must obtain a qualified written appraisal of the property.

Full rules for safeguarding deductions can be found in IRS Publication 526, *Charitable Contributions*, available free at *www.irs.gov* or by calling 800-829-3676.

Source: IRS News Release IR-2003-134.

Chapter Four

MAKE CHARITY SWEETER WITH INNOVATIVE DONATION TECHNIQUES

When you make a substantial gift to charity—more than $10,000, say—there are better ways than simply writing a check. Sophisticated "planned giving" strategies can provide you with lifetime income or use of valued property, as well as tax savings.

In the planned giving area, there are many vehicles from which you can choose.

Charitable gift annuities

How they work: You make a gift to a charity and receive an annuity, a guaranteed stream of income at a fixed rate that can go on for your lifetime or for a specific term.

Some charities stipulate a minimum amount for gift annuities, such as $10,000.

The older you are when you make the donation, the greater the periodic income you can receive.

Examples: With Charity A, a 60-year-old donor might receive 5.7%, or $5,700 per year on a $100,000 gift. An 80-year-old making that same $100,000 gift might receive 8%, or $8,000 per year.

A couple will receive lower payments than a single recipient because of their longer joint life expectancy. If that 80-year-old donor has a 75-year-old spouse, and payments are to continue until they both die, the annuity rate might drop from 8% to 6.6% per year.

Tax treatment: In all of these situations, part of the income stream will be taxable and part will be a tax-free return of capital.

Loophole: When the gift annuity is funded with appreciated assets, the capital gains obligation is tax deferred—the taxable gain is spread across the annuity payments. With any gift annuity, donors get partial tax deductions as well.

Example: A 75-year-old might be entitled to a deduction equal to 40%—the difference between the value of what was given away and the value of what is expected to be paid back.

Key: Gift annuities offer fixed income as well as security because the obligation to pay the annuity is a claim on all the assets of the issuer.

Payments from charitable gift annuities may be deferred.

Example: You make a gift at age 55 but stipulate that annuity payments not begin until you reach 65. The payment stream will be greater, to take into account 10 years of growth in the interim.

Loophole: With this strategy, you may obtain a charitable deduction now, while you're in a high tax bracket, yet defer the income until you're retired and your tax rate is lower.

Charitable remainder annuity trusts

An annuity trust is similar to a charitable gift annuity.

How they work: You make a donation and then your "income beneficiaries" (often, you and your spouse) receive fixed payments for life or for a specific term. After the income interest terminates, the remainder (what's left in the trust) goes to charity. Again, by giving away appreciated assets you can defer capital gains tax.

How does an annuity trust differ from a gift annuity?

• Expenses. If a trust must be created, some legal expenses will be involved. Gift annuities tend to be simpler and cheaper.

• Control. You have more control with an annuity trust. You set the income you wish to receive. It must be at least 5% of the initial trust principal.

Example: If you donate $100,000 to a charitable remainder annuity trust, you must receive at least $5,000 per year.

Trade-off: The more income you decide to receive, the less will be left to charity and the smaller your up-front charitable deduction.

Charitable remainder unitrusts

How they work: A unitrust resembles an annuity trust with one key difference. You receive a payout that's based on a percentage of the value of the trust assets rather than a fixed amount. Again, the minimum is 5% a year.

Key: Your income will grow if the trust fund earns more than the payout percentage you set. A unitrust provides inflation protection if the income stream grows in time.

Variation: A net-income-makeup charitable remainder unitrust allows donors to give now and receive income after waiting a period of years, often after retirement.

Drawback: For all types of remainder trusts, donating appreciated assets has been a popular strategy. This approach is less popular now that the tax on capital gains has been reduced.

Moreover, lower interest rates reduce the appeal of unitrusts because they effectively place upper limits on payout percentages.

Comparison: Unitrusts are more flexible than annuity trusts because, with the former, additional contributions can be made after the trust is created.

On the other hand, annuity trusts are easier to administer and provide a dependable income stream.

When you set up a charitable remainder trust, you can serve as trustee, which gives you some ongoing control over the trust funds. You can also decide to change the charitable beneficiaries.

Caution: Serving as a trustee can involve a great deal of work. There are records to keep, tax returns to file, and fiduciary rules to follow. Trustees fees can vary, depending on circumstances.

Charitable lead trusts

Such trusts are the opposite of remainder trusts.

How they work: The charity gets a stream of income first and the trust assets eventually are distributed to someone you designate.

Advantage: Lead trusts can be useful if you want to fulfill annual charitable obligations yet you want to transfer assets to your children or grandchildren while minimizing gift taxes.

Example: Suppose you have pledged to contribute $10,000 per year to a favorite charity for the next 15 years. You might set up a 15-year lead trust with $250,000 worth of securities. After 15 years, any of the remaining assets will go to your children or grandchildren.

Loophole: Depending on interest rates at the time you establish the trust, the value of the taxable gift might be zero, or near zero. That's true even if the securities appreciate and turn out to be worth $300,000, $400,000, or more by the time the trust expires and the beneficiaries receive the assets in the trust fund.

Key: Low interest rates boost the appeal of charitable lead trusts. The lower the interest rate, the lower the value of the taxable gift to the trust beneficiaries.

Pooled income funds

How they work: These are essentially mutual funds run by a charity. Net earnings are paid out to participants on a pro rata basis.

Result: A donor's income depends upon the investment success of the fund's manager.

Benefits: Pooled income funds may appeal to those making gifts too small for a unitrust but who do not want to lock themselves into a fixed income stream. You can increase your contribution to a pooled income fund over time, increasing your income.

Bargain sales

Suppose you bought real estate several years ago for $75,000 and it has appreciated in value to $250,000. You would like to give it to charity, avoiding the capital gains tax, but you're not eager to make a $250,000 gift.

Strategy: Sell the property to the charity at a bargain price, perhaps $125,000. Thus, the charity would gain $125,000 while you put $125,000 in your pocket.

Result: Half of the appreciation ($87,500) would be a taxable gain for you while you are entitled to a $125,000 tax deduction. This deduction may wipe out your tax obligation from disposing of the property and give you an additional write-off.

Retained interest gifts of real estate

You can give property (including your home) to a charity now but retain the right to use the property for your lifetime, and perhaps your spouse's lifetime as well.

Loophole: You'll get a partial tax deduction now for a future gift. The deduction depends on your life expectancy and the interest rates in effect at the time.

Bottom line: No matter which type of planned gift you choose, you can expect recognition once the gift becomes irrevocable, even though the assets may not go to the charity for many years.

Source: David Scott Sloan, Esq., deputy chair, Private Wealth Services, Holland & Knight LLP, 10 St. James Ave., Boston 02116, and a member of the firm's board of directors where he chairs the strategic planning committee. He has served as chairman of the Taxation Section and the Tax Legislation Committee of the Massachusetts Bar Association as well as the Estate Planning Committee of the Boston Bar Association.

Chapter Five

YEAR-END CHARITABLE STRATEGIES

Year-end holidays may have you thinking about contributing to your favorite causes. With some savvy planning, you can enjoy substantial tax savings—so you can do well while doing good.

Know the limits

If you itemize deductions on Schedule A of your federal tax return, you can deduct charitable donations. There are some restrictions, though...

• AGI limits. Cash gifts that you make to public charities cannot exceed 50% of your adjusted gross income (AGI).

Donations of appreciated property, such as stock, can't exceed 30% of AGI for gifts to public charities.

Example: You expect your AGI this year to be $100,000. You can deduct charitable donations of up to $30,000 worth of appreciated property.

If you donate the maximum $30,000 worth of appreciated property to charity, you also can donate up to $20,000 in cash and get a full $50,000 first-year write-off.

Excess deduction: Any charitable donations you can't deduct this year because of the limitations can be carried forward for up to five years. Each year, the same percentage-of-AGI limits apply.

• Alternative minimum tax (AMT) limits. Charitable deductions are permitted under AMT rules. However, high-bracket taxpayers deducting large charitable contributions may reduce their regular income tax by so much that the AMT will come into play.

Strategy: Have your tax pro crunch some numbers to see how much you can effectively donate to charity this year and still avoid the AMT.

Don't write checks

Suppose you intend to make $30,000 worth of charitable contributions by year-end and your tax adviser tells you that amount will be fully deductible. You can simply write $30,000 worth of checks to your favorite charities.

Better way: Instead of writing checks, donate appreciated securities to your favorite charities.

Loophole: For assets that are held more than one year before the donation, you can get a deduction for their full current market value. The unpaid capital gains obligation disappears.

Example: You hold stock you bought many years ago for $5,000. The stock is now trading at $30,000. Thus, you have a $25,000 unrealized gain.

At a 15% federal tax rate on long-term gains, you would owe $3,750 in tax if you sold all the shares. Thus, this holding is really worth only $26,250 to you, after tax. By donating the shares, you can get the full $30,000 deduction.

How to do it: Here's a simple procedure for donating appreciated stocks, mutual fund shares, or other securities...

• Call the charity and get its brokerage account number.

• Call your own broker or your mutual fund company and explain what you want to do, providing the charity's account number.

• Follow up by fax or phone to confirm the transaction.

Trap I: Don't donate securities held in an IRA, SEP, or other tax-deferred retirement plan. Under current tax law, the value of the shares donated to charity will be considered taxable income to you, at ordinary income rates.

Instead, donate appreciated securities held in a taxable account, which won't trigger any income tax.

Trap II: Don't donate securities selling at a loss. Instead, sell those securities

174

to take the tax loss yourself, and donate the cash to charity.

Donor advised funds

The above procedure for donating appreciated securities probably will work fine if you're making one $30,000 donation, or even two or three large donations.

However, if you intend to make donations to, say, 10 different charities of $3,000 each, the paperwork involved can be daunting.

For multiple donations of this nature, use a donor advised fund.

How they work: You make an up-front contribution (cash, securities, or other assets) to the donor advised fund. At the time of the contribution, you can deduct this contribution as a donation to a public charity.

At your own pace, you can specify "grants" from the donor advised funds to various charities of your choice. In essence, you can deduct now and deal with the paperwork later.

Example: You donate $30,000 worth of appreciated securities to your local community foundation's donor advised fund on December 30, 2005. The fund can sell the shares without owing any tax so you'll have the full $30,000 in your fund account.

Assuming that you don't run afoul of the percentage of AGI limits, you can take a $30,000 deduction for 2005.

Making grants: You might notify the fund in January that you would like to donate $3,000 to your alma mater and $3,000 to a disabled veterans' group. Grants will be made to the specified recipients in your name so that you'll get the appropriate recognition.

Other grants can be made in the future, perhaps years from now. You can add to the account, if you want.

Key: Funds that are yet to be donated will be invested. Investment earnings will be untaxed and can add to the amount available for future contributions.

Strategy: Contributing to a donor advised fund may be particularly effective if you have unusually high taxable income this year. You get the up front write off to offset the extra income while fulfilling your charitable commitments over a period of years.

Caution: Some donor advised funds impose a management fee for assets yet to be given to charity. Before donating, make sure the advantages you'll enjoy justify the fees you'll pay.

Many local community foundations sponsor donor advised funds. They also are offered by major financial firms such as Fidelity, Vanguard, and Charles Schwab.

Stocking stuffers

Besides cash and securities, other items may be donated before year-end to generate tax deductions for 2005.

Examples: Clothing, collectibles, even life insurance policies that you no longer need.

Trap: Be cautious about donating autos to charity. New rules apply to cars valued at over $500.

Again, you're probably better off selling the car and giving cash to charity.

Substantiation

For small gifts of goods, you can assign your own valuations without having to show receipts. Larger gifts require a paper trail...

• For a contribution worth $250 or more, you must get a written receipt of your donation from the charity.

• For a donation of more than $500 worth of goods, you must include Form 8283, *Noncash Charitable Contributions*, with your tax return, providing details about your gift.

• If you claim a deduction of more than $5,000 for any one item, you must have a qualified appraiser provide a valuation that you attach to Form 8283.

Caution: If you're donating art or other types of collectibles, you'll need to have a record showing that the items are being used for the charity's primary purpose, to get a full deduction.

Example: Donate a painting that the university uses in art appreciation courses.

Give yourself some time so that a year-end rush won't keep you from gathering together all of the necessary records.

Source: Kathy Stepp, CPA, CFP, founder, Stepp & Rothwell, Inc., 7300 College Blvd., Overland Park, KS 66210. She has frequently been on *Worth* magazine's list of top financial advisers.

NEW AUTO DONATION RULES AND EXCEPTIONS

The new law effective in 2005 limits deductions for autos valued over $500 that are donated to charity. Now a deduction can generally be claimed only for the amount the charity receives when it sells the donated auto to raise funds.

There are three exceptions. The full market value of a car is deductible if the charity...

• Makes significant use of the car itself, or...

• Improves the car to increase its value, or...

• Donates the car or sells it at a below-market price to a needy individual, in furtherance of its charitable purpose.

For a full explanation of the new rules, see IRS Notice 2005-44.

Chapter Six

SELLING YOUR COMPANY? USE A CHARITY TO SWEETEN THE DEAL

Selling the company that you've developed over many years can be emotionally trying. It can be a taxing time—literally—too.

Chances are, you have a low basis in your company's shares. You may owe nearly 15% of the proceeds to the IRS as a long-term capital gain. In some states, the total tax bill—both federal and state—can be around 20% (15% federal and 5% state).

Strategy: Transfer your shares in the company to a charitable remainder trust (CRT) well before the terms of the sale are finalized. This maneuver will allow you to defer the tax, paying it over many years.

Added benefits: You will receive a large up-front income tax deduction, lifetime payments, and recognition from your favorite cause.

Putting charity first

Scenario: You have built your company from scratch into a thriving business, but now you're ready to retire. You find a buyer willing to pay $2 million.

With a low basis in your company's shares—check with your accountant—you would have a long-term capital gain of almost $2 million and might owe about $400,000 (20%) to your state and to the IRS.

Charitable intent: Instead of selling directly to the buyer, you transfer shares in your company to yourself as the trustee of a CRT that you create.

Have an unrelated third party professional appraiser put a value on the shares. Your tax professional should be able to advise you on where to find an appraiser.

As trustee, you handle the final negotiations, enter into the final agreement, and ultimately sell the shares to the buyer for $2 million.

If the deal falls through for some reason, the independent appraisal may be necessary to demonstrate the value of your contribution to the CRT.

Outcome: If the sale goes through, the buyer winds up owning your company and the CRT has $2 million in cash.

Loophole: As an exempt entity for income tax purposes, the CRT will not owe tax on the sale of your company's shares. It will have the entire $2 million in cash to invest in a diversified portfolio of stocks, bonds, mutual funds, etc.

If you had sold the shares to the buyer personally, you would have had only $1.6 million, net of taxes, to reinvest.

Caution: You need to work closely with a tax adviser to steer clear of pitfalls in the private foundation rules and possible unrelated business taxable income (UBTI) for the CRT. A tax pro also can confirm whether you're better off with a CRT, versus paying tax on an outright sale. If the sale doesn't happen, the stock will be stuck in the CRT.

Cash flow

With a CRT, you can specify a stream of payments to a beneficiary or beneficiaries you name.

You can name yourself and your spouse as the individual beneficiaries. The trust can be instructed to make payments as long as either is alive. (See below for details.) Thus, the cash might flow for decades.

Finish line: When the beneficiaries die, the assets left in the trust (the "remainder") go to a charity or charities you've named.

Deductions: more or less

With such a strategy, you stand to gain multiple benefits.

Tax deduction: The present value of your future charitable donation will be calculated by your tax pro in accordance with actuarial tables issued by the IRS. You'll get an immediate tax deduction, even though the charitable gift might not occur until many years in the future.

Running the numbers: The older you are, and the lower the payment to the individual beneficiaries, the greater your charitable tax deduction.

Conversely, if you're relatively young and you desire a substantial payment from the CRT, your charitable deduction will be reduced.

Limit: You must structure the arrangement so that the present value of the future charitable gift is at least 10% of the amount transferred.

In the above example, with a $2 million transfer, your charitable gift (and the resulting deduction) must be at least $200,000.

Caution: If you are relatively young (under, say, age 45), this 10% rule might prevent you from creating a CRT. Even if you specify the minimum payment (see below), less than 10% would go to charity. On the other hand, in some circumstances, the charitable deduction you get from a CRT may not be fully deductible right away, if it's too large in relation to your income. For property donations, the deduction limit is generally 30% of adjusted gross income per year.

Charitable deductions you can't use immediately generally can be carried forward for up to five years.

Calculating the payments

You have considerable flexibility in setting up your payment stream from a CRT. Options...

• Annuity trust. You will get regular fixed payments.

Minimum: Each year, you must receive at least 5% of the amount you contributed. In the previous example, with a $2 million transfer to the CRT, your fixed payment must be at least $100,000 a year.

• Unitrust. Here you get a fixed percentage of trust assets, determined each year. Again, that percentage must be at least 5% of trust assets.

Key: With a unitrust, payouts can grow or decrease if the trust assets earn more or less than the unitrust payout percentage.

Waiting period: If you do not need current income, a NIMCRUT (net income with makeup charitable remainder unitrust) might be used. A NIMCRUT can be designed to pay out little now but more later, perhaps after you retire.

Upper limit: For all types of CRTs, the IRS has indicated it does not like annual payouts to be extremely high, such as 50%.

As a practical matter, the 10% charitable-gift rule puts a cap on the size of the payment. Often, though, if you wish to receive ample cash flow, an 8% or 9% payout will work.

Tax treatment: Payouts to the individual beneficiaries are taxed in a manner that reflects the trust's income, first as (1) ordinary income, then (2) capital gains, then (3) tax-exempt income, and finally, (4) return of principal. The trustee files a tax return for the CRT, and the composition of the payouts is determined by a Schedule K-1, copies of which are filed with the CRT's tax return and provided to the individual beneficiary.

Strategy: You might invest the CRT funds in municipal bonds and growth stocks that generate little ordinary income.

Result: You'll pay tax mostly at long-term capital gains rates.

In our example, with a long-term gain around $2 million, you would pay tax at capital gains rates over a period of years until you recognized $2 million worth of gains.

Giving back

The CRT strategy works only if you have some charitable intent. Ultimately, a significant amount likely will go to a charity or charities of your choice, rather than to your family or other beneficiaries.

Even though the charity won't receive a benefit until sometime in the future, you will get some recognition now for your philanthropic efforts.

"S" stands for sorry

The benefits of this strategy are limited to owners of companies run as C corporations, partnerships, or limited liability companies (LLCs).

Trap: If your business is an S corporation, only certain types of trusts are eligible shareholders—and CRTs don't qualify. Therefore, transferring S corporation shares to a CRT will cause your company to lose its status as an S corporation and will likely have adverse tax consequences.

Tactic: Have your tax pro run the numbers to see how much tax you would owe if you were to abandon your S corporation election. Then you can decide whether the CRT tax deferral is worthwhile.

Using a CRT to defer the tax on the sale of your company involves many technical rules that must be followed precisely. Check with a competent tax adviser before proceeding.

Source: B. Dane Dudley, Esq., partner in the law firm Day, Berry & Howard LLP, CityPlace 1, Hartford 06103. He specializes in estate planning, trusts and estate administration.

Section 3: Charitable Contributions and Helping the IRS

Chapter Seven
A BOOST FOR YOUR HEIRS

If you plan to leave a gift to charity when you die, it may be better to do it with life insurance than with a bequest.

How: Make a gift to charity now of funds to buy a single-premium life insurance policy ($300,000, for instance) that will pay off when you die ($1 million).

Advantages: You get a tax deduction for your gift—in this case, $300,000—while you are alive. And the tax-free death benefit ($1 million) from the policy payable to the charity will let you fund a much larger bequest to the charity with a smaller gift now. This leaves more in your estate for heirs. Consult with an expert about details.

Source: Irving L. Blackman, CPA, founding partner, Blackman Kallick Bartelstein, LLP, 10 S. Riverside Plaza, Chicago 60606. *www.taxsecretsofthewealthy.com.*

Section 3: Charitable Contributions and Helping the IRS

Chapter Eight
CHARITABLE-GIFT ANNUITY

A charitable-gift annuity gives you an immediate tax deduction plus income for life. As with regular immediate annuities, you invest a lump sum in return for guaranteed payments. If you die prematurely, the charity—not an insurance company—keeps the money.

More information: Consult your favorite charity, or go to the American Council on Gift Annuities, 317-269-6271, *www.acga-web.org*.

Source: Martin M. Shenkman, Esq., CPA, attorney specializing in estate planning, Teaneck, NJ.

Section 3: Charitable Contributions and Helping the IRS

Chapter Nine

HOW TO TURN IN A TAX CHEAT (AND MAYBE EVEN GET A REWARD)

If you know someone or some business that is cheating on taxes, you can report the fact to the IRS and seek a reward equal to a percentage of any tax the IRS collects as a result of the information you provide.

But be aware of the risks—and don't count on getting the money.

Here's what to know about the IRS informant rewards program...

The process

IRS rules allow informants to be paid awards as large as $10 million. The amount of any award is based on the value of the information provided and the amount of tax the IRS collects as a result of receiving it. An award can be...

- 15% of the tax collected when the information provided is specific and a direct factor leading to tax recovery.

- 10% of tax collected when the information causes or materially assists an investigation of a specific issue that leads to tax recovery.

- 1% of tax collected when the information causes an investigation that leads to a tax recovery, but does not assist the investigation of specific issues.

So, the more detailed the information provided, and the more directly it identifies specific wrongdoing, the greater the potential reward will be.

To seek a reward, first report the wrongdoing by calling the IRS tax fraud hotline at 800-829-0433, or by reporting it to an agent at your local IRS office.

Then, fill out IRS Form 211, *Application for Reward for Original Information*, and mail it to the Informant's Claim Examiner at the IRS Service Center for your area (the address is on the form).

To claim a reward, you must divulge your name on Form 211. The IRS keeps the names of informants confidential.

For more details, obtain IRS Publication 733, *Rewards for Information Provided by Individuals to the Internal Revenue Service*, at www.irs.gov or by calling 800-829-3676.

Pitfalls

Turning in a tax cheat to get a reward may sound attractive, but before you do it, be aware that there are pitfalls...

• Your identity may be revealed. The IRS keeps the names of its informants confidential, but in practice, it often is not difficult for the person who is informed upon to figure out who provided the information to the IRS.

The nature of the information is the first clue—it may be that no one but the informant had it.

The motive of the informant is another clue. Most IRS informants are aggrieved individuals—spouses, employees or business partners who feel they were treated wrongly by the party about whom they are reporting—and the informed-upon party usually knows who has a motive to give the information to the IRS.

• You, too, may be investigated by the IRS. Since most informants are exercising grudges, the IRS may wish to verify an informant's credibility. Also, when an informant displays detailed knowledge of a spouse's or business partner's tax cheating, the IRS may suspect that the informant has participated in such schemes as well.

These considerations can lead the IRS to take a look at the informant's own tax situation—so a would-be informant who has himself/herself engaged in dubious tax practices might think twice about signing a Form 211. It might be better to inform anonymously and not ask for a reward.

Uncertain payoff

However, probably the biggest problem for informants seeking rewards from the IRS is how chintzy the IRS tends to be.

In practice, the IRS pays few awards, and those that it does pay usually are small. The IRS says that typically fewer than 8% of claims for rewards are allowed—and in cases where they are, the average reward has been only 2.74% of the tax collected.

While the maximum of any single reward can be $10 million—during 2003, the last year for which data are available—the IRS paid out a total of only $4.1 million to 190 informants out of 4,765 who applied for the entire year.

Moreover, there is no way for an informant to enforce the payment of a reward from the IRS, even if the information provided does lead to a big tax recovery. This is because the law says rewards are entirely discretionary with the IRS, and gives the IRS sole authority to decide how valuable the information provided to it proved to be.

Example: If the IRS decides that it would have learned of a tax cheating scheme on its own, it can decline to pay a reward even if it actually learned of the scheme from an informant.

In fact, informants who seek to collect a percentage of a tax recovery under the IRS's 15% (or 10% or 1%) of recovery guidelines can't even find out how much tax the IRS collected from the informed-upon party, because the Tax Code's confidentiality rules prohibit the IRS from revealing this information.

Courts have repeatedly held that informants can't successfully sue the IRS to collect rewards it doesn't want to pay, even when the IRS has made large tax recoveries after receiving an informant's information—and that the IRS doesn't even have to explain why it refuses to pay.

Example case: Gregory Krug provided the IRS with information that led to its collecting millions of dollars of tax. But the IRS denied his claim for a reward, saying by letter that the amount of tax involved in the case was too small to grant a reward, that it had already possessed the information Krug had provided, and that the information did not lead to an investigation.

Krug then sued, and the IRS admitted in court that the reasons it had given for not paying any reward were false—his information did cause an investigation and the IRS did collect millions of dollars of tax.

But the IRS then simply refused to disclose its real reason for not paying any reward, citing taxpayer confidentiality rules.

Court: For the IRS. It need not pay anything "because the IRS is not obligated to pay a reward even to eligible applicants." [*Gregory C. Krug*, Fed. Cl., 81 AFTR2d ¶98-666.]

Bottom line

While you can turn in a tax wrongdoer to the IRS in the hope of collecting a reward, don't count on getting one. Realize that there will be nothing you can do about it if the IRS refuses to pay.

If you have any concern about the IRS investigating you as the result of providing a tip, and wish to keep your identity secret, pass up on the idea of getting a reward. Instead, provide information anonymously to the IRS through its tax fraud hotline.

Source: Randy Bruce Blaustein, Esq., senior tax partner, R.B. Blaustein & Co., 155 E. 31 St., New York City 10016. Mr. Blaustein is author of *How to Do Business with the IRS: The Complete Guide for Tax Professionals* (Prentice Hall).

Section 4: Business

Much Wiser Tax Return Filing for Business Owners 191

Loopholes in Working Abroad 195

Advertising Loopholes 198

The Too, Too Common Mistake Made with Employer Stock...
    How to Keep More Profit 201

When to Lease Business Equipment...and When to Buy 205

Loopholes for Foreigners Working in the US 209

How to Get a Bigger Tax Refund for Your Business 212

The Key Information Returns for Your Business 216

Avoid the Tax Bite When You Pay for Employees' Meals 220

For Free Answers to Your Business Tax Questions...Look On-Line 224

FUTA and SUTA—The Ins and Outs of Unemployment
    Taxes for Small Business 229

Cut Your Company's Building Costs with Clever Use of the Tax Code 233

Business Owners: Tax-Saving Moves to Make Before Year-End 237

Why It's So Useful to Set Up Your Business as an LLC 241

A Microbusiness Can Create Tax-Sheltered Wealth, Cut Other
    Taxes, and Help You Start a New Career, Too 245

12 Easy High-Tech Ways to Simplify Business Tax Chores 249

Beware: Incentive Stock Option Trap 253

Risks and Benefits of Borrowing from—or Lending to—
    Your Own Company 254

Independent Contractors Are Still Under IRS Scrutiny—How to Protect
    Your Business 258

Challenge for Businesses...Collecting Tax on On-Line Sales 262

AMT Protection for Employees 266

Section 4: Business

Chapter One
MUCH WISER TAX RETURN FILING FOR BUSINESS OWNERS

If your private business—like most today—is organized as a proprietorship or "pass-through entity" (S corporation, limited liability company, or partnership), its income is reported on your personal tax return, due April 15.

Smart filing strategies to cut taxes and your audit risk...

K-1 filings

Every business organized as a pass-through entity files a Schedule K-1 that reports how much income it distributed to its owners, much as a Form 1099 or W-2 reports income to income recipients. A copy is sent to both the IRS and the owners.

More than $1 trillion dollars is reported on K-1s annually but in the past, the IRS never matched K-1s against individual tax returns as it does 1099s and W-2s.

The IRS believes this income may be underreported on unmatched personal returns by as much as 20%—more than $200 billion!

Result: The IRS has made it a top priority to begin matching K-1s to personal returns. It started a test matching program last year but ended it due to computer problems. It says it will resume K-1 matching in the near future.

What to know: Basically, two kinds of income are reported on K-1s...

• Interest and dividends. These will be easy for the IRS to match using systems similar to those used for 1099s.

• Profits and losses. These will be difficult to match because numbers shown on a K-1 may not match those reported on the corresponding personal return even when reported correctly.

Example: An S corporation's owner can deduct his/her share of its losses on his personal return, but only up to the amount of his basis (investment in plus personal loans to the corporation) in its shares. Beyond that, losses aren't deductible but may be carried forward to offset future income.

So, if an owner who has already deducted the maximum amount of losses receives a K-1 showing an additional loss, it won't be reported on his personal return. The next year, if he receives a K-1 showing a gain, it will be offset by the carryforward loss and won't be reported on the return either. In both years, the K-1 and return will not match—even though both are correct.

Risk: In the case of such a mismatch, an IRS auditor must examine the taxpayer's return personally to assure proper reporting.

Smart filing: Since the IRS intends to resume and expand K-1 matching soon...

• Be sure that interest and dividends reported on a K-1 match the numbers on your return to avoid having it flagged.

• If a profit or loss shown as distributed on a K-1 does not match the number shown on your personal return, add a brief explanation why. If the IRS notices the mismatch, the explanation may satisfy it—and avert a call from an auditor.

More filing strategies

• IRS audit guides. Before filing your return, get the IRS audit guide for your business. The same audit guides IRS auditors use are available free on the IRS Web site for more than 50 different kinds of businesses. Knowing in advance what an auditor will look at on a return will help make it audit-proof.

To find the guides, go to *www.irs.gov*, then click on "Businesses" and "Market Segment Specialization Program."

The audit guide on partnerships is especially recommended if your business is organized as one.

• Equipment deductions. To spur the economy, Congress increased the maximum amount of newly purchased business equipment that can be fully deducted under "Section 179 expensing" to $108,000 in 2006 (it had been just $24,000 in 2002).

Planning: To make best use of Section 179 expensing, use it on equipment that otherwise would be depreciable over the longest period.

Reverse tactic: If business income will be subject to a low tax rate this year, you may not want to use these new tax breaks but prefer to save deductions for later years when taxes will go higher.

In that case, don't make any 179 election—and do make a written election on your tax return choosing not to use bonus depreciation. Normal depreciation rules will then apply, deferring deductions into future years.

• Retirement plan contributions. Maximize deductible contributions to your Keogh or other employer-sponsored retirement plan. By filing an extension for your tax return, you can extend the time to do so until the return's new due date. If you don't have a plan open yet, a simplified employee pension (SEP) plan can be opened as late as then.

Cash-saving tactic: File an extension for your return to get extra time to make a plan contribution. Then file the return and deduct the contribution on it—before you make the contribution—using the deduction to get a larger refund. Then, when you get the refund, use it to help fund the plan contribution.

• Refunds and estimated taxes. If you file an extension for 2005, both it and your final tax payment for 2005 will be due on April 17, 2006—the same date your first estimated payment for 2006 is due.

Snag: When you file an extension, you may not know your final tax bill for the year. That could leave you incurring an underpayment penalty—even though you make an estimated payment for the next year on the same date.

Tactic: Take the funds you would send to the IRS with your estimated payment for 2006 and pay them with the extension for 2005 instead. Then, on your return, elect to have any overpayment applied to 2006.

Result: If you estimated your 2005 tax correctly, you will be credited for a tax payment for 2006 just as if you made an estimated payment. But if you underestimated your 2005 tax bill, your payment with the extensions will avert an underpayment penalty. You may then owe interest on an estimated tax underpayment—but that will cost less than interest plus a penalty on the 2005 underpayment.

• Loss carryforward or carryback. If you suffer a business loss for 2006, you can carry it back two years to get a tax refund for it. File IRS Form 1045, Application for Tentative Refund, to get a "quick refund."

Alternative: If you think you will be in a higher tax bracket in coming years than you were in the last two years, elect to forgo the carryback and carry the loss forward instead.

• Bad debts. If your business uses accrual accounting, examine its receivables to find any that have become uncollectible and deduct them from income. The business will accrue them in taxable income—and pay tax on income it doesn't receive—if it fails to deduct them.

Note: Bad debts must be specifically identified, not estimated.

• Independent contractor reporting. This is another top audit issue for the IRS. Verify that all workers who are treated as contractors have been properly identified and issued 1099s. Two reasons...

☐ There is a $50 per form penalty for failing to file.

☐ If the IRS later decides contractors are employees, the potential defenses against steep penalties will be lost if 1099s have not been filed.

• Meal, entertainment, and auto deduction records. An IRS auditor will always look at these during a business audit, no matter what the audit's primary focus.

Why: It is "easy money" for the IRS—it always expects records to be inadequate, and it's often easy to find personal expenses deducted among the business ones.

Safety: Fully organize these records now so that if an IRS auditor calls, they will stand up to inspection.

Source: Martin S. Kaplan, CPA, Martin S. Kaplan, CPA, PC, 11 Penn Plaza, New York City 10001. He is author of *What the IRS Doesn't Want You to Know*. (Wiley).

194

Section 4: Business

Chapter Two
LOOPHOLES IN WORKING ABROAD

Americans working abroad run the risk that their income will be taxed twice —first in the country where they work and again in their home country. But with careful planning, they can shelter some worldwide income from tax.

Foreign income exclusion

Loophole: A provision in the Tax Code permits Americans who live and work in other countries to exclude up to $80,000 of wages, salary, professional fees, and moving expenses from US income tax. The exclusion is not automatic and must be claimed on Form 2555, Foreign Earned Income.

When married couples work overseas, each spouse is entitled to exclude up to $80,000 of income.

Limitation: This exclusion does not cover dividends, capital gains, interest, pensions, and other unearned income.

To qualify for the exclusion, you must be a bona fide resident of a foreign country for a full tax year. Whether you are a bona fide resident depends on your intention and the length and nature of your stay.

Example: When you go abroad with a definite purpose for a temporary period and return to the US after you accomplished it, you're not a bona fide resident of that country. But if accomplishing the purpose requires an extended, indefinite stay and you make your home (i.e., establish permanency, also including your family) there, you may be considered a bona fide resident.

Loophole: Satisfy the physical presence test. People who are not bona fide residents of foreign countries may qualify for the foreign income exclusion by meeting the "physical presence" test. To satisfy the test, you must be physically present in the country for at least 330 days of 12 consecutive months. To figure the minimum 330 full days, add up all the separate periods you were present in a foreign country during the 12 months. The 330 days do not need to be consecutive.

Note: Residents of Guam, Northern Mariana Islands, American Samoa, Puerto Rico, and the Virgin Islands might be exempt from US tax for income earned in those possessions. These exemptions are claimed on IRS Form 4563 or 8689 or 1040-PR. Check with your tax adviser.

Foreign housing costs

Loophole: Housing reimbursements or payments as a result of foreign employment are excluded from income subject to the limits in the foreign income exclusion. This amount can exceed $80,000. The excluded housing costs are the excess of annual expenses over 16% of the salary of a US federal employee paid at the annual rate for a grade GS-14. These amounts are prorated and calculated daily.

Loophole: You can carry forward unused (not deducted) foreign housing costs—subject to that year's limitations.

Foreign tax credit

Loophole: Claim a foreign tax credit on your US return when you pay tax in a foreign jurisdiction on income earned in that country. Do this by filing Form 1116 with your 1040.

The credit is limited to the lesser of the foreign taxes paid or the US tax on the income.

Example: You paid $45,000 in foreign taxes on $100,000 that you earned in that country. US tax on that same income is $35,000. Your foreign tax credit is limited to $35,000.

Please note: Starting in 2005, the full foreign tax credit can offset alternative minimum tax (before 2005, there was a 90% limit on the use of the credit for this purpose).

196

More loopholes

Loophole: Do not pay Social Security taxes when you work abroad. They should not be deducted from your earnings because you are not required to pay them. You might be required to pay the foreign country's version of Social Security taxes, depending on the US tax treaty with that country.

Self-employment tax, on the other hand, is treated differently...depending on the tax treaty that the US has signed.

Example: The treaty with Australia does not provide for an exemption of self-employment tax. So even though the money you earn in Australia is exempt from US income tax, you pay US self-employment tax on 100% of your foreign earnings.

Loophole: Avoid filing overseas. The US has treaties with many foreign countries limiting the tax rate that the country assesses on foreign earned interest and dividend income. The tax is withheld by the company paying the dividend or interest.

Example: You get a dividend check from a Dutch company, which withholds 15% in taxes. You do not have to file a tax return with the Netherlands. And you can take a tax credit on your US return for the 15% tax that was withheld in the Netherlands.

Loophole: If you have, or are a signatory of, a foreign bank or securities account, you must check the box on the bottom of Form 1040 Schedule B and report this on Form TD F 90-22.1, Report of Foreign Bank and Financial Accounts. If the aggregate value of the accounts at no time during the year was more than $10,000, you do not have to file the form. You also do not have to file the form if the account was maintained in certain facilities operated by a US financial institution.

Source: Edward Mendlowitz, CPA, shareholder in the CPA firm WithumSmith+Brown, 120 Albany St., New Brunswick, NJ 08901. He is author of *Estate Planning* (Practical Programs).

Section 4: Business

Chapter Three
ADVERTISING LOOPHOLES

Businesses use advertising to build new markets and increase revenues from current customers. Generally, reasonable advertising expenses are deductible in the year incurred for businesses that operate on the accrual basis of accounting. Cash-basis businesses deduct advertising expenses in the year the expenses are paid.

Deductible advertising can be used for obtaining new business, image enhancement, public relations, or "help wanted" solicitations.

Use these tax strategies to stretch your advertising budget even further...

Loophole: Advertising done to create long-term advantages can be fully deducted, even though the benefits will be reaped in subsequent years. These include the costs of creating the advertising materials as well as the advertising campaign. Specifically...

• Logo, trademark, brand, and image-building materials are immediately deductible.

• Vanity book (ghost-written tomes about the company, its founder, or CEO) publishing costs are accumulated and deducted when the book is published and distributed.

• "Shelf-space bonuses" paid to have products prominently displayed are deductible as incurred.

Loophole: Sponsoring local athletic teams is deductible advertising when you play, coach, or manage a team and your sponsorship buys some form of company recognition. These include your company name, logo, or marketing on team uniforms, signs, programs, or score cards, or in the team's media ads.

Loophole: Costs of creating content for Web sites can be deducted by a company.

Caution: The IRS could very well contend that cost to create the permanent parts of the site (its structure, functionality, and appearance) is a capital cost. One argument against capitalizing such costs is the changing nature of Web sites. Purchased Web site designs can be amortized over three years; purchased software is Section 179 property, with elective expense deductions up to $108,000 in 2006.

Loophole: Mailing-list development costs are deductible even though a mailing list has an extended life. On the other hand, if a mailing list is sold, the income is considered capital gain and purchasers recover the cost by amortizing this "intangible asset" over 15 years.

Loophole: Business promotion costs—such as when establishing new product lines, setting up new sales territories, or opening branches in new areas—are fully deductible by existing businesses. When these same costs are incurred by someone who wants to get into a new business, they are considered nondeductible capital costs that may be amortized as "start-up" costs. However, they are not deductible if the project is abandoned and you never actually went into business.

Loophole: Advertising specialties and promotional products are deductible when they include your company name or message and are of minimal value ($4 or less). Items costing more are considered business gifts, which carry an annual deduction limit of $25 per recipient.

Loophole: Catalogs, brochures, and other advertising literature are all deductible as advertising expenses even though they will be distributed by the company and used by customers in future years.

Note: Federal circuit courts disagree with the IRS on the proper tax treatment of catalog costs. The IRS contends that such costs must be capitalized and deducted over the expected benefit periods. If you publish catalogs, check with your tax adviser.

Loophole: Package graphic design costs are currently deductible according to the Tax Court. The IRS disagrees. But both the Tax Court and the IRS do agree that display cases, billboards, and similar tangible items need to be depreciated and deducted.

Loophole: Advertising to express a company's views on current but indirect business issues—such as the economy—can be deducted.

Note: Political advertising to promote or defeat legislation or a candidate cannot be deducted, nor can advertising in political journals, meeting or convention programs, books, or media announcements.

Loophole: Circulation costs to obtain subscribers are fully deductible even though the subscription revenue covers more than one tax period. These include mailing costs, sales commissions, binders, and premiums.

You can elect to capitalize and amortize circulation costs.

Trap: To the extent the costs are deducted and not capitalized, they might subject noncorporate and certain other taxpayers to the alternative minimum tax.

Note: Subscription revenue is fully taxed when received by cash-basis taxpayers and is picked up ratably by those using accrual-basis accounting.

Source: Edward Mendlowitz, CPA, shareholder in the CPA firm WithumSmith+Brown, 120 Albany St., New Brunswick, NJ 08901. He is author of *Estate Planning* (Practical Programs).

Chapter Four
THE TOO, TOO COMMON MISTAKE MADE WITH EMPLOYER STOCK... HOW TO KEEP MORE PROFIT

If you hold appreciated employer stock in your tax-deferred retirement plan, you're entitled to a key tax break when you leave the company. But you must know the fine points to make the most of this shelter.

How it works

Most people will roll the balance of their account in an employer-sponsored plan into an IRA, maintaining the tax deferral. Down the line, all withdrawals will be fully taxed, at ordinary income rates.

Loophole: If you withdraw employer stock rather than rolling it over, you'll owe tax on your basis (tax cost) in the stock, not on its full market value. The difference, known as the net unrealized appreciation (NUA), will remain untaxed until the shares are sold.

What's more, sales of the NUA shares will immediately receive favorable long-term capital gains treatment.

Example: Paul Williams retires from his company with $600,000 in his employer-sponsored retirement plan, including $420,000 of employer stock. Paul's basis in those employer shares (the value of the shares when contributed to the plan) is $90,000.

Paul can withdraw all of his employer shares from his retirement plan and owe tax on just $90,000 worth of ordinary income. The other $330,000

($420,000 minus $90,000) is considered NUA.

Key: Paul can sell his NUA shares right away. If he does, he'll have a $330,000 long-term capital gain, taxed at only 15%.

Devilish details

What else do you need to know about this tax break?

Required: The NUA rules apply only if you take a lump-sum distribution from your employer-sponsored plan. That is, all the assets in your account must be withdrawn.

Key: Even though you must take all of these assets from your employer plan, it's not necessary to pay full tax right away. Assets that are not NUA may be rolled into an IRA.

Example: As above, Paul Williams has $600,000 in his employer plan, including $420,000 in employer stock.

When he withdraws his employer stock, he can roll the other $180,000 ($600,000 minus $420,000) to an IRA, for ongoing tax deferral.

You don't have to transfer all of your employer stock outside of the plan. If you wish, you can transfer some shares into an IRA and transfer the other shares into a taxable account.

Trap: If you roll some employer shares into an IRA, the NUA tax break will be lost on those shares when they are sold. Withdrawals from your IRA will be taxed as ordinary income.

Holding pattern: As mentioned, you can sell your NUA shares right away, for long-term capital gains. But what if you decide to retain some or all of your NUA shares?

Any further appreciation will be taxed as short-term gains up to a year, or as long-term gains after more than a year has elapsed. Your NUA always will qualify as long-term gain.

Early birds: What about the 10% early withdrawal penalty that usually occurs before age 59½?

Loopholes: You'll avoid this penalty on withdrawals from an employer-sponsored plan if you leave your job in or after the year of your 55th birthday.

And even if you are liable for the penalty, it will be applied only to the tax basis of the withdrawn shares.

Example: If Paul Williams is 53 years old when he changes jobs and withdraws employer shares with a market value of $420,000 and a basis of $90,000, the 10% penalty tax will be only $9,000.

There will be no penalty on the $330,000 worth of NUA, in our example, and no penalty on the $180,000 that's rolled into an IRA.

Covering the basis

As mentioned, partial withdrawals of NUA shares are permitted. This may be a savvy move if your company keeps thorough records and you have some high-basis as well as low-basis shares.

Example: Suppose, in the above example, Paul Williams has $420,000 worth of employer stock in his retirement plan but his basis in these shares is $300,000. Withdrawing all the shares will trigger $300,000 worth of ordinary income, which is not an attractive prospect.

However, Paul is able to identify $155,000 worth of employer shares in his account, held for many years, with a basis of only $20,000.

Strategy: Paul can direct those specific shares, now worth $155,000, to be distributed from his account when he leaves the company.

He'll owe tax on only $20,000 worth of ordinary income (and a 10% penalty of only $2,000, if applicable). The $135,000 NUA ($155,000 minus $20,000) will qualify as long-term gain.

Key: In this situation, the other $265,000 worth of employer stock ($420,000 minus $155,000) can be rolled into an IRA, along with Paul's other plan assets. Tax deferral can continue inside the IRA.

Know how to hold them

You may choose to hold onto NUA shares after withdrawing them from the plan and paying tax on the cost basis.

Trap: You shouldn't hold onto these shares until you die, though. If you do, the NUA portion will be taxable to your heirs, as long-term gains, when they sell the shares.

Any subsequent gain after the initial distribution from the plan will receive a step-up in basis, under current law, if the shares are held until your death.

Similarly, other securities get a basis step-up to fair market value when they're inherited. Thus, it makes more sense to liquidate NUA shares if you need spending money in retirement and hold on to other appreciated securities.

Example: Suppose Paul Williams pulls $420,000 of employer stock from his employer's plan and pays tax on $90,000 worth of basis. At his death, that stock is worth $500,000. The NUA of $330,000 ($420,000 minus $90,000) will be subject to tax, as long-term capital gains, when Paul's heirs sell the shares.

Strategy: Paul's heirs would be better off if Paul had sold the NUA shares during his lifetime and held on to a different $500,000 worth of appreciated securities.

Assuming current law remains in effect, Paul's heirs could have sold the other inherited securities without owing any tax on prior appreciation.

Important: Whether or not your securities get a basis step-up at death, the current value will be included in your taxable estate and possibly subject to estate tax.

Also, it isn't smart to liquidate securities solely on the basis of tax planning. It's also wise to keep investment considerations in mind, maintaining a well-balanced portfolio.

Strategy: Assuming such donations fit in with your overall investment plans, use NUA shares for charitable contributions.

Benefits: You'll get a full deduction for the market value of the shares without parting with any cash.

Giving away NUA shares allows you to retain other assets, which you can decide either to liquidate or to bequeath to heirs with a basis step-up.

Source: Mark Cortazzo, CFP, senior partner, MACRO Consulting Group, 1639 Route 10 E., Parsippany, NJ 07054. A member of the Financial Planning Association and the Estate Planning Council of Northern New Jersey, he has been named one of the best financial advisers in the US by *Worth, Registered Rep,* and *Research* magazines. He has written a guide to net unrealized appreciation planning, available at *www.macroconsultinggroup.com.*

Chapter Five

WHEN TO LEASE BUSINESS EQUIPMENT ...AND WHEN TO BUY

No matter what type of business you run, it probably requires some sort of equipment. For most business owners, the first impulse is to buy needed items.

Tax law makes buying equipment more attractive than ever. This year, many companies can expense (deduct immediately) up to $108,000 worth of equipment purchases.

Moreover, purchasing equipment on an installment basis is more affordable with interest rates so low.

Although buying equipment has appeal, there are times when leasing equipment makes more sense, for tax and financial reasons.

Taxing matters

If your company cannot fully take advantage of the tax benefits of equipment ownership, leasing may be a better choice.

Frequently, business equipment is obtained via a "fair market value" lease, also known as a true lease.

With this type of lease, your company has the option to return the equipment at the end of the term at no further obligation. Or, the lease may be renewed. As a third option, the equipment may be purchased at fair market value —hence the name.

Loophole: The payments on such leases are fully tax deductible as a business expense.

While these lease payments are deductible, your company's outlays for purchased equipment may have to be written off over several years. Leasing may accelerate tax deductions, compared with lengthy depreciation schedules.

Example: With a three-year lease, you may get faster write-offs than you would if you bought equipment that is depreciated over five years.

Trap: In some cases, the alternative minimum tax (AMT) may limit your depreciation deductions for purchased equipment.

Loophole: Equipment leasing expenses are not "preference items" so they don't increase your AMT liability.

Attraction of leasing

Aside from taxes, there may be other reasons to lease equipment rather than buy it.

• Preservation of capital. When your company purchases equipment, a 10% to 20% down payment may be required.

On the other hand, equipment leases often require much smaller amounts of cash up front. "Soft costs," such as warranties, shipping, and installation may be built into the lease payments rather than paid immediately.

Key: By leasing equipment, your company may retain scarce capital for other purposes. Credit lines can be maintained. With leasing, you pay for equipment over time and avoid a large initial outlay.

• Expected obsolescence. If there is a substantial risk that equipment will become obsolete before the end of its useful life, it may not make sense to purchase it.

If you lease equipment, you can decide at the end of the lease term whether to keep the property (via release or purchase) or to upgrade to state-of-the-art items. Regular replacement can reduce repair and maintenance costs.

• Limited use. If your company only expects to need an item for a short period of time, why buy it? You'll soon have to worry about reselling the equipment.

• Questionable resale value. When your company buys equipment, it assumes the risk of finding a buyer when that item no longer is useful. If you have doubts about its future market value, you can avoid that risk by leasing.

• Availability. Certain types of equipment may be more easily obtained from a leasing company than from other sources.

• Urgency. If you need equipment right away, leasing may be indicated. For inexpensive items, your company might not have to provide financial statements and the approval process may be expedited.

• Seasonal business. Companies with revenues that are skewed toward certain times of year may be able to arrange a flexible lease, with payments scheduled to be in sync with the flow of business.

• Balance sheet concerns. Some leases may not have to appear on your balance sheet. This can improve crucial financial ratios and help you obtain additional financing, providing more capital for growth.

Bottom line: It doesn't pay to buy depreciating assets, or those that are likely to become outdated soon. For such assets, leasing can provide 100% financing with relatively low payments over an extended time period.

The case for buying

Equipment leasing isn't for everyone. As mentioned, current tax law and low interest rates favor equipment purchases. Buying equipment may also pay off if the economic expansion continues in 2006. As the threat of insolvency due to poor business conditions declines, your company may want to put its cash flow to work by buying productive equipment. Purchasing equipment eliminates worries about releasing essential business property.

Moreover, buying equipment allows your company to gain from any appreciation.

Example: Some river barges are now worth more than when they were originally purchased 10 years ago.

Generally, if you think you'll be using equipment for most of its useful life, purchasing it may be cost effective. Also, buying may offer tax advantages now...

• Expensing. In 2006, equipment purchases of up to $108,000 can be written off immediately. Therefore, if your equipment purchases will be below that level, buying may offer the greatest tax advantage.

Loophole: You can take this deduction for the year the equipment is placed in service, not when it's paid for.

Required: To get the full $108,000 write-off, your company can purchase no more than $430,000 worth of equipment that year. Also, there must be taxable income for this deduction to offset.

The tax law certainly will have an impact on your buy-or-lease choice. Nevertheless, you should consider other factors, such as your need for capital and the prospect of obsolescence before deciding how to acquire equipment.

Source: Richard M. Contino, Esq., managing partner, Contino + Partners, 70 W. Red Oak La., White Plains, NY 10604. He is author of *The Complete Equipment-Leasing Handbook* (Amacom).

Section 4: Business

Chapter Six

LOOPHOLES FOR FOREIGNERS WORKING IN THE US

People who work in the United States but live abroad must pay US tax on their earnings here plus taxes to their home countries. Here are some smart ways to whittle down your payments to the IRS...

Loophole: Work in the US under a visa rather than a green card. Legal resident aliens (green-card holders) are treated as if they were US citizens and must pay US tax on all of their worldwide income.

As a general rule, nonresident aliens are taxed on income connected with a US business and capital gains from sale of US real estate. Other income, including interest and dividends, is taxed at a flat rate of 30% (or lower, depending on the tax treaty). Foreigners report US income on IRS Form 1040NR, *US Nonresident Alien Income Tax Return.*

Strategy: Forgo applying for a green card if you have substantial non-US income (other types of visas permit US investing and business activity). Reason: People who hold work visas must pay US tax only on income earned in the US and do not owe any Social Security tax. The rate of tax and withholding from earnings depends on the tax treaty between the foreign country and the US government.

Trap: Even if you do not have a green card but meet a complicated test—including 183 days of physical presence in three years—you will be taxed as a resident.

Loophole: Resident aliens who claim a foreign tax credit reduce the US tax owed on income that was taxed in another country. Because tax rates abroad typically are higher than rates in the US, the credit often eliminates virtually all

US tax.

Report the income on Form 1116, Foreign Tax Credit, with your US tax return. The credit is limited to the lesser of the foreign taxes paid or US tax on the income.

Loophole: Nonresident aliens do not owe self-employment tax on income from a business or profession. But they still must pay income tax on their earned income.

Loophole: Nonresident aliens should own real property in a trust or limited liability company (LLC) but not directly in an individual's name.

Reason: The state probate process will no longer apply. (US income tax on net earnings, or the capital gains tax, is still owed.)

Caution: Avoid a regular C corporation because of separate US and state corporate taxes, and double taxation when the corporation is liquidated. Nonresident aliens cannot be shareholders of S corporations.

Loophole: Set up a revocable living trust. It will facilitate many of the decisions and actions that are needed after a person's death. It cannot save income or estate taxes but does reduce much of the probate process.

Loophole: Create a single-person LLC. Income and expenses are reported on your individual income tax return. No separate US tax applies to LLCs but some states tax them, so consult an attorney in the state where you own the property. Also, LLCs may offer an element of asset protection.

Loophole: US tax treaties with many foreign countries limit the tax rate that the US assesses on interest, dividend, and original issue discount (OID) income. US tax returns do not have to be filed if the payer of the interest, dividend, or OID withholds the tax and the amounts are the only US transactions. (Capital gains from securities are not taxed.) Withholding tax is required by the payer on any income paid to a nonresident alien individual, partner, or corporation that is not connected with a US trade or business.

Loophole: If you have, or are a signatory of, a foreign bank or securities account, you must check the box on the bottom of Form 1040, Schedule B, and report it on Form TD F 90-22.1, *Report of Foreign Bank and Financial Accounts.*

If the aggregate value of the accounts never exceeded $10,000 in the year, the form is not required. Exceptions also are made for certain accounts maintained in certain facilities operated by US financial institutions.

Loophole: Foreigners do not have to obtain a Social Security number for income earned in the US or for bank accounts. Form W-7, Application for IRS Individual Taxpayer Identification Number, is used to obtain a number that is used for tax purposes instead of a Social Security number or employer's identification number. Obtaining this number creates no inference about US immigration status or the right to work in the US.

A note on expatriates: US citizens who renounce their citizenship and leave the US do not have to file and pay US taxes. But people leaving in 2006 who previously had five-year annual incomes averaging more than $131,000 or net worth exceeding $655,000 must file tax returns for 10 years after they leave the US. To renounce citizenship, file IRS Form 8854, *Expatriation Initial Information Statement*.

Source: Edward Mendlowitz, CPA, shareholder in the CPA firm WithumSmith+Brown, 120 Albany St., New Brunswick, NJ 08901. He is author of *Estate Planning* (Practical Programs).

Chapter Seven

HOW TO GET A BIGGER TAX REFUND FOR YOUR BUSINESS

April 17, 2006 will be here before you know it, but there are still a number of steps you can take to reduce your 2005 tax bill and even get an early refund.

Reduce taxable income

Hopefully, you've been taking steps all year long to keep your taxable income as low as possible. But it's not too late to take additional steps after year-end. These include...

• Adopt LIFO inventory. In times of rising prices, using the "last-in, first-out" method to compute the cost of goods sold can lower your income from sales. If you've been using FIFO (first-in, first-out), you have until the time you file your return to make the switch.

• Set up and fund a qualified retirement plan. If 2006 has been profitable, shelter income while saving for your retirement by putting money into a qualified retirement plan...

• If you already have a plan, you have until the extended due date of your return to fund it.

• If you haven't yet set up a plan, it's not too late to create a simplified employee pension (SEP) plan. You have until the extended due date of the return to set up and fund the SEP. If you qualify and your income is high enough, you can shelter as much as $44,000.

Strategy: Get Uncle Sam to pay for the contribution. File your return, reporting a deduction for your intended contribution. Then use the refund generated by the deduction to finance the contribution.

• Use the most favorable depreciation write-offs. Increased first-year expensing ceiling of $108,000 in 2006, gives you great flexibility over the equipment write-offs you can claim.

You may be able to use accelerated depreciation on building components if they are classified separately from the structure itself.

Example: If you were to install special wiring in your office building, it could be depreciated over seven years using accelerated depreciation, as opposed to straight-line depreciation over the 39 years applicable to the building.

Strategy: Use a real estate depreciation expert to help you devise a cost segregation study, which is a formal analysis of depreciation for building components.

Reduce taxes

If your tax bill seems overwhelming, you can offset your tax liability dollar for dollar with tax credits. The federal tax law has an ever-growing list of credits for business, including credits for...

• Adopting a retirement plan if you don't have one.

• Providing child-care services for your staff.

• Undertaking research and development.

• Hiring certain types of workers, such as veterans or food stamp recipients.

• Modifying your facilities to accommodate disabled people.

• Doing business on American Indian reservations.

• Doing business in other economically disadvantaged areas.

Strategy: Check whether any of these or other business credits apply to your situation.

State tax opportunities

Using federal tax breaks is not the only way to reduce your annual tax bill. Carefully review your state income tax rules for business. There may be deductions, credits, and tax abatements available. Each state has different rules.

Many incentives relate to creating jobs, hiring certain disadvantaged workers, and doing business in economically depressed areas.

Strategy: Contact your state revenue department or consult with your tax adviser to determine whether actions you've already taken may entitle you to state tax breaks.

Reclaim taxes you've paid

• Overpaid estimated taxes. If you've overpaid estimated taxes for the year, you don't have to wait until you file the return to get a refund. C corporations can obtain one by filing Form 4466, Corporation Application for Quick Refund of Overpayment of Estimated Tax. File the return after the start of the year but before you file the corporation's return. You should hear from the IRS within 45 days of the application and receive the funds to meet other company expenses.

Strategy: Don't assume that the overpayment can be applied to 2006 estimated tax payments.

Reason: If 2006 is a losing year, you won't be able to recoup your 2006 estimated tax overpayment until 2007!

Caution: Owners of pass-through entities and sole proprietors who have overpaid personal estimated tax on their share of business income can obtain a refund only by filing their personal tax returns.

Strategy: Individuals should take a good look at income and expenses for the year before making their fourth installment of estimated taxes for 2005 (due January 17, 2006). You may be able to reduce or forgo the payment, thus avoiding a larger overpayment—that won't be refunded until the return for 2005 is filed.

• Net operating losses (NOLs). If your business lost money in 2005, you may be able to use losses to obtain a refund of taxes going back two years.

Note: Certain situations entitle you to a longer carryback period...

• If your business had average annual gross receipts of $5 million or less during the three prior years, you have a five-year carryback for NOLs arising from government-declared disasters.

• Farmers and ranchers have a five-year carryback.

• Businesses with NOLs created from product liability have a 10-year carryback.

Obtain a quick refund from the carrybacks by filing the appropriate form...

• For C corporations—IRS Form 1139, *Corporation Application for Tentative Refund.*

• For other taxpayers—IRS Form 1045, *Application for Tentative Refund.* Usually, you'll hear from the IRS within 90 days.

• Prior returns. Generally, you can go back three years to amend returns and claim refunds of overpaid taxes.

Example: In 2004, you made renovations to your office building, depreciating them over the remaining useful life of the building, which was 25 years. You now recognize that some of those renovations, such as movable partitions and wiring, qualify as components that can be separately depreciated much more rapidly, generating a sizable refund for 2004 and 2005. Use the more rapid depreciation write-offs on the 2006 return and file amended returns for 2004 and 2005 to reflect the proper depreciation treatment.

Source: Jacob Weichholz, CPA, tax partner, Ernst & Young LLP, 5 Times Square, New York City 10036.

Chapter Eight

THE KEY INFORMATION RETURNS FOR YOUR BUSINESS

Information reporting goes beyond furnishing data on wages to the IRS and the Social Security Administration. Your reporting obligations extend to the following areas...

Retirement plans

If you have a qualified retirement plan, such as a profit-sharing plan, you must report annually on the plan's activities—annual contributions, distributions, number of participants, etc. Forms to use...

• Form 5500, *Annual Report/Report of Employee Benefit Plan*, if you have any employees.

Exception: You do not have to file if your plan is a SEP or a SIMPLE-IRA plan.

• Form 5500-EZ, *Annual Return of One Participant (Owners and Their Spouses) Retirement Plan*, if you are self-employed and the only participant is you (or you and your spouse...or you and your partners and spouses).

Exception: You do not have to file if plan assets did not exceed $100,000 in any year after 1993.

This IRS form is not filed with the IRS—it is filed with the Pension and Welfare Benefits Administration (now called the Employee Benefits Security Administration). If you do not receive a form in the mail, request one. (It cannot be downloaded because it is a scannable form.)

Due date: The last day of the seventh month following the close of the plan year (for example, July 31, 2006, for the 2005 plan year for calendar-year plans). If additional time is needed, request an automatic two-and-a-half-month extension by filing Form 5558, *Application for Extension of Time to File Certain Employee Plan Returns.* If you obtained an automatic six-month filing extension for your personal income tax return, you have until October 16, 2006, to file Form 5500 or 5500-EZ for 2005 (attach a copy of the extension when you file the form).

Penalties: As much as $25 a day (up to $15,000) for late filing.

For more information, go to *www.efast.dol.gov* or call 866-463-3278.

Cash transactions

• Large cash transactions. If you receive more than $10,000 in cash in one or more related transactions in the course of doing business, you must report the transaction to the IRS and give a written statement to the person who paid you in cash. "Cash" is not limited to currency—it includes cashier's checks, money orders, bank drafts, and traveler's checks.

How to file: Use Form 8300, *Report of Cash Payments Over $10,000 Received in a Trade or Business.* The form must be filed with the IRS within 15 days of receiving the cash.

Example: If the transaction occurred on January 1, you must report it to the IRS by January 15. You have until January 31 of the following year to give a written statement to the person who paid you in cash.

Penalties: If you cannot show reasonable cause for your failure to report the transaction on time, you may be subject to penalties. A minimum penalty of $25,000 can be imposed for a willful failure.

And criminal prosecution can result. Recently, a self-employed business owner sold 34 electric generators for cash—each costing more than $10,000— and did not report the transactions. She pleaded guilty to a charge of failing to file an information return, the maximum sentence for which is six years in jail and a fine of $250,000.

• Small cash transactions. Businesses, such as convenience stores, groceries, liquor stores, travel agencies, courier services, and gas stations, that sell or redeem money orders or traveler's checks in excess of $1,000 per customer per day or issue their own value cards must report "suspicious" activities that exceed $2,000. The government estimates there are about 158,000 such businesses handling $200 billion annually. Suspicious activities may include...

☐ Customers attempting to keep the transaction from being reported or asking how to avoid reporting.

☐ Customers providing false or expired identification.

☐ Individuals splitting up a transaction that equals more than $3,000 combined.

☐ Customers who refuse to proceed with the transaction once told that a form must be completed.

☐ Customer attempts to threaten or bribe you.

☐ Customers buying multiple money orders in even hundred-dollar denominations or in unusual quantities.

Use Form TD F 90-22.56, *Suspicious Activity Report by Money Services Businesses*. The form must be filed with the US Treasury Department's Money Services Business Division within 30 days of the suspicious activity.

Legal note: The person that you report cannot sue you for damages.

Paying contractors

If you use independent contractors or subcontractors in your business and pay them $600 or more annually, you must report payments to the IRS. (In most cases, payments you make to corporations do not have to be reported.)

How to file: Use Form 1099-MISC, *Miscellaneous Income*.

Obtain the form from the IRS (800-829-3676) or from office supply companies. You cannot download these triplicate forms.

You must furnish the form to the contractor no later than January 31 of the year after the year of payment. The IRS copy of the form must be filed no later than February 28. The filing address depends on where your business is located. If you file electronically, you have until March 31 to file with the IRS (although there is no additional time for furnishing the necessary form to the independent contractor).

You can request a filing extension by filing Form 8809, Request for Extension of Time to File Information Returns.

Penalties: The penalty for late filing depends on how late you are. The faster you correct the nonfiling, the smaller the penalty. For example, $15 per information return if you file within 30 days (up to a maximum of $25,000 for small businesses)...$50 per return if you file after August 1 (up to a maximum of $100,000 for small businesses).

Source: Barbara Weltman, Esq., small-business expert and author of *J.K. Lasser's Small Business Taxes* (Wiley). One of her books is *The Complete Idiot's Guide to Starting an eBay Business* (Penguin). *www.barbaraweltman.com.*

Chapter Nine

AVOID THE TAX BITE WHEN YOU PAY FOR EMPLOYEES' MEALS

Chances are that you provide at least some meals for your employees. Ideally, the cost of those meals is deductible by your company and not taxable for the employees.

Trap: Unless you meet specific standards, you and your employees could be looking at a very stiff bill.

Exclusions for eating

For meals to be excluded from income, the Tax Code [Section 119(a)] provides some shelter. Meals furnished to an employee are excluded from income if your company provides the meals on its premises and for its convenience.

This exclusion also applies to meals provided to employees' spouses and other dependents.

To show that a meal is provided for your convenience, you must prove that there's a solid reason for bringing in pizza, sandwiches, etc. It cannot be done to reward your staff. Acceptable reasons include...

• Making employees available during meal periods.

• Meal periods so short that it is impractical for employees to go out for meals.

• No suitable places to buy meals near your business.

• Employees have to work extended hours, missing a meal, so meals are provided immediately afterward.

Trap 1: Meals furnished merely to promote employee morale or goodwill must be included in their income. Providing free bagels daily to employees before work probably wouldn't qualify for an exclusion. Most employees could eat breakfast at home or on the way to work.

Trap 2: Cash allowances for meals or cash reimbursements do not qualify for this exclusion.

Exception: Meal money paid on an occasional basis to an employee working overtime can be excluded from income.

Majority rule

Some employees might be entitled to meal inclusion, while others won't. Keeping track can be a headache.

Helpful: If more than half of the employees receiving meals qualify for the exclusion, all meals furnished to employees will be considered as being provided for the employer's convenience.

So, the value of all the meals received under these circumstances would be excluded from employees' income and deductible by the employer.

The 100% solution

Your company can take a deduction whether or not employees must include meals as compensation.

In general, meals that you provide for your employees are treated as business entertaining. Your company's deduction is limited to 50% of the cost.

However, there are certain circumstances under which a 100% deduction is allowed. If you provide meals primarily for the benefit of rank-and-file employees rather than highly compensated executives, a 100% deduction will be permitted.

A 100% deduction is also allowed for meals that are excludable from an employee's gross income as a "de minimis" fringe benefit. A *de minimis* fringe benefit is one that is so small and infrequent that accounting for it would be unreasonable or impracticable.

Meals or meal money a company provides to an employee may qualify as a *de minimis* fringe benefit if...

• The amounts paid are reasonable, and...

• Meals or meal money are provided occasionally, not regularly or routinely, or...

• Your company provides meals or meal money to employees working overtime.

Example: You sometimes bring in dinner from a nearby restaurant for employees who work late. The employees need not report any income from such meals and your company can take a 100% deduction for the costs.

•The cost of the on-site meal you provided was "for the convenience of the employer," so it qualifies for a 100% deduction.

Example: You want your company's sales reps to be around as much as possible in order to deal with buyers, so you limit their lunch break to 30 minutes. Providing sandwiches for their lunch makes it more likely they will conform to this schedule. The sales reps don't have to include any income, while you can take a 100% deduction.

Cafeteria plans

Another part of the Tax Code [Section 132(e)(2)] applies if you maintain a subsidized eating facility for employees.

Benefits: You can deduct the operating expenses and your employees can avoid recognizing taxable income. Required...

• The facility must be on or near your business premises.

• Your company must own or lease the facility and operate it as well.

• Meals must be furnished during or immediately before or after the employees' working hours.

In addition, the facility's revenues must equal or exceed its direct operating costs.

Key: It may be necessary to charge all employees for meals, enough to cover the direct costs, to preserve the tax benefits.

Note: Nondiscrimination rules apply. Thus, you can't get favorable tax treatment if you operate a dining room solely for top executives.

Stiff payroll tax

If you can't meet the requirements previously described, the taxable value of the meals must be included in your employees' gross income. Such income will be subject to payroll tax and income tax withholding. Furthermore, your company will have to comply with payroll tax requirements.

This can be expensive. And determining the amounts to include as income can be a nightmare. Worse still, your expenses might be only 50% deductible if there's no rationale for a 100% deduction.

In the case of a subsidized facility, Treasury regulations call for the direct operating costs to be increased to 150% to determine the meals' value. Therefore, the extra payroll tax your company would have to pay could be enormous.

Paper trail

Because the downside risks are so significant, your company should take steps to sustain the tax benefits of any meal program...

• Have a written policy on employee meals.

• Record the rules in the corporate minutes and disseminate it, if practical. Notices explaining the policy should be sent to all employees as well as to managers.

• Keep separate records. If 50%-deductible meals for entertaining clients are lumped with 100%-deductible meals, confusion will result. If you are challenged, it's possible that no 100% deductions will be allowed.

Strategy: Separately identify and report meal expenses that qualify for a 100% deduction. The extra administrative hassle likely will be well worth it, given the added tax benefits.

Source: John B. Truskowski, Esq., CPA, of counsel to Lord, Bissell & Brook LLP, 115 S. LaSalle St., Chicago 60603, where he heads the tax practice group. He formerly chaired the State and Local Tax Interest Group of the Illinois CPA Society and chaired the Federal Taxation Section Council of the Illinois State Bar Association.

Chapter Ten

FOR FREE ANSWERS TO YOUR BUSINESS TAX QUESTIONS...LOOK ON-LINE

The Internet can help you find answers to your business tax questions—at no cost. You can use the information you find there to support the tax positions you take on your returns. Areas of greatest concern to business...

Reasonable compensation

Compensation is one of the most frequently litigated issues between taxpayers and the IRS. Businesses need to know what is considered "reasonable" compensation for two important reasons...

• Only reasonable compensation is deductible. Amounts in excess of that are not deductible.

• Businesses want to pay competitive wages to attract and retain good workers. But they need to know what's competitive.

The tax law doesn't set a dollar amount. What's reasonable pay in your business depends on the facts and circumstances, including location, job responsibilities, what other companies pay, and company profitability, too.

On-line help: You can learn what's reasonable by seeing what similar companies are paying their employees. This information can help you fix your pay scale and avoid litigation with the IRS. To review pay levels, visit...

• Career Info Net at *www.careernet.org* (click on "Employment").

• WorldatWork, The Professional Association for Compensation, Benefits and Total Rewards at *www.worldatwork.org*.

Classification of workers

Workers are either "employees" or "independent contractors." Are those working for you properly classified? The answer affects your obligation to pay employment taxes and provide fringe benefits (e.g., health insurance and retirement plan contributions).

If you treat workers as independent contractors but the IRS later reclassifies them as employees, the consequences can be very serious for your business. You can be liable for back taxes plus substantial interest and penalties. These sums could be steep enough to put you out of business.

What's more, if you owe these reclassified workers back benefits, your retirement plan could lose its qualified status.

Caution: Worker classification is currently a top audit target of the IRS since there are billions of tax dollars at stake.

On-line help: On its Web site, the IRS provides criteria you can use to check your worker classifications. These factors may be found in an IRS audit guide created for its personnel to use in examining employers. Visit *www.irs.gov/tax pros/article/0,,id=98941,00.html*.

Travel and entertainment expenses

You can cover employee travel expenses by reimbursing them for their actual costs or at a standard per diem rate. Using the per diem method eliminates the need for employees to substantiate to the company the actual costs of lodging, meals, and incidental expenses. These costs are covered by the per diem rates.

Per diem rates are fixed on the government's fiscal year starting October 1. You may use the rates in effect for the first three quarters of the year in the fourth quarter, or you can use the new rates in effect for the fourth quarter.

On-line help: To find the rates, look at...

• IRS Publication 1542, *Per Diem Rates (for Travel Within the Continental United States)*, at *www.irs.gov*.

• Per diem rates at the U.S. General Services Administration site at *www.gsa.gov*.

Charitable contributions

Regular C corporations can claim an enhanced charitable contribution deduction for gifts of property. They can deduct the property's adjusted basis—typically cost—plus one-half of its unrealized (not taken) appreciation for certain donations. Included...

• Property, including inventory, donated to a charity for the care of children, the ill, or the needy.

• Donations of scientific property used for research by certain educational institutions or scientific research organizations.

• Donations of computer equipment to schools, grades K–2, and public libraries.

Note: The deduction for computer equipment expired on December 31, 2005, unless Congress extends it, retroactively.

Other inventory donations, including donations by other types of businesses, are deductible at the inventory's basis (i.e., cost).

Donations of other types of property, such as securities of other companies, may be deductible at fair market value.

On-line help: Use the Internet to learn where to make your donations and what to value them at.

Where to donate excess inventory: To find a charity interested in receiving your excess inventory, visit these clearinghouses...

• Gifts in Kind International at *www.giftsinkind.org*.

• World Vision's Gifts-in-Kind Program at *www.worldvision.org*.

Where to donate used computer equipment: In addition to the clearinghouses above, try...

• www.Recycles.Org at *www.recycles.org*.

• Computers for Children at *www.computersforchildren.com*.

• EducateUSA.com at *www.educateusa.com*.

Valuing property donations: One of the key problems in donating property to charity is determining the correct value of the donation. Some suggestions for help...

• IRS Publication 561, *Determining the Value of Donated Property*, at *www. irs.gov*.

• UsedComputer.com, at *www.usedcomputer.com*, for determining the value of old PCs.

Multistate operations

Thinking about doing business in another state? Before you do, find out the tax implications. Learn about...

• Income taxes, including special tax incentives for businesses that are new to the state.

• Employment tax obligations for workers in the state.

• Sales and use taxes.

• Property taxes.

For the reasons just mentioned, you may decide a new location is too costly from a tax perspective. Or large tax breaks may prompt you to locate in economically distressed areas.

On-line help: All key tax information is provided on state Web sites. For links, click on the Federation of Tax Administrators at *www.taxadmin.org*. Other helpful resources...

• TaxSites.com at *www.taxsites.com/state.html*.

• Tax Foundation at *www.taxfoundation.org*.

Selling a business

Whether you are selling your company or buying another company, you need to know the value of the business.

To find a qualified appraiser, click on...

• American Society of Appraisers at *www.appraisers.org*.

• Institute of Business Appraisers at *www.go-iba.org*.

• International Society of Appraisers at *www.isa-appraisers.org*.

• National Association of Certified Valuation Analysts at *www.nacva.com*.

Note: You can also use these sites for valuing portions of your interest in a business for purposes of making a gift. Even if you plan to give shares in your company to children or grandchildren worth less than the annual gift tax exclusion (currently $11,000, or $22,000 if a spouse joins in the gift), you should get a correct appraisal of the company's worth. This will pinpoint the value of the interests you give if the transfers are ever examined by the IRS. Use the information above to find a qualified appraiser.

Source: Barbara Weltman, Esq., small-business expert and author of *J.K. Lasser's Small Business Taxes* (Wiley). One of her books is *The Complete Idiot's Guide to Starting an eBay Business* (Penguin). *www.barbaraweltman.com.*

Section 4: Business

Chapter Eleven

FUTA AND SUTA—THE INS AND OUTS OF UNEMPLOYMENT TAXES FOR SMALL BUSINESS

Employers must pay taxes to the federal government, as well as their states, to cover unemployment obligations. Tax to the federal government is called FUTA (Federal Unemployment Tax Act), which creates the tax obligation.

Tax to the state generally is called unemployment insurance (UI), even though you do not obtain coverage through an insurance company and payments are not called premiums. (It is also referred to as SUTA—state unemployment tax.) On the state level, your payments are not determined by a flat tax rate, but rather depend on your "experience"—how many employees have made claims against you—so your UI rate may change from year to year.

Figuring the federal tax

FUTA is calculated on wages up to $7,000 per employee. Wages include not only cash wages, but also commissions, fees, bonuses, vacation allowances, sick pay, the value of goods, clothing and noncash fringe benefits, employee contributions to 401(k) and SIMPLE plans, and payments to adoption programs.

Note: If your business is incorporated, you must pay FUTA even if you are the only employee.

If you have a state experience rate lower than 5.4%, you can take a 5.4 percentage point credit against the federal rate. Generally, this means that the effective rate you pay to the federal government is only 0.8%, rather than 5.4%. As such, the maximum tax for each employee usually is just $56 per year

($7,000 x 0.8%).

Caution: The full credit for contributions to a state fund applies only if UI is paid on time.

Credit reduction states: States may be forced to borrow from the federal government to pay unemployment benefits. If the funds have not been repaid, then employers in such states must pay additional federal unemployment tax. For example, due to economic conditions, New York was such a "credit reduction" state for 2004 because it failed to repay borrowed funds. As a result, employers in New York had to cut their 5.4 point credit by 0.3, for a top credit of 5.1 percentage points.

Figuring the state tax

In contrast to the modest federal unemployment tax, states may levy substantial sums, depending on your experience. New employers typically are assigned a rate for their first year or two (depending on the state) because they do not yet have any prior experience with claims.

Caution: Don't assume your UI rate for 2005 is the same as it was for 2004. Your experience may affect your rate. And law changes may increase or decrease your UI rate. For example, Illinois has increased its top rate for 2005 to 9.8% on a total wage base of $10,500 (up from 8.6% on a total wage base of $9,800 in 2004).

Dumping: Because of the high cost to employers of state unemployment coverage, some employers have used a tax evasion scheme in which shell companies are formed and manipulated to obtain low tax rates. Once the low rates are obtained, the payroll from high-rate companies is "dumped" into the low-rate company.

Caution: The federal SUTA Dumping Prevention Act of 2004, requires states to enact anti-dumping legislation. California is one of the first states to do so— starting on January 1, 2005, significant penalties are imposed on employers that engage in dumping. Their UI rate will be fixed at the highest state rate, plus two percentage points. And there is a penalty of the greater of $5,000 or 10% of underreported contributions, penalties, or interest imposed on anyone who advises employers about dumping. Michigan has also started to crack down on dumping.

Deposit requirements

In the past, employers were required to deposit FUTA taxes if accumulated taxes exceeded $100, an amount fixed in 1970. The Treasury has increased the deposit threshold so that starting in 2005, employers are required to deposit FUTA taxes if accumulated taxes exceed $500. This increase in the deposit threshold is expected to provide relief to about four million small businesses.

Caution: A late payment penalty can be assessed for not paying taxes on time or not paying via the Electronic Federal Tax Payment System (EFTPS) when required.

Electronic deposits: If your total tax deposits from all sources were more than $200,000 in 2004, or if you were required to deposit via EFTPS in 2005, you have to deposit FUTA taxes electronically in 2006. Even if this does not apply to you, you can opt to deposit FUTA taxes electronically using EFTPS. For information, go to *www.eftps.gov* or call 800-555-4477. Check with your state about electronic deposits for unemployment insurance.

Annual filing for FUTA

While the federal tax burden may be low, employers cannot overlook filing requirements. There are substantial penalties for failing to file on time.

Employers are required to report unemployment taxes to the federal government only annually. This is done on Form 940, Employer's Annual Federal Unemployment (FUTA) Tax Return or Form 940-EZ, Employer's Annual Federal Unemployment (FUTA) Tax Return. (Household employers use Schedule H of Form 1040 to report FUTA taxes on household employees.)

Note: The IRS is in the process of revamping the Form 940 for 2006 annual returns filed in 2007. At that time, there will no longer be a Form 940-EZ.

The simplified form—Form 940-EZ—can be used if you paid unemployment contributions to one state only and if all wages were taxable for state unemployment purposes. For example, if you paid wages to corporate officers, such amounts are taxable for FUTA but may be exempt from state unemployment insurance. If so, Form 940-EZ cannot be filed in this case. The same may be true for certain types of fringe benefits subject to FUTA but exempt from state unemployment insurance.

Important: Employers in credit reduction states may not file Form 940-EZ.

You must file a federal return if you paid wages of $1,500 or more in any calendar quarter in either the current or previous year, or you had one or more employees for at least some part of a day in any 20 or more different weeks in the current or previous year.

In the case of household employees, the filing threshold is cash wages of $1,000 or more for all household employees in any calendar quarter this year or the prior year.

Special rules apply to agricultural employers.

Electronic filing: The annual filing of the unemployment tax return can be done electronically.

Quarterly filing for UI

While the FUTA return is filed annually, state UI returns typically must be filed quarterly. Check with your state to determine filing deadlines as well as opportunities to file electronically.

Source: Joanne Mitchell-George, Esq., senior managing editor, Aspen Publishers, 111 Eighth Ave., New York City 10011. She is author of *American Payroll Association Basic Guide to Payroll* and *Payroll Answer Book* (both from Aspen).

Chapter Twelve

CUT YOUR COMPANY'S BUILDING COSTS WITH CLEVER USE OF THE TAX CODE

When your company undertakes any construction, put tax planning into the blueprint. You can cut building costs by accelerating depreciation deductions.

Trap: Commercial real estate must be depreciated over 39 years. Thus, the money you spend on construction will be recovered at a snail's pace, based on deductions at a rate of around 2.5% per year.

Loophole: Many of the dollars you put into, say, a new warehouse or a renovated headquarters will be spent on building components rather than on the base building—and such property can qualify for five- or seven-year depreciation.

Examples: Process equipment (such as pipes used in chemical plants), electrical components (such as cables, wires, connectors, conduits), and plumbing items (such as faucets and valves) may qualify for faster depreciation. Creative planning can expand this list.

Land improvements: Money spent on landscaping, parking lots, etc., may be recovered over 15 years, much faster than the 39-year depreciation schedule for real estate. Plus, allocating various "soft costs" (for instance, architectural and materials testing services, such as for radon gas, and construction period interest) according to their function can lead to a portion of these soft costs being depreciated as shorter-lived property.

Payoff: The faster you take depreciation deductions, the greater their present value and the lower your net cost, after tax.

Moving parts

Some preconstruction planning can help you maximize the shift from 39-year real estate outlays to five- or seven-year depreciation of building components. For more details, see IRS Publication 946, *How to Depreciate Property.*

Key: IRS Revenue Ruling 75-178 states that an element's "attachment" to the property is more important than its "nature and use," when it comes to Tax Code classification. This ruling can support the use of a rapid depreciation schedule, as long as the item is not a structural component of the building.

Strategy: Design building components as movable furnishings rather than parts of the basic structure, whenever possible. The depreciation period is shorter. Examples...

• Premanufactured products. Freestanding, movable shelves are considered furniture when it comes to depreciation. Use them rather than built-in shelves, which might be subject to real estate depreciation.

• Partitions, not walls. Non-load-bearing partitions that include doors and windows can qualify for seven-year depreciation—tax treatment you won't get with permanent walls.

• Relocation, relocation, relocation. Another tactic for accelerating real estate depreciation is to have relocatable furniture (such as removable cabinets), lights, certain plumbing fixtures (such as toilets), and possibly even ceilings (such as acoustical tile), rather than permanent built-ins.

• Individual air-conditioning units. Central air-conditioning will be depreciated over the full 39-year schedule. Individual units are depreciated over five to seven years.

Bottom line: With thorough planning, a large portion of the money you spend on a construction project can be recovered via five- or seven-year depreciation.

Important questions

Here are a list of questions that you should ask yourself (and answer truthfully) when you're planning construction. The answers will help you sort out whether the money is being spent on a structural component, which would make it real estate, or on personal property, which qualifies for faster depreciation.

- Has the property been moved or can it be moved?

Tactic: Have your architect design a method of attachment that will permit removal, even if the item must be fastened to the building frame.

- Is the element designed for permanence? If you can show that something can be easily disassembled and reassembled, you will have a much stronger case for classifying that component as a furnishing.

- Is there evidence that the element will someday be disassembled or moved? Plans to prepare for future relocation should be included in the architect's notes.

- How expensive and time-consuming will it be to move the element? The easier and more feasible it will be to move, the more likely that it can be counted as a furnishing.

- How much damage will the element sustain if it is detached from the building? Less is better, for tax as well as practical purposes. A thoughtful design can facilitate future detachment.

- How is the property attached to the land? Even a building's foundation can be designed for easy removal, which may permit seven-year depreciation.

Standard fare

For the best tax results, tell your architect to avoid custom building components.

Strategy: Buy materials in standard sizes. If your return is examined by the IRS, the ability to easily reassemble or replace elements will enhance the appearance of impermanence needed for favorable tax treatment.

Impress upon your architect the importance of tax-wise nomenclature throughout the plans.

Example: Avoid use of the term "structure." That word will signal 39-year depreciation to an IRS agent, even if it doesn't refer to part of a building.

Two for the money: To maximize tax savings, engage an architect to draw up two separate contracts.

One contract can cover the base building, which will be depreciated over 39 years. The other can cover as many elements as can be designed for impermanence, which will be depreciated as five-, seven-, or 15-year property.

Tactic: Negotiate and price each of these contracts separately. This will show your tax preparer which elements can be classified as shorter-lived property and will support your allocation in an IRS examination.

Beyond taxes

Using the strategies above has advantages beyond lower taxes...

• Standard components are cheaper to buy and install than custom ones.

• Designing components for impermanence rather than permanence increases flexibility. The price of changing your plans won't be as great, if that becomes desirable.

• Building in flexibility now will make future maintenance and repair less expensive.

Lessons for lessors

The above strategies also work for real estate that you lease, if you plan leasehold improvements. Design for impermanence to gain faster depreciation deductions.

Strategy: If you think you might spend substantial amounts on leasehold improvements, be thorough when you review a lease for real estate space. Avoid agreements in the lease that force your company to share tax savings with the landlord.

Loophole: Whether you own or lease property, try to speed real estate depreciation using the strategies above.

Source: David Kahn, CPA/PFS, managing director, American Express Tax and Business Services Inc., 1185 Avenue of the Americas, New York City 10036.

Section 4: Business

Chapter Thirteen

BUSINESS OWNERS: TAX-SAVING MOVES TO MAKE BEFORE YEAR-END

Now is the time for business owners to plan their year-end tax moves. Enough of the year has passed to project results for the entire year, while enough time remains to implement smart strategies...

Dividend distributions

The top tax rate on dividends is at an historic low of 15%. It may never be lower. If you own a regular (C) corporation, consider taking funds from it through dividend distributions at the current low rates.

Strategy: If the owners of a family business want to shift ownership of it to the younger generation, consider redeeming shares of stock held by the older generation before year-end. When share ownership is concentrated within a single family, the redemption will probably be treated as a dividend under the Tax Code, rather than as a stock redemption subject to capital gains treatment—but the same low 15% top tax rate now applies either way.

Thus, there's an opportunity to shift ownership while the older owners take money out of the business at a very low tax rate.

If cash needed to pay such a dividend isn't available in the business, the cash can be borrowed. Today's very low interest rates make such borrowing inexpensive, and the interest paid on it is deductible. If dividend recipients invest the distributions and then earn more on the investments than the after-tax cost of the company's borrowing, they may benefit from this "rate play" as well.

Alternative minimum tax

The alternative minimum tax (AMT) is a growing problem for every high-income individual—but it poses a special trap for owners of "pass-through entities," such as S corporations, partnerships, and limited liability companies.

Trap: Items on such a business entity's tax return that can create AMT liability pass through to the personal tax returns of its owners. Owners who are passive investors in the business may not be aware of these items at all until they are reported on the business's tax return, after year-end. At that point, if AMT liability is created, it will be too late to undo the damage.

Examples: If you are a member of an investment partnership, its investment expenses will pass through to be included among your miscellaneous itemized deductions—which aren't deductible under the AMT. If you are an owner of an operating business, its accelerated depreciation can create AMT liability.

Important: AMT rules are complex and every situation is different. If you are an investor in a pass-through entity, consult your tax adviser about how its tax attributes may create AMT risk—and what to do about it before year-end.

Equipment purchases

The Tax Code allows up to $108,000 of business equipment acquired in 2006 to be deducted immediately (subject to income limitations). The $108,000 is reduced dollar for dollar for acquisitions over $430,000.

Important: The equipment must be purchased and placed in service by year-end to be deductible on tax returns.

Last-minute equipment purchases can be big tax savers—and may even boost short-term cash flow when the equipment is financed and the immediate tax savings exceed the up-front financing cost.

Be sure to make purchases early enough to meet the "placed in service" deadline of December 31.

S corporation basis

Losses incurred by an S corporation are deductible on the personal tax returns of its owners—but only up to the amount of their basis for this purpose. This basis equals the amount they have invested in the corporation as payment for their stock shares, plus adjustments, plus the amount of funds they have personally loaned to the business.

If you are an owner of an S corporation and plan to take a deduction for corporate losses on your 2006 tax return, be sure your basis in the corporation is adequate to do so. If not, take steps to increase your basis before year-end. Talk to your tax adviser.

Newly acquired buildings

If your business purchased, constructed, or expanded a building or new office space during 2006, maximize depreciation deductions for it by having an expert conduct a "cost segregation analysis" of its component parts.

Nonresidential business real estate generally is deductible over 39 years, but equipment is deductible over much shorter periods, such as five or seven years. And many components of a building may, surprisingly, qualify to be depreciated as equipment.

Examples: Decorative features of a building, such as special lighting, finishes, or movable partitions. Also, items constructed into the building to support equipment, such as wiring for a computer room or piping for machinery.

Expert analysis is a must, and may produce big tax savings through faster depreciation deductions. Conduct your component analysis while the premises are new and those who worked on the project are available to answer questions.

Compensation planning

Owner/employees of businesses must receive reasonable salaries—but "reasonable" may cover a significant range, and a higher or lower salary may be desirable tax-wise under particular circumstances. Considerations...

• Owners of C corporations may elect to take high salaries because they are deductible at the corporate level, while dividends are not.

• Owners of S corporations, which don't pay corporate-level tax, may want to take low salaries because salary is subject to payroll taxes while nonsalary distributions are not.

Consider business and personal tax rates, and adjust compensation accordingly before year-end.

Inventory write-downs

If a business owns inventory that has declined in value, it can take a corresponding deduction. But it can't just estimate the decline—a lower value for the inventory must be documented by taking steps to sell it at the lower price. Do so by year-end.

Similarly, if the business holds excess inventory or equipment that it intends to abandon, it can take a corresponding deduction. It must physically abandon the deducted items and be able to show that it has—a mere entry in the books is not sufficient.

Bad debts

When a business using accrual accounting holds receivables that have become uncollectible, it can deduct them. Their amount cannot be estimated—specific receivables must be identified and written off the books, and there must be proof documenting their worthlessness. Look for such receivables now.

Receivables that have declined in value but aren't worthless can't be deducted, and neither can those whose value is subject to dispute. However, if you can document a receivable to be partially worthless and it is partially written off the books (to its value), a deduction can be claimed.

A business can obtain a deduction for these by selling them for their market value before year-end and deducting the loss incurred.

Source: Steven Hurok, CPA, director, BDO Seidman, LLP, 90 Woodbridge Center Dr., Woodbridge, NJ 07095.

Chapter Fourteen

WHY IT'S SO USEFUL TO SET UP YOUR BUSINESS AS AN LLC

When setting up a new business—or expanding an existing one—one of the most important decisions to make is the choice of legal entity.

Today, few new businesses are formed as regular (C) corporations, and even S corporations are becoming less popular—as limited liability companies become the entity of choice.

Tax issues to consider

Some of the key tax issues when selecting a form of business entity are...

• How its operating income will be taxed, and...

• How its owner(s) will be taxed in the future when they "exit" the business by selling it.

In addition, a business's founders will want to have flexibility in managing it, arranging its ownership structure, and allocating income among themselves.

On all of these points, C corporations now generally are inferior compared with the "pass-through entity" alternatives available today.

Key: A C corporation is a separate taxpayer subject to corporate level taxes. But a pass-through entity has its income taxed directly on the personal tax returns of its owner(s)—avoiding the corporate level tax. The pass-through entity alternatives...

• S corporations. These are corporations organized in the normal manner under state law, which provide their owners with corporate protection against personal liability for the business's obligations. S status is obtained by filing an election, Form 2553, *Election by a Small Business Corporation,* with the IRS.

Snag: The IRS imposes important restrictions on S corporations.

Examples: They can have only one class of stock...profits must be distributed to owner's pro rata...with stock ownership, there can be no more than 100 shareholders.

• Partnerships. These are unincorporated business entities. They are not subject to the restrictions that the IRS applies to S corporations and so are much more flexible to use.

Catch: At least one partner who is active in the business must be personally liable for its obligations as a "general partner." Others who are passive investors may attain limited liability as "limited partners."

• Limited liability companies (LLCs). Available in all 50 states, they are a cross between a corporation and a partnership, offering the best aspects of both.

Like a corporation, an LLC provides protection to all its owners against personal liability for a business's obligations. But an LLC's owners are taxed by the IRS as a partnership (unless they elect otherwise)—avoiding the restrictions imposed on S corporations.

Pass-through pluses

Advantages of pass-through entities to consider...

• Operating income. Because C corporations are subject to their own corporate-level tax...

☐ Profits paid to shareholders as dividends are subject to double taxation—first as income to the corporation, then to the dividend recipient. The reduction of the top tax rate on dividends to 15% reduces, but does not eliminate, this double tax.

☐ Capital gains realized by the corporation do not receive the new low 15% tax rate paid by individuals—they are taxed at ordinary corporate rates.

☐ Losses incurred by a business, such as during a start-up phase, are locked in the business and can't be used by its owners to offset other income.

Contrast: The income of a pass-through entity is taxed directly on its owners' personal tax returns. Thus, double taxation of profits is avoided, capital gains receive the lower personal tax rate, and business losses can be deducted by the firm's owners personally, subject to limitations.

• "Exit" taxes. Corporate level taxes also create problems when the owner of a private C corporation wants to sell the business.

Conflict: The owner probably will want to sell the stock of the business to obtain tax-favored capital gains. But the buyer probably will want to buy the business's assets so the purchase price will be attributed to them and they can be depreciated from a higher basis.

If the seller insists on a stock sale, the buyer will want to pay less because he/she obtains smaller depreciation deductions. But if the seller accepts a sale of assets, gain will be taxed to the corporation at normal rates, and profits distributed from the sale will be subject to double tax.

Pass-through entities are able to avoid these problems because of the lack of entity-level tax—a sale of either the business or its assets will have the same basic result on its owner's tax return.

Comparisons

Differences among pass-through entities...

For many years the choice of pass-through entity was only between an S corporation and a partnership. The trade-off was that an S corporation provides protection against personal liability for business debts, while a partnership provides much more tax-planning flexibility. Examples...

• Two founders of a new business, one of whom contributes money and the other expertise, can readily be 50-50 owners of a partnership.

But if the same two persons form an S corporation, the one who contributes expertise may be deemed by the IRS to have received his stock as taxable compensation for services.

• A partnership can make "special allocations" of earnings. For instance, partners can agree that a "money" partner will receive a larger share of earnings than others until his investment is recovered. But an S corporation can distribute profits only pro rata with stock ownership.

Possible LLC catch: The details of the law that apply to LLCs vary by state, and LLC status may not be available for all kinds of businesses or in all circumstances. Check your state's law.

Strategy: If you own a business that is already operating as a C corporation, consider expanding it through subsidiary or "sibling" firms organized as pass-through entities.

Example: If new office space is needed by a regular corporation, its shareholders can organize an LLC or partnership to acquire the space and lease it to the corporation.

Pass-through snags

Possible problems with pass-through entities...

• Profits are taxed to owners even when not distributed to them. So if profits are retained in the business to fund growth, the owners may not have cash with which to pay the tax.

Solution: Have the business always distribute enough funds to cover the tax on its total profits.

• Owners of pass-through entities are subject to restrictions on tax-favored benefits and "perks" that do not apply to owner-employees of C corporations. For example, an owner of a pass-through entity cannot participate in the company's life insurance plan.

Consult a benefit specialist to see if this matters to you, and if so, how to work around it.

• Owners of partnerships and LLCs are not salaried employees who receive W-2s, and IRS rules governing their compensation are complex.

Source: Eric Kea, CPA, national director of partnership taxation, BDO Seidman, LLP, 330 Madison Ave., New York City 10017.

Chapter Fifteen

A MICROBUSINESS CAN CREATE TAX-SHELTERED WEALTH, CUT OTHER TAXES, AND HELP YOU START A NEW CAREER, TOO

Recent tax law changes make starting a home-based "microbusiness" a better way than ever to obtain extra income that is fully or largely tax sheltered, as well as new deductions for expenses you couldn't deduct before.

How it can help

A microbusiness is a small, low-cost unincorporated business run from its owner's home. It may be used to...

• Earn extra income through a sideline activity, such as after-hours consulting in one's regular line of work, or freelance writing about a favorite subject.

• Step toward a new career. If you have an idea for a new business of your own, you may be able to start and test it as a microbusiness. If your avocation is photography or collecting and you would like to turn it into a second career after retiring from your current job, developing it as a microbusiness may help you prepare the way.

New technology and the Internet make it much easier to run such home-based businesses.

Increased tax breaks may provide the subsidy needed to help get the business off the ground.

Tax savings

• Start-up help. When you run a business from home, you can claim all the expense deductions that are available to any other kind of business.

Deductible: Supplies, travel, meals and entertainment, business use of a car, business phone calls, publications, software, business equipment, advertising, interest on business debts, and so on.

Tax boost: If these expenses produce a loss—as is common during a business's start-up stage—it is deductible against other income, such as salary from a regular job. The tax savings that result can serve as a subsidy from the IRS that helps you get the new business started.

• Bigger tax shelter. Once the business turns profitable, the biggest new change in the tax law helping small business kicks in. This is Congress's dramatic increase in the amount of profits that may be sheltered from tax in a qualified retirement plan—in some cases, 100%.

Formerly, an owner of an unincorporated business could save up to 20% of its income tax free in a defined-contribution Keogh retirement plan.

But the newly authorized "solo 401(k)" lets 100% of the first $15,000 of income be sheltered for 2006 (or 100% of the first $20,000 for persons age 50 or older), plus 20% of all self-employment income, up to a maximum amount of $44,000 ($49,000 if age 50 or older).

Example: A person over age 50 has $20,000 of income from a micro-business. Under old rules, he/she could save up to $4,000 (20%) in a Keogh. With a solo 401(k), he can now save the entire $20,000—100% of $16,000 plus another $4,000 (20% of the entire $20,000).

This change lets even a modest sideline business greatly add to retirement wealth—and can make its profits almost or entirely tax free!

The solo 401(k) is just one example of many new retirement plan options. An expert can help you find the best among them for you.

• Home deductions. Working from home saves the cost of renting an office. And if you follow the rules for deducting a home office, you can save even more by deducting home ownership costs you couldn't deduct before.

Examples: Utilities, maintenance, insurance premiums, depreciation.

Basic rule: To qualify as a deductible home office, a portion of your home must be used exclusively and on a regular basis as...

• The principal place where you conduct a business or...

• A location required for administrative and record-keeping tasks relating to work conducted elsewhere, because you have no other office.

The deduction is limited to the net income from the business, but an unused deduction can be carried forward. Full rules are in IRS Publication 587, *Business Use of Your Home.*

• Easier equipment deductions. Because a home office is used exclusively for work, equipment located in it—computers, phone lines, etc.—is fully deductible. Without the office, home-based equipment is deductible only to the extent you document its business use.

• Commuting deductions. Travel between two places of work is a deductible business expense. So having a qualified work location in your home may convert what was nondeductible commuting from home to other work locations into deductible business travel.

• Home sale exclusion. New IRS rules say a space used as a home office does qualify as residential property eligible for exclusion of gain when the home is sold. So having a home office won't cost any of the potential exclusion of up to $250,000 ($500,000 on a joint return) on a home sale.

Note: When a home is sold for a gain, depreciation taken on an office after May 6, 1997, is taxed back as income, but at a favorable top rate of 25%.

• Family benefits. More savings are available by hiring your children and low-tax-bracket family members.

If you hire your child to work for you, the child's salary is deductible by you at your top tax rate, while the child's salary will be taxed to him at his low (or zero) rate, lowering the family tax bill. The child can also use the earned income to fund an IRA that may earn decades worth of tax-free investment returns.

The Tax Court has allowed deduction of reasonable salaries for children as young as seven years old who performed basic tasks, such as taking messages and cleanup chores.

No Social Security tax is due on the salary of a child under age 18 who is employed by a parent's proprietorship.

Audit risk

Contrary to popular perception, starting a home-based business does not create any special risk of audit.

What does increase audit risk is using a home-based business as a long-term tax shelter—deducting losses from it year after year against other income, such as salary from a regular job. In that case, the IRS may conclude the business has no profit motive, treat it as a "hobby," and disallow all loss deductions. Self-defense...

• If a business earns a profit in three of five years, it is presumed by the IRS to have a profit motive, so loss year deductions are allowed.

Key: The profits can be small and losses large, so if the business is run to report small gains in three years, losses much larger than the gains may be deductible in the other two.

• Even if a business incurs continuous losses, showing it is run with a profit motive will keep the losses deductible.

Indicators of profit motive: Keeping detailed business books and records, having segregated business bank accounts, obtaining all required business permits and licenses, consulting with experts about operations, having and following a credible business plan, revising the business plan in light of results to improve profitability, and similar steps.

With such evidence present, the courts have found "profit motive" in spite of periods of losses running 10 years and longer—allowing the deduction of all the losses.

Source: Frederick W. Daily, Esq., a tax attorney based in Incline Village, NV, and author of *Stand Up to the IRS* and *Tax Savvy for Small Business* (both from Nolo.com).

Chapter Sixteen

12 EASY HIGH-TECH WAYS TO SIMPLIFY BUSINESS TAX CHORES

Time is money to small-business owners, so tax-related time-savers put money in your pocket and boost your bottom line. Here are some tech-based processes you can integrate into your business to operate more efficiently and save money...

Accounting

Chore: Keeping payroll records. Use Web-based systems to upload employee time records to your accountant or a payroll company (such as ADP or PayChex). The accountant or payroll company processes the information—then checks can be printed in the accountant/payroll company's office or the small business's office. This process relieves the small business of the in-house cost for payroll processing, which saves money even with the outsourcing cost.

Chore: Distributing payroll checks. Set up direct deposit with your bank or your employees' banks. This eliminates the time and cost of generating paper checks, and employees appreciate the convenience of not having to make a trip to the bank. And you may save bank fees—ask your banker about incentives for employees who set up accounts in your bank.

Caution: You cannot require an employee to accept direct deposit and must make paper checks available to those who prefer them.

Chore: General ledger. Like payroll, company data on income and expenses can be transmitted to your accountant, who can maintain general-ledger account information. You save on the cost of an in-house bookkeeper—you only need someone to input income and expenses in your accounting software.

Record keeping

Chore: Substantiating travel and entertainment costs. Employees usually are required to document their travel and entertainment (T&E) costs to the company. Doing so is mandatory if the company maintains an accountable plan so that employees are not taxed on company advances or reimbursements of T&E costs. Substantiation can be simplified if employees are issued company credit cards that can be used only for company-related T&E. The statements generated by the credit card company act as substantiation for the T&E expenses.

Chore: Administering HRA/FSA disbursements. If the business has a health reimbursement arrangement (HRA) or flexible spending arrangement (FSA) for medical costs, employees must substantiate their medical payments to the company to obtain reimbursement. Substantiation and reimbursement can be collapsed into one step if a company issues employees credit or debit cards that can only be used to pay medical expenses. The employees do not have to seek reimbursement—they're automatically covered for their expenses because the credit or debit card has a spending limit equal to the HRA/FSA reimbursement limit. The statements generated by the credit card company act as substantiation for the medical expenses.

Important: Businesses that rely on these cards for these expenses must review monthly statements from the credit card company to make sure there is no employee abuse (e.g., charging nonmedical expenses).

Communication

Chore: Getting information to your accountant. Income and expense information can be easily sent on-line. This enables the accountant not only to prepare returns, but also to monitor activities throughout the year and advise accordingly. The accountant does not have to travel to the business as often, saving you money.

Example: In viewing information on-line, your accountant notices that expenses for inventory are growing at an alarming rate compared with sales and can recommend cutting back.

Receipts and other paper documents can be scanned and sent on-line to the accountant.

An accountant can more easily e-mail prepared documents to the business if the documents are needed by a third party (e.g., a bank, if the business is applying for a loan).

Chore: Getting information from the IRS. The IRS's new Transcript Delivery System (TDS) enables practitioners to obtain tax return transcripts and account information of their clients in minutes over a secure line, saving clients the time of finding the information in their files.

Note: Only practitioners who have e-filed five or more returns can use TDS.

Tax payments

Chore: Paying taxes. Businesses can pay their federal taxes electronically using the Electronic Federal Tax Payment System (EFTPS) on-line. Payments by individuals can be scheduled up to 365 days in advance (180 for businesses), a convenience that is especially appreciated by business owners who travel and may not be at the office when a tax payment is due.

Note: Tax payments can be charged to any major credit card, but this is a more costly alternative. While the IRS does not assess a fee for credit card payments, credit card companies charge a convenience fee of 2.5% of the tax charged on the card.

Electronic forms

Chore: Furnishing W-2 forms to each employee. Instead of creating paper forms, generate electronic forms that can be E-mailed to employees. Payroll information already in a business's computer system can be easily tapped to create W-2 forms.

Chore: Preparing 1099-MISC forms for each independent contractor. Computer accounting systems enable sorting of disbursement information to make the preparation of these forms much easier.

Bonus: If you file 1099s electronically, you receive an additional month to file them with the IRS (e.g., a deadline of March 31, 2006, instead of February 28, 2006).

Chore: Receiving 1099s from investments. You can access Form 1099 information on-line from your brokerage firm and transmit the information to your tax preparer. Contact your broker for instructions.

Bonus: If corrected 1099s are issued, as happened dramatically last year because of errors made by investment firms, the information is available more quickly to preparers.

Filing returns

Chore: Filing quarterly and annual returns. E-filing is an easy way for businesses to meet their many filing obligations...

• Income tax returns—all types of business returns (including corporate returns) can now be filed electronically with the IRS.

• Payroll tax returns—Form 941, Employer's Quarterly Federal Tax Return, and Form 940, Employer's Annual Federal Unemployment (FUTA) Tax Return, can be filed electronically with the IRS. W-2 information can be filed electronically with the Social Security Administration (for information about W-2 on-line, visit *www.ssa.gov/bso/bsowelcome.htm*).

• Employee benefit plan return—the annual information return for qualified retirement plans and certain other employee benefit plans—can be e-filed with the Department of Labor's Employee Benefits Security Administration. For information about EFAST, the ERISA filing acceptance system, visit *www.efast.dol.gov.*

Source: Lisa N. Collins, CPA/PFS, former vice president and director of tax services, Harding, Shymanski & Co., PC, Evansville, IN. She is author of *The Complete Idiot's Guide to Tax Deductions* (Alpha).

Chapter Seventeen

BEWARE: INCENTIVE STOCK OPTION TRAP

The alternative minimum tax (AMT) sets a big trap for those who exercise incentive stock options (ISOs) to buy stock shares at a discount.

A person who exercises ISOs will acquire shares while paying a price less than their full value. Under regular tax rules, no gains tax is due on shares acquired with ISOs until the shares are sold. But under AMT rules, gain—equal to the difference between the value of the shares and the price paid for them—is taxable when the ISOs are exercised.

Trap: A person who's not aware of the AMT may simply buy shares and hold them. If the shares later fall in value, he/she may end up owing tax on gain he no longer has.

Example: You use ISOs to pay $10 for shares worth $60. Under regular rules, no tax is due until you sell the shares. But under AMT rules, you have a gain of $50 and, at a 28% tax rate, owe AMT of $14. If you make no provision for the AMT and hold the shares past year-end, and they later drop in price to less than $24, your AMT due on them may be larger than your gain, depending upon your other items of income and expense and the related AMT consequences.

This trap proved costly to many during the stock market boom and bust.

Important: There are ways to plan around this trap, and it is vital to get expert advice before exercising ISOs.

Source: Allyson Hayes, senior tax manager, BDO Seidman, LLP, 330 Madison Ave., New York City 10017.

Chapter Eighteen

RISKS AND BENEFITS OF BORROWING FROM— OR LENDING TO— YOUR OWN COMPANY

Many business owners make loans to—or take loans from—their corporations. But if care isn't taken, such loans can cause costly tax or legal problems even when they are made for perfectly legitimate purposes. How to make loans safely...

Loans to the business

Common reasons loans are made to a business...

• Owners of an S corporation may loan funds to it, so that they have sufficient basis in it to be able to personally deduct its losses.

Key: While an S corporation's income and losses are deducted on the personal tax returns of its owners, losses are deductible by them only to the extent of their basis in the company. Basis generally equals the amount paid to purchase stock shares plus the amount of loans made to the business.

Timely: Owners of S corporations who intend to deduct losses in 2005 should check now to be sure they have sufficient basis to do so. If not, they may want to loan funds to the company by year-end to increase it.

• The owners of any corporation that needs funds may prefer to loan funds to it rather than make a capital contribution in exchange for more stock. Reasons...

☐ When the need for funds passes, the owner can get the money back from the company tax free through loan repayments—only to the extent of the owner's basis in the loan. (Amounts repaid in excess of the basis will be taxable.)

In contrast, if the company later "repays" the same amount to the owner through a dividend, it will be taxable.

☐ Advancing funds to the business through a loan is less risky since the claims of lenders receive higher priority than those of shareholders, and get paid off first.

Example: In bankruptcy, lenders to a business may be fully or partially repaid while its shareholders have the lowest priority.

☐ If nothing is repaid, a larger loss deduction may be available from a loan than a capital contribution. Why: If you loan funds to your company to protect your job by keeping the company running, and it fails anyhow without repaying you, the full amount of the loan may be deductible against ordinary income as a bad debt under employee business expense rules, although the courts have ruled inconsistently on this point.

In contrast, if you advanced the same funds to the corporation as a capital contribution, your loss of them would be a less valuable capital loss used to offset capital gains, with only $3,000 deductible against ordinary income annually. However, there is a $100,000 ordinary loss available on a married-filed-jointly tax return for Section 1244 stock, if the stock qualifies.

The major risk when making loans to your corporation is that at a later date the IRS—or a bankruptcy court, if the business fails—may rule that the loans were not genuine but were, in fact, a disguised contribution to capital.

Results: All the advantages described above of making a loan are lost. Loan repayments may be deemed taxable dividends. And if the business hits hard times, priority status as a creditor is lost, as are potentially larger deductions for unrepaid amounts.

Trap: Two mistakes company owners frequently make when loaning funds to their businesses are being careless with documentation and "forgetting" the loans—not following through on the loan terms. But formalities are important in transactions between related parties, such as a corporation and its owners.

If loan terms are not fully documented and followed in practice, the IRS and courts may decide there was no genuine loan at all.

Safety: Fully document any loan with a note and in the corporate minutes. Set a market rate of interest and a repayment schedule. Then follow the terms of the loan, making scheduled payments.

If the company has financial hardship and falls behind on making repayments, act as any creditor would—make formal demand for payment and take legal action to obtain it—to protect your creditor status.

If you fail to do so, and instead act like a shareholder facing a stock loss, the IRS and courts may decide that's what you are.

Loans from the business

There's an easy-to-understand attraction to taking a loan from one's own corporation when it possesses ready cash—it is a legal, tax-free way of taking money out of the business. Loan proceeds are not taxed in income as are compensation and dividends.

Catch I: Once again, the IRS is suspicious of loans between "related parties," such as a corporation and its owner. If it concludes a loan isn't genuine, it can deem the proceeds to be taxable as a dividend or compensation—applying back taxes and penalties.

Again, the way to protect a loan's status is to fully document it, set market terms, and follow the terms.

Catch II: With loans from a business, there is a second trap that owners of private corporations often fall into.

After first receiving legally tax-free money from their business, owners often want more. After all, why pay tax on money from a business when it is perfectly legal to take the money out tax free?

Loans from a business can become a kind of "Devil's candy," with one leading to another, distributing tax-free funds among the business's owners and their family members until total loan amounts equal a significant portion of the value of the business and/or wealth of the borrowers.

This can result in...

• Inability to sell the business. Excessive loans may complicate a future attempt to sell the business. Large debts owed to the business by a selling owner may be of dubious value on the business's balance sheet in the view of potential buyers—and the seller may not be able to afford to pay them off.

• Loss of creditworthiness. Large loans to owners who have limited ability to repay them may impair the business's general credit standing and its ability to borrow should the need arise.

• Accumulated earnings penalty tax. When a regular corporation accumulates more than $250,000 in earnings that aren't used in the business, the IRS may impose a penalty tax. Large personal loans made to shareholders represent just such earnings, if the company can't prove that the retained earnings are needed for valid business purposes.

Moreover, the fact that loans are made in excessive amounts can by itself turn legitimate loans into disallowed ones, for tax purposes. As a federal Court of Appeals said in just such a case...

"[W]hereas withdrawal of reasonable amounts are countenanced as a loan if other loan factors are present, excessive and continuous diversion of corporate funds into the controlling shareholder's pocket takes on a different character. There is a principle of too much; phrased colloquially, when a pig becomes a hog it is slaughtered." [Roger Dolese, CA-10, 605 F.2d at 1154.]

So, even if the form of genuine loans is followed, excessive borrowing can result in loans being deemed to be dividends or compensation, with big income tax bills resulting to borrowers—and in the case of compensation, a bill for back employment taxes imposed on the business as well.

Safety: When taking loans from a business, document and follow the terms —and resist the temptation to make too much of a good thing.

Source: Christopher J. Loiacono, CPA, partner and cochairman, tax department, Eisner LLP, 750 Third Ave., New York City 10017.

Chapter Nineteen

INDEPENDENT CONTRACTORS ARE STILL UNDER IRS SCRUTINY—HOW TO PROTECT YOUR BUSINESS

Businesses may sometimes prefer to use independent contractors rather than employees.

Objectives: To save on payroll taxes and fringe benefit costs...to keep the flexibility of easily expanding or contracting the workforce as business demand dictates.

Unfortunately, businesses continue to face IRS scrutiny on this issue. Are the workers really independent contractors or are they employees? The IRS wants them labeled employees because it's easier to collect taxes from businesses than from independent contractors.

Section 530 defenses

Section 530 of the Revenue Act of 1978, as amended by the Small Business Job Protection Act of 1996, gives businesses a way to defend against IRS charges that they should have classified workers as employees and withheld payroll taxes.

Employers can escape employment tax liability if there is a reasonable basis for classifying workers as independent contractors. Reasonable basis includes...

• Judicial precedent, published rulings, or technical advice from the IRS given specifically to the company.

• A past IRS audit in which no assessment was made on account of improper worker classification.

• Demonstrating a long-standing, recognized practice by a significant segment of the industry in which the individual works.

Businesses are protected in their worker classification if they meet any of these three bases, have been consistent in their treatment (i.e., treated all workers doing the same job as independent contractors), and issued Form 1099s to the contractors.

Example: A cable installation company demonstrated that it had a reasonable basis for treating its installers as independent contractors because there was a long-standing industry practice, it always treated them this way, and it filed all tax returns in a way consistent with independent contractor status [KM Systems, Inc., DC NJ, 2004-2 USTC ¶50,295]. Company owners testified that they had been in the industry since 1980 and did not know of any company that treated installers as employees.

Important: You don't need to prove worker status under a common law analysis involving dozens of factors centered on the issue of control over the worker—just rely on a Section 530 defense.

Homework

Don't wait for the IRS to inquire about your worker classification. Get your defenses ready. Have your tax professional research whether there are precedents or rulings supporting your treatment of workers. Have him/her write an opinion supporting your worker classification. Courts view these opinions more favorably if they're obtained before an audit is conducted.

Check on the worker classification practices of your industry. You are not required to show that more than 25% of your industry follows the same practice —you can rely on statistics readily available from the Bureau of Labor Statistics (*www.bls.gov*).

Some industries have historically high rates of using independent contractors. For example, typically two-thirds to three-quarters of workers in the construction industry are independent contractors. Other industries with high use of contractors include cosmetology as well as trucking.

Note: There is no set time frame for showing that a practice is "long-standing." Ten years is the usual standard, unless your industry is too new—such as dot-com consulting—for 10 years to be reasonable.

Compliance checks

A compliance check is a type of checkup that the IRS conducts to look at your worker classification. It is not a term that's found in the Tax Code, regulations, or case law—the IRS created it for its own protection so that it's not bound by the "prior audit" defense of Section 530.

Strategy: If the IRS asks to do a compliance check, you should request an audit of your worker classification (provided you have your defenses ready). If you withstand the audit, you are protected from any future IRS inquiry on your worker classification, as long as you are consistent in your treatment and reporting.

Burden of proof

As long as you can demonstrate a reasonable basis for your worker classification and you cooperate with the IRS, you are deemed to have established a prima facie case and it becomes the IRS's burden to prove you wrong. Since you already established a reasonable basis, it becomes very difficult for the IRS to meet its burden of proof in court, and you are likely to win.

Classification settlement

The IRS may ask you to reclassify workers under its Classification Settlement Program (CSP), with the promise of waiving penalties on back taxes you should have paid. Don't agree before assessing your Section 530 defenses. There may be no reason to reclassify workers under this program and pay back taxes.

Don't try to obtain prior IRS endorsement of your classification by submitting Form SS-8, *Determination of Worker Status for Purposes of Federal Employment Taxes and Income Tax Withholding.* Despite your supporting information on the form, the IRS is more likely than not to rule your workers to be employees.

Reclassifying workers prospectively won't impact your prior classification.

Just because you now choose for business reasons to treat workers as employees does not mean that your past treatment of them as independent contractors was incorrect.

Paper trail

Making a written agreement with a worker to treat him as an independent contractor is no guarantee that the classification will hold up, but it can be extremely helpful to your case. The contract should specify the existence and terms of the independent contractor arrangement and that the contractor understands he is responsible for employment taxes and is not covered by workers' compensation or unemployment insurance or any benefit plans.

Work with professionals

Small businesses can be easily convinced by an IRS agent that cooperating with the agency and agreeing to settlements is the best course of action. It may be the worst. If there is any hint of a worker classification challenge, hire an attorney or CPA who is knowledgeable in this area of the law.

Important: Make sure your professional is skilled in state issues—states may have their own standards for worker qualification.

Professionals are advised to review IRS training materials on worker classification (*www.irs.gov/taxpros/article/0,,id=98941,00.html*).

Source: Edgar H. Gee, Jr., CPA, 300 Montvue Rd., Knoxville, TN 37919. His testimony before Congress led to the enactment of favorable legislation regarding independent contractors. Mr. Gee is coauthor of *Guide to Worker Classification Issues* (Practitioners).

Chapter Twenty

CHALLENGE FOR BUSINESSES ...COLLECTING TAX ON ON-LINE SALES

The volume of business conducted over the Internet is skyrocketing. And no wonder. Small companies can easily reach around the world for business. Sellers on eBay, who number in the millions, may have buyers in all 50 states and in numerous countries abroad, too.

Question: What are your sales tax obligations on on-line sales?

Sales tax collection

Today, 45 states and the District of Columbia have sales taxes—only Alaska, Delaware, Montana, New Hampshire, and Oregon do not. In addition, there are more than 7,500 counties, cities, towns, and other local jurisdictions that impose their own sales taxes. Which ones must you know about? In which jurisdictions are you obligated to collect tax?

The general rule for sales tax collection is that you are responsible for collecting the tax on sales you make to buyers who are located within your state. Generally, the state in which you are physically located is the jurisdiction you must contend with. But you may be considered to operate in more than one state—for instance, if you have a sales force working in another state. Selling on-line does not, by itself, create a presence in another state that would subject you to sales tax obligations there.

Example: You have an office in New York and sell DVDs on-line. You must collect sales tax only from buyers located in New York. You do not have to collect the tax from buyers in other states.

If your business operates in more than one state, you must collect sales tax from buyers in each of these states.

Getting started: If you are opening a business, contact your state tax authority (the department of revenue, finance, or tax). Find your state's Web site by going to *www.entrepreneur.com*. Obtain a sales tax package, which includes a guide to sales tax and a state tax number under which you remit your tax collections. Be sure to observe state rules regarding when to deposit the tax collections and file sales tax returns.

Important: Continue to monitor your state's Web site to learn about new developments affecting your sales tax obligations.

Exemptions

Even if you are subject to sales tax collection rules, the items you sell may be exempt from tax. These exemptions include...

• Clothing. There may be dollar limits. For example, in Connecticut, clothing and footwear selling for less than $50 are exempt.

• Computer software. Different rules may apply to custom software, off-the-shelf software, as well as software that is downloadable from your computer.

• Machinery. Items used in manufacturing or agriculture may be exempt.

• Medicines and medical devices. These exemptions may require doctors' prescriptions.

• Newspapers and periodicals. These may be exempt.

• Casual sales. Some jurisdictions exempt individuals not engaged in business from collecting sales tax. For example, someone in New York who uses eBay to sell a vase that she has owned for years, and who is not in the business of selling, is not required to collect sales tax even if the buyer is in New York.

Resale

While collecting sales tax and remitting it to the state is certainly a burden on business operations, there's a bright side—you do not have to pay any sales tax on items purchased for resale.

Example: Ordinarily, a seller must collect sales tax on a purchase if the buyer is located within the same state. But an in-state buyer is exempt from tax if items are purchased for resale. The buyer must provide the seller with a resale number—the one assigned to the buyer by the state tax authority and which the buyer uses to report sales tax collections when the items are sold from the buyer's inventory.

Note: Some resale certificates remain valid indefinitely, but some must be renewed. For instance, in Florida, they are valid only for one year and must be renewed annually.

Special situations

As business becomes more complex, so do sales tax rules...

• Shipping and handling. Do you have to collect sales tax on these charges? The answer varies from jurisdiction to jurisdiction. Usually, these charges are considered to be part of the cost of an item and therefore subject to sales tax.

However, shipping charges may be exempt where the buyer assumes liability during shipment, called "F.O.B. (free-on-board) origin." Some states exempt shipping charges if separately stated. Vermont, for example, exempts shipping charges if separately stated and delivery is made by US mail or common carrier (e.g., FedEx).

• Drop shipments. These arrangements, which are shipments of items directly from a manufacturer or wholesale distributor at the direction of a seller, are increasingly common. A great deal of commerce on eBay works this way: An eBay seller conducts an auction for an item that is never in his/her possession. When someone wins the bidding, the seller directs a third party, called a "drop shipper," to mail the item to the winning bidder. The seller may be in one state, the buyer in another, and the drop shipper in a third.

In drop shipping, there are two sales going on...

1) Between the seller and the manufacturer or wholesaler (drop shipper)—even though no goods change hands—and...

2) Between the seller and the buyer.

For sales tax purposes, the rules vary in each state. Usually, the sale between the seller and the drop shipper is exempt from sales tax even if the parties are located in the same state. This is a resale that is exempt from sales tax if the seller furnishes a resale number to the drop shipper. But state law may collapse the two sales into one, so that tax is due if the drop shipper and buyer are located in the same state. Neither the drop shipper nor the seller may be required to collect the tax. Instead, the buyer remains responsible for it (the buyer owes a use tax to his state).

Source: Barbara Weltman, Esq., small-business expert and author of *J.K. Lasser's Small Business Taxes* (Wiley). One of her books is *The Complete Idiot's Guide to Starting an eBay Business* (Penguin). *www.barbaraweltman.com.*

Section 4: Business

Chapter Twenty-one
AMT PROTECTION FOR EMPLOYEES

If you are an employee who expects to take a large deduction for employee business expenses, beware. The alternative minimum tax (AMT), which hits a number of moderate-income taxpayers, may hold a surprise trap for you.

The number one cause of AMT liability at moderate income levels is high state and local taxes—they are not deductible on the federal return under AMT rules. But another leading cause is the deduction for unreimbursed employee business expenses. Examples...

- The cost of providing one's own equipment, tools, and supplies.
- Driving/transportation costs and meals and entertainment.
- Costs of books, publications, and professional education.
- Membership fees in professional organizations.

Trap: Employee business expenses are deducted as "miscellaneous itemized deductions," which also are not deductible under AMT rules, and a large amount of these expenses can help cause AMT liability.

Self-defense: Avoid deducting such expenses by negotiating to be reimbursed for them by your employer under an accountable plan. Even if you won't be subject to AMT, you may still come out ahead—because miscellaneous itemized deductions are allowed only to the extent that they exceed 2% of adjusted gross income (AGI).

Source: Sidney Kess, attorney and CPA, 10 Rockefeller Plaza, New York City 10020. He is coauthor/consulting editor of *Financial and Estate Planning* and coauthor of *1040 Preparation and Planning Guide, 2006 Edition.* (CCH). Over the years, he has taught tax law to more than 710,000 tax professionals.

Section 5: Family Loopholes

How to Save Big on Taxes If You're Divorced or Separated 269

When It Pays to File Separate Returns 273

Dependency Exemptions for Parents and Nonrelatives 277

Defensive Divorce—Avoid the Tax Traps 279

Hidden Risks of Tax-Favored College Savings 283

Six Ways to Save on Taxes When Children Move Back Home 287

Tax Traps and Opportunities in Making Loans to Your Kids 291

"Family Support" Payments Qualify As Deductible Alimony 295

Shift Income for Tax Savings 296

Generous Tax Breaks that Help Support Your Aging Parents 301

Protect Against Spousal Liability 306

Section 5: Family Loopholes

Chapter One

HOW TO SAVE BIG ON TAXES IF YOU'RE DIVORCED OR SEPARATED

The new tax law makes marital breakups a lot easier on the pocketbook. To save on taxes if you are divorced or legally separated...

File as head of your household. In many cases, your tax bill will be lower than if you file as a single person or married filing separately.

The 15% bracket covers up to $30,650 in taxable income in 2006 for single filers and married people filing separately this year. For heads of household, the 15% bracket covers income up to $41,050. Beyond those thresholds, the tax rate jumps to 25% for all categories.

You and/or your spouse can file as head of household if you meet four tests...

• Your home was the principal residence of a qualifying child for more than half the year.

• You file a tax return separately from your spouse.

• Your spouse did not live with you during the last six months of the year.

• You paid more than half of your household's costs during the year.

Tax rates on joint returns are the most favorable, but you might not want to file jointly if your marriage is in trouble. If the IRS audits a joint return and finds a shortfall, it usually can dun either spouse for the entire amount of additional taxes, interest and penalties.

You can be a head of household even though you can't claim the child as a dependent because you signed IRS Form 8332, *Release of Claim to Exemption for Child of Divorced or Separated Parents.*

Loophole: Even if you're not divorced or legally separated, you can qualify for favorable head-of-household tax rates if you meet the four tests.

Use prior years' tax returns to help locate hidden assets. In property settlement negotiations, your spouse might hide assets. Look at these forms to get your fair share...

• Schedule B, Interest and Ordinary Dividends, requires the names of mutual funds, brokerage firms, banks and other sources of dividends and interest if the amounts involved are substantial—more than $1,500.

• Schedule D, Capital Gains and Losses, allows you to more easily track sales of securities and investment property.

• Schedule E, Supplemental Income and Loss, discloses income or loss from rental real estate, royalties, trusts, partnerships and S corporations.

Strategy: If this information is on a joint return that you signed, ask your tax preparer for copies. You are entitled to see copies, even if your spouse provided all the income. If you filed a joint return without a preparer, submit IRS Form 4506, *Request for Copy or Transcript of Tax Form,* to get copies. This form doesn't have to be signed by your spouse. The IRS generally keeps copies of returns for five years, so you'll have access to information as you negotiate a property settlement.

Value assets on an after-tax basis. Divorce and separation agreements typically involve horse-trading—you get the house, I keep the stocks, etc. But an asset might not be worth its face value to you after taxes.

Example: An asset with a current face value of $100,000 was purchased for $40,000, its cost basis for tax purposes. A $60,000 unrealized gain will carry over after the property distribution. At a 15% capital gains rate on a sale, you will pay $9,000 in tax. This asset will be worth $91,000 to you, not $100,000.

AMT trap: If you liquidate assets that have gone up in value, you may have to pay state and local income taxes on the sale, which could make you subject to the alternative minimum tax (AMT).

270

Use the home exclusion. You owe no tax on gains of up to $250,000 on the sale of your principal residence. For married couples, the exclusion is as much as $500,000. Formerly, a spouse who moved out after a divorce or legal separation lost this break because the home was no longer his/her "principal residence." Thanks to a change in tax law, the ex-occupant now can retain the $250,000 exclusion.

To qualify: The ex-occupant must remain an owner...a divorce or separation agreement must grant him use of the home...the ex-spouse must have lived in the home for at least two years at any time before the sale. The ex-occupant can claim the $250,000 exclusion even if the sale occurs years after the divorce.

If one ex-spouse ceases to be a joint owner: In most cases, the spouse who gets the home will be able to sell immediately and claim a $250,000 exclusion. A two-year wait won't be necessary.

However, if the owner-spouse remarries, the new husband or wife has to live in the home for at least two years for this couple to qualify for the full $500,000 exclusion.

Factor in dependency exemptions. In 2006, you can deduct $3,300 for each dependent you claim. In a divorce or separation, dependency exemptions now go to the parent specified in the divorce or separation agreement or, if neither parent is specified, the custodial parent.

Strategy: A low-income custodial parent can sign over the dependency exemptions to the higher-income parent on IRS Form 8332. These exemptions may result in greater tax savings for the higher-income parent.

Example: For those in the 33% bracket, each $3,300 exemption saves more than $1,000 in federal income tax. For those in the 15% bracket, each $3,300 exemption saves about $495.

Factor in child tax credits. The child tax credit has been fixed through 2010 at $1,000 per child under age 17. This increase makes dependency exemptions more valuable, so negotiating these exemptions is more important.

Caution: Again, income limits restrict taxpayers' ability to claim the child tax credit. Congress now is debating legislation that might affect these limits. The credit starts to phase out when AGI exceeds $110,000 for married couples filing jointly...$75,000 for single individuals or heads of household...and $55,000 for married couples filing separately.

Source: Julian Block, Larchmont, NY–based attorney and syndicated columnist.

Chapter Two

WHEN IT PAYS TO FILE SEPARATE RETURNS

Don't assume that filing a joint return is always the best thing for a married couple to do. Recent tax law changes should prompt some to think again about filing separate returns.

New tax breaks

As a general rule, the tax law discourages separate filing for married couples—separate filers are usually not treated as well as single individuals. But the new law continues key tax breaks that equate the benefits for joint filers to twice the amount for singles. Separate filers have also been given some breaks—equating them to single filers.

• Tax brackets. The 15% tax bracket for married persons filing jointly is one-half that for joint filers (the same as for single taxpayers).

Impact: More married persons will not be penalized for filing separately.

• Standard deduction. The standard deduction amount for joint filers has been doubled to twice that of unmarried persons filing separate returns. Again, married persons filing separately now have the same standard deduction as single individuals.

Example: Both spouses have income of $25,000 and claim the standard deduction. It makes no difference to the couple's federal income tax bill if they file jointly or separately. In 2006, they would each pay $2,105 on separate returns or $4,210 on a joint return.

The tax law changes effectively have made filing for married couples with income up to a certain level tax neutral—the tax bill comes out the same for the couple whether they file jointly or separately. With this tax neutrality as a base, there are now key instances when filing separately can produce an overall tax savings for the couple.

Testing the waters

There is no magic formula to use in determining whether filing separate returns makes sense. Filing jointly usually saves taxes, especially where one spouse has little or no income. But there are some situations where it may pay to file separately...

• Capital gains and dividends. Suppose one spouse with capital gains and/or dividends is in the 10% or 15% tax bracket. This means that this income will be taxed at only 5%, compared with a 15% rate that would apply on a joint return if combined income pushes the couple into a tax bracket above 15%.

Example: A married person filing a separate return can have taxable income in 2006 up to $30,650 while still falling within the 15% bracket. Assume that a spouse has $5,000 from a part-time job, dividends of $10,000, and interest of $10,000. Since this spouse is in the 15% tax bracket, the dividends are taxed at only 5%. If the couple had filed jointly and were in a tax bracket of 25% or higher, the couple would pay 15% on the same dividends, or $1,000 more in taxes.

• Medical expenses. If the spouse with the smaller income has the greater share of medical expenses, separate filing may save taxes. This is because it may be easier for expenses to exceed the 7.5%-of-adjusted gross income (AGI) threshold for deducting medical expenses.

Example: A spouse with $20,000 of income has $10,000 of unreimbursed medical expenses. Filing separately means that only the first $1,500 in medical expenses is nondeductible ($10,000 − [$20,000 x 7.5%]). Thus, $8,500 of medical expenses is deductible. If the couple's combined AGI is $100,000, and the other spouse has no medical expenses, the deductible portion drops to just $2,500.

Separate filing should be considered to maximize deductions for casualty and theft losses and miscellaneous itemized expenses. Also, if one spouse itemizes deductions, the other must do so as well and cannot use the standard deduction.

• Child tax credit. The adjusted gross income threshold for claiming the $1,000 child tax credit is $110,000 on a joint return and $55,000 for married filing separately. (Proposed legislation would increase these thresholds.) If the couple's combined AGI exceeds the $110,000 limit, one spouse may be able to claim the credit by falling under the $55,000 limit. That spouse must meet the other requirements for claiming the credit (i.e., be your dependent).

Important: Run the numbers both ways—filing jointly and separately—to determine which alternative is better. Tax preparation software allows for these "what if" calculations. Cautions...

• Even if the numbers show joint filing to be better, separate filing should still be used by a spouse who is concerned about liability for the tax related to the joint return. Separate filing is the only way to guarantee freedom from the other spouse's tax debt.

• Once you file jointly, you cannot change your filing status for that year. But if you file separately, you generally have three years to change your status and file a joint return.

Special issues

There are two traps to avoid in separate filing. Even though separate filing may save regular federal income taxes, it could wind up costing more in overall taxes by increasing alternative minimum tax (AMT) or state income taxes.

• AMT. Regular income taxes are not the only factor to consider in choosing filing status. An increasing number of taxpayers are falling subject to the AMT by reducing their regular taxes.

For AMT purposes, married persons filing separately have half the exemption amount of joint filers ($29,000 versus $58,000*). The smaller exemption for married persons filing separately may subject them to AMT, reducing or eliminating any savings that resulted for regular tax purposes from choosing this filing status.

*The exemption amount for 2005; the exemption amount for 2006 is uncertain.

• State income taxes. In many states, filing status for federal income tax determines your state filing status—if you file separately on your federal return, you must also file separately for state tax purposes. And state taxes may not necessarily provide any benefit for this filing status—it may even impose an added tax cost that can wipe out federal income tax savings.

When to avoid separate filing

Don't opt to file separate returns if you want to take advantage of certain tax benefits that require joint filing. These tax benefits include...

• $25,000 rental loss allowance.

• Credit for the elderly.

• Education credits.

• Dependent care credit.

• Earned income credit.

• IRA deduction for a contribution on behalf of a nonworking spouse.

• Converting a traditional IRA to a Roth IRA.

• Savings bond interest exclusion.

• Opportunity to exclude all or half of Social Security benefits (if income permits).

Note: Some of the above benefits may be claimed on a separate return if spouses live apart for the last six months of the year, or the entire year (depending on the benefit).

Bottom line: The decision on filing status is a complex one. If you have questions, consult a tax adviser.

Source: Marc A. Aaronson, Esq., CPA, partner, Eisner LLP, 750 Third Ave., New York City 10017.

Chapter Three

DEPENDENCY EXEMPTIONS FOR PARENTS AND NONRELATIVES

Although there are brand-new rules for the dependency exemption for children starting in 2005, the other exemption rules for dependents remain the same. Don't overlook the fact that it's possible to claim dependency exemptions for persons who aren't children or even relatives—as well as for relatives who don't live with you. You can even claim as dependents persons who have ample wealth of their own.

You can claim as a dependent a person who meets *all* of five tests by...

• Being either a member of your household for the entire year or a relative (relatives do not have to live with you).

• Being a US citizen or resident of the US, Canada, or Mexico.

• Not filing a joint tax return (except to claim a refund).

• Receiving more than half of his/her support from you.

• Not having income exceeding the dependency exemption amount ($3,300 in 2006).

Surprises

• Wealth doesn't count. If a person has substantial wealth but low income and you pay for more than half of the person's support, you meet the support test. This is true even if the person has substantial savings—savings are not income.

• The fair rental value of your home counts in determining the amount of support that you provide.

- "Support" includes such things as housing, food, clothing, medical care, and education. So, a dependent can spend substantial sums on nonsupport items while you still provide most of his/her support.

These rules can create some unexpected planning opportunities.

Example: A person has substantial assets but arranges to have little income (perhaps by investing in non-dividend-paying, appreciating assets). You pay for most of the person's support items. The support test is met, so the person qualifies as your dependent.

Medical deductions

You can deduct the medical expenses that you pay for persons who do not qualify as your dependents solely because they fail to meet the income test.

Example: A retired parent has income of more than $3,300 and large medical bills. You can pay the parent's medical bills and deduct them on your own tax return provided you pay most of the parent's items of support and the other dependency tests are met—even though the parent does not qualify as your dependent because of his income.

Multiple support

Sometimes several people combine to support another—such as children supporting a parent. In that case, they may still be able to claim a dependency exemption even though no one person pays more than half of the person's support.

How: File IRS Form 2120, *Multiple Support Agreement.* Those providing the support then can obtain a dependency exemption and assign it to one among them.

Details: See IRS Publication 501, *Exemptions, Standard Deduction, and Filing Information,* available at *www.irs.gov.*

Source: Joseph W. Walloch, CPA, president of Walloch Accountancy Corporation in San Bernardino and Redlands, CA. He is professor of advanced accounting and taxation at the University of California, Riverside.

Chapter Four

DEFENSIVE DIVORCE—AVOID THE TAX TRAPS

When a marriage is on the rocks, most Americans know they need a good divorce lawyer. Far fewer know they also need good tax counsel.

Many people assume a divorce is a tax-free event. Under Federal tax law [Code Section 1041], they are technically right—the splitting up of assets is tax free. But all too often, the trap has been baited for future tax liabilities.

The most common tax traps are created by the divorce decree, specifically the division of assets between spouses and provisions concerning custody of children. Another common tax trap stems from past joint tax returns that are challenged by the IRS. One spouse feels that the other caused the tax problems, and that he/she is an "innocent spouse" entitled to relief under the Tax Code.

In this age of specialization, do not expect a divorce lawyer, even the best one available, to know all the nuances of tax law, or how the provisions of the decree can trigger future tax liabilities. If you or members of your family are in the throes of a divorce, have the documents reviewed by a competent tax lawyer or accountant before you go to court.

Division of assets

The spouse who receives an asset also receives the old marital tax basis in that asset. Say a couple have both a $100,000 certificate of deposit (CD) and a $100,000 stake in a mutual fund, which they purchased in the early 1990s. The fund's tax cost basis, including reinvested dividends, is $10,000. The couple splits up and agrees that one gets the fund shares and one gets the CD.

Tax consequences if each needs the cash to start life anew: The person with the mutual fund must sell the shares and pay capital gains taxes on $90,000. Even at today's low 15% rate on long-term capital gains, that is $13,500, and in a high-tax state like New York or California, the total taxes approach $20,000. Compare: The spouse with the CD simply cashes it in with no tax liability.

The situation can get even more complicated if the asset is subject to liabilities exceeding the basis in the asset, as may happen when appreciated property has been refinanced.

The transferor of property under Code Section 1041 is required, at the time of the transfer, to supply the transferee with records sufficient to determine the adjusted basis and holding period of the property.

Important: No sanctions are specified if the transferor fails to comply with these rules. As a result, consideration should be given to incorporating these rules into the divorce decree.

Child support vs. alimony

Alimony is deductible by the spouse who pays it and taxable to the spouse who receives it. Child support is not deductible, but only one spouse is entitled to tax breaks—a personal exemption for the child, and possibly head of household status, which means lower taxes than paid by a single filer with the same income. The breaks belong to the spouse named in the divorce or separation agreement, or in the absence of this, the custodial parent.

Which parent derives the greater benefits from being able to claim a child on a tax return will depend on individual facts and circumstances. The issue ought to be considered and addressed in the divorce decree, lest the benefit automatically go to the custodial parent (the parent the child lives with for the greater portion of the year).

Furthermore, the decree or separation instrument must clearly state a fixed amount for child support, or the entire payment to the ex-spouse may be deemed alimony.

When a parent falls behind in alimony and child support, catch-up payments are applied first to child support.

To be deductible, alimony must be paid in cash or cash equivalents, not services. When a taxpayer transfers property to a trust or buys an annuity to pay alimony, the trust income or annuity proceeds are included in the former spouse's income, but are not deductible by the taxpayer. Payments of trust principal are not taxable to the receiving spouse, but trust income is taxable to the beneficiary spouse.

Innocent spouse

Most married couples file joint tax returns. Doing so nearly always results in lower overall taxes than filing separately. It also means that both spouses are liable for the taxes owed and for any liabilities that result from errors, omissions, or fraud that the IRS might find on their returns.

All too often after a divorce, that joint liability comes back to haunt a spouse —usually a wife but sometimes a husband—who feels she/he was as much a victim of a former mate's duplicity as was the IRS. If that is indeed the case, that person may be entitled to "innocent spouse" relief from having to pay back taxes, interest, and penalties.

Such relief has traditionally been exceedingly difficult to get. The IRS tends to view many people who seek such relief as negligent rather than innocent. To take two extreme examples, a spouse who signs a return without reading it, saying only, "Do we get a refund?" is negligent. One whose spouse engaged in lucrative criminal activities that she took extreme measures to conceal from both him and the IRS is an innocent spouse.

Prior to 1997, tax law [Code Section 6013] provided only limited relief to innocent spouses. Basically, a spouse had to show lack of knowledge, economic benefit, or reason to know, and the issue had to exceed certain thresholds for adjusted gross income.

In 1997, the criteria were expanded and liberalized under Code Section 6015 and Code Section 66. Form 8857, *Request for Innocent Spouse Relief*, was introduced to allow a spouse who did not know or have reason to know of an error to claim relief from tax, interest and penalties. The changes [Code Section 6015(c)] also provided for allocating, based on earnings, tax deficiencies to individuals who were divorced, legally separated, or had lived apart for 12 months.

Current law also provides for "equitable relief." The IRS may grant relief where, "taking into account all the facts and circumstances, it is inequitable to hold an individual liable for all or part of any unpaid tax or deficiency arising from a joint return." There is a list of such factors in Revenue Procedure 2000-15.

Examples: Hardship, abuse, spouse's legal obligations.

Issues after divorce

There can be tax consequences if...

• A couple owned a business or an investment, like real estate, that is considered a passive activity.

• A home must be sold.

• One former spouse sells property to the other.

• A former spouse is entitled to a share of one's pension.

The potential snares are numerous. Before starting life anew as a single taxpayer, seek tax advice to avoid costly surprises.

Source: Danny C. Santucci, tax attorney and owner, Santucci Publishing, a tax and financial publisher, 1011 Brioso Dr., Huntington Beach, CA 92648. He is a frequent lecturer before bar associations, CPA societies, and other tax professional groups across the country, and the author of more than 25 books, including *Defensive Divorce* (Santucci).

Section 5: Family Loopholes

Chapter Five
HIDDEN RISKS OF TAX-FAVORED COLLEGE SAVINGS

Tax-favored college savings accounts are being marketed aggressively by financial institutions.

Big trap: Those who sell these accounts rarely warn that they may cause you to lose college financial aid. You might even lose more aid than your savings account is worth. What you must know...

The aid formulas

If there is any chance your child will qualify for college financial aid, you must know the aid formulas when you save. Basics...

• The federal formula is used for federally financed aid and by public colleges and universities. Under it...

☐ 35% of a student's own assets are deemed available to pay his/her education costs. This 35% is applied during each year of college, so after four years, 82% of the original amount of assets is depleted (assuming no other change to them).

☐ Up to 5.6% of parental assets are deemed available for college costs. After four years, 21% is depleted.

• The institutional formula is used by some private schools to award aid from their own resources. Here, 25% of a child's assets and 5% of parental assets are deemed available to pay college costs annually.

Note: Under both formulas, outside scholarships and third-party payments, such as those from grandparents, etc., reduce eligibility for aid dollar for dollar.

Example: A school costs $30,000 and a student qualifies for $14,000 of aid, leaving $16,000 still to be paid. If the student wins a $10,000 scholarship, other aid is reduced to only $4,000, so $16,000 must still be paid by the family.

Tax-favored options

Various tax-favored saving options are treated differently under the college aid formulas...

• Section 529 plans allow large tax-deferred savings that remain tax-free if used for college costs. Two kinds...

☐ Prepaid plans. These allow you to purchase tomorrow's academic credits at today's prices. But the dollar value of any credits redeemed reduces aid dollar for dollar—except for the federal Pell Grant.

This is currently the worst 529 option from an aid standpoint, and should be avoided by families who are likely to qualify for aid.

☐ Savings plans. Here, contributions are invested, usually without any guarantee on the rate of return. This kind of plan is treated as an asset of the owner. If a parent owns it, it is deemed a parental asset, with up to 5.6% counted against aid eligibility each year. If the child owns it, there is an aid reduction of up to 35% of the child's assets per year.

Best option: Under the current federal formula, a 529 savings plan owned by a grandparent or other third party, such as a trusted relative or friend, is deemed that person's property and not considered in the aid formula. So it does not reduce tuition aid.

However, some private colleges ask about such plans and may count them when awarding their own aid.

• Coverdell ESA accounts. Formerly known as Education IRAs, these have smaller contribution limits (currently $2,000 per year per beneficiary from all sources) than Section 529 plans but let tax-deferred savings be applied to a wider range of costs (such as high school tuition and purchases of computers).

A recent announcement by the Department of Education has clarified that these accounts will be treated the same as 529 savings plans for aid purposes.

Trap: Many Coverdell accounts can convert to being the property of the child at the age of majority, 18 in most states. So, when opening the plan, the parent should choose to remain the owner even after majority.

• Uniform Gifts to Minors Act (UGMA) accounts, and Uniform Transfers to Minors Act (UTMA) accounts. These hold investments in the name of a child, and their income is taxed at the child's rate (when the child is over age 14) rather than at the higher rate of the child's parents.

Snag: These accounts always are deemed the property of the child—so they are significantly worse for college aid purposes than 529 savings plans and Coverdell accounts that are owned by the parent.

• Gifts from grandparents. Payments by grandparents (or other third parties) toward a student's tuition made directly to the college are totally free of gift tax and don't count toward the annual $12,000 gift tax exclusion. Snag: Such payments reduce aid dollar for dollar.

Best: A grandparent should make gifts to the student's parents, so they reduce aid by no more than 5.6% of their value, rather than by 100%.

Important: Gifts to the parents are gift tax free only up to $12,000 per person per year. Don't exceed it or you'll eat into your $2 million estate tax exemption.

• Trusts. The biggest mistake may be placing funds in a trust for a child with the provision that the child cannot touch trust principal until a post-college age—such as 25. The intent is to keep the child from squandering the money beginning at age 18, the age of majority.

Trap: The trust assets reduce aid eligibility even though the student can't use them.

Example: A trust holds $20,000 of principal for a child who can't tap it until age 25. The 35%-of-assets assessment reduces the child's eligibility for aid by $7,000 every year—$28,000 total. That's $8,000 more than is in the trust!

Better: Set up the trust to benefit the student's parents so that it is deemed a parental asset.

Better choices

Another complication is that the tax law and aid formulas are both likely to change in coming years. So parents planning now to pay college costs in 10 or 15 years can't know what the rules will be.

Self-defense: Consider first saving in a tax-favored retirement account—such as an IRA, 401(k), or Keogh plan. Advantages...

• Retirement accounts are not counted in aid formulas—so putting savings into them won't reduce eligibility for aid the way saving outside one in a taxable account, 529 plan, Coverdell ESA, or UGMA/UTMA account will.

• By saving for your retirement you'll be in a much better financial position to pay for college without worrying about what you will live on once you retire.

Trap: While funds from some IRAs can be withdrawn penalty free to pay for qualified higher education costs, all the funds withdrawn will be considered income in the financial aid formulas.

Source: Kalman Chany, president, Campus Consultants, New York City, and author of *Paying for College Without Going Broke* (Random House).

Chapter Six

SIX WAYS TO SAVE ON TAXES WHEN CHILDREN MOVE BACK HOME

It's becoming increasingly common for grown children who have left home to move back in with their parents.

Such a return may cause an unexpected financial burden on the parents. But tax breaks can reduce the strain. Here are the tax savers for parents hosting adult children...

Dependency exemptions

When a child moves back in with you, you may be able to claim the child as a dependent on your tax return. In fact, if a married child moves in with you, you may be able to claim the child's entire family as dependents. Key requirements...

• The dependent must not provide more than half of his own support during the year.

• The dependent, if married, cannot file a joint tax return.

• Your child is under age 19 or is under 24 and a full-time student for at least five months during the year.

A dependent's own income and savings aren't counted in his support unless spent for support. So, if an individual has income, and even substantial savings, it won't keep the support test from being met if the funds aren't spent on his support.

Note: Different rules apply for other relatives, including your own children who are older than 19/24.

The full rules for dependents can be found in IRS Publication 501, *Exemptions, Standard Deduction, and Filing Information*, available at *www.irs.gov* or by calling 800-829-3676.

Medical expenses

You can deduct medical expenses paid for a dependent—and also those paid for persons who would qualify as dependents except that they have income exceeding the $3,200 amount or they filed a joint return.

Example: An adult child moves back in with you due to illness. The child has income exceeding $3,200 for the year from a job, but you pay most of the child's support for the year. You can deduct on your own return the medical expenses you pay on the child's behalf.

Such expenses you pay also count as support in determining whether you paid more than half the person's support.

Note: Medical expenses are deductible only to the extent that they exceed 7.5% of adjusted gross income.

Dependent care credit

The dependent care credit is available if, to be able to work, you must pay someone to care for a dependent while you are away from home. The dependent can be a child under age 13 or one of any age who is incapable of self-care.

Example: A child of yours who is a single parent becomes ill and moves in with you together with your grandchild who is under age 13. If your child must be attended to during the day for you to be able to work, you can take the credit for both your child and grandchild. Expenses are limited to $3,000 for one dependent or $6,000 for two or more. The credit is up to 35% (depending on your income level) of allowable expenses.

More: Many employers provide tax-favored dependent-care benefits, such as flexible spending accounts that use pretax dollars taken to pay for dependent-care expenses—providing the same tax benefit as if they were tax deductible. Check your employer's benefit plan.

288

Head of household status

If you aren't married, having a child move in with you can entitle you to lower tax rates by making you eligible to file your tax return using head of household status.

To qualify, you must provide a household for the child and pay more than 50% of the household's cost. The child does not have to qualify as a dependent.

Income shifting

When children who are in a lower tax bracket than you move back into your household, it creates a prime opportunity to shift income into lower tax brackets to reduce the family tax bill.

Examples: You can make gifts to move interest-paying assets from your high tax bracket into the child's lower bracket. Or you can shift stocks to the child so dividends are not taxed at the 15% rate but at only the 5% rate that applies to persons in the 10% and 15% tax brackets—or even the 0% rate that applies to the first $850 (for 2006) of income of a dependent.

Planning points...

• Take care not to shift so much income as to violate the $3,300 income limit if you are planning to claim the gift recipient as a dependent.

• If the support test is key, correspondingly limit the amount of the gifted wealth that the recipient spends on his own support.

• Avoid these problems entirely by gifting appreciated assets and having the recipient cash them during a later year.

You can make gifts of up to $12,000 per recipient tax free each year using your annual gift tax exclusion. The limit is $24,000 when a gift is made jointly by a married couple. It is considered as made half by each.

Home rental

A child returning home doesn't always have to be a sign of trouble or ill fortune—it can be a welcome money- and tax-saving opportunity.

Suppose your children grow up, leave home and do well—and leave you with a largely empty house. But after college, one of them gets a job near your home.

Opportunity: The child can rent a room in your home instead of renting an apartment.

Rewards: In addition to the pleasure of the child's company...

• The child can pay less rent than he would on a full apartment, saving money.

• You receive supplemental income.

• You receive tax deductions for expenses related to generating income from a portion of your home for otherwise nondeductible items—such as insurance and utilities—which shelter a portion of your rental income from tax.

In fact, when including depreciation as an expense, it may be possible to generate a deductible tax loss—making all your rental income tax free and obtaining an extra tax deduction, too.

Required: The child must pay a "fair rent"—although the Tax Court has suggested this may be as much as 20% below market rent for comparable property because of the reduced risk of renting to a family member compared with renting to a stranger. [Case: Lee Bindseil, TC Memo 1983-411.]

Bottom line: The child pays reduced rent and you receive tax-favored supplemental income.

Planning ahead: If you sell the home for more than its depreciated basis, the depreciation will be recaptured and taxed. But you may be in a lower tax bracket than you are now, and the maximum tax on recaptured depreciation is 25%.

Moreover, if you own the home until you die, it will pass to heirs with stepped-up basis, and the depreciation will never be recaptured and taxed.

Source: Sidney Kess, attorney and CPA, 10 Rockefeller Plaza, New York City 10020. Mr. Kess is coauthor/consulting editor of *Financial and Estate Planning* and coauthor of *1040 Preparation, 2006 Edition* (CCH). Over the years, he has taught tax law to more than 710,000 tax professionals.

Chapter Seven

TAX TRAPS AND OPPORTUNITIES IN MAKING LOANS TO YOUR KIDS

Many parents want to help their children buy a house, start a business, or meet some other need for cash. Sometimes, a loan is more practical than an outright gift.

Today's low-interest-rate environment makes intrafamily loans attractive, not only to borrowers, but to parents who can make below-market loans to kids at a time when the alternative is a meager return from a CD.

However, care should be taken to avoid tax traps.

When loans equal gifts

If you make a formal loan to a child and collect a market rate of interest, you probably won't incur tax problems.

Trap: Many parents make interest-free or low-interest loans to their children. Such loans may have gift and income tax consequences.

Under the Tax Code, foregone interest must be "imputed" (implied) on loans between family members at the applicable federal rate (AFR).

Example: In April 2006, Joe Brown loaned $200,000 to his daughter Ann, payable in nine years. No interest is being charged.

Loans of three to nine years are considered midterm loans. In April 2006, assume that the AFR rate used by the IRS for midterm loans was 4.09%.

Result: The imputed interest is $8,180 (4.09% of $200,000) per year. Each year, Joe must recognize for tax purposes $8,180 worth of interest income. He also is deemed to have made an $8,180 gift to Ann each year on which she pays no interest.

Tax break: Ann may get an $8,180 interest deduction each year.

Example: Ann uses the $200,000 to buy a business (an S corporation with $200,000 of assets). If she had paid her father interest on the loan, and itemized her deductions, she could have deducted that interest.

Therefore, she can deduct interest she never actually paid.

What if Ann pays, say, 2% interest on this loan—$4,000 per year? This is still 2.09 percentage points below the AFR, so $4,180 worth of imputed interest would have to be recognized by Joe and, perhaps, could be deducted by Ann in addition to the $4,000 of interest actually paid.

Exceptional treatment

With interest rates currently at modest levels, the tax consequences of below-market loans aren't as harsh as they would be with higher rates.

Nevertheless, you may benefit by avoiding some of the tax consequences if you qualify for either of two exceptions.

Exception 1: If the cumulative amount of below-market loans to a given child doesn't exceed $10,000 at a given time, no interest will be imputed.

Required: The loan can't be used to buy income-producing investments.

Example: Joe Brown also lends his son Bob $10,000 so Bob can buy a car. No interest is charged.

Since this loan falls within the $10,000 limit, no interest must be imputed, so there will be no tax consequences.

Caution: Say Bob uses only $5,000 to buy the car and puts the other $5,000 into a bond fund. There will be imputed interest on the $5,000 that's invested.

Assuming the AFR is 4.09%, as above, the annual imputed interest would be $205 (4.09% of $5,000).

Joe (the lender) would have to recognize $205 of taxable income while Bob (the borrower) might have a $205 deduction.

Exception 2: This exception applies to larger loans. If the loans from one family member to another don't exceed $100,000, there will be no income tax consequences.

Required: The child's net investment income must be no more than $1,000 each year. Generally, this refers to interest and dividends.

Example: Suppose Joe lends Ann only $100,000 to buy a condo. For the year, Ann reports $150 in income from interest on a bank account and mutual fund dividends. She's under the $1,000 allowance, so this loan has no tax consequences.

But what if Ann's investment income is above the $1,000 limit? Suppose she has $2,500 in interest and dividend income this year. Since she's over the limit, interest will be imputed, but will total no more than her investment income.

In this example, only $2,500 worth of interest income would be imputed to Joe, the lender. (Ann has $2,500 of investment income, so that's the maximum for imputed interest.)

That's true even if Ann pays no interest on the loan and the foregone interest, based on the AFR, is $4,090, or 4.09% of $100,000.

Trap: If loans to a given borrower total more than the $100,000 exception even by a few dollars, the exception won't apply. On a $110,000 loan, for example, all the foregone interest would have to be added to Joe's taxable income.

Key: The amount of interest income that's imputed to the lender can be deducted by the borrower, if the requirements for deducting interest are met.

Gauging the gift tax

The two exceptions (for loans of up to $10,000 and $100,000) relate to income tax consequences, not to gift tax consequences.

The foregone interest on a below-market loan is treated as a gift. Fortunately, the annual gift tax exclusion applies to such gifts.

Current level: Everyone can give up to $12,000 per person in 2006 to any number of recipients. (The dollar limit may be adjusted for inflation in the future.) With interest rates at current levels, this exclusion might eliminate the need to pay gift tax.

Example: As above, if no interest were paid on a $200,000 loan that was made when the AFR is 4.09%, the imputed interest would be $8,180 per year. If no other gifts were made by the lender to the borrower, the $12,000 exclusion would cover all the foregone interest.

Result: No gift tax need be paid.

Trap: If the lender makes gifts to the borrower that year of $12,000, besides making the loan, the foregone interest would not be fully covered by the exclusion—creating a taxable gift.

Savvy strategies

The lower the level of interest rates, the less painful the tax consequences of making a below-market loan to your child. Nevertheless, certain steps can avoid tax traps...

• Formalize the loan. Both parties should sign an agreement spelling out the terms of the loan, and those terms should be followed.

Trap: Without a formal loan agreement, the IRS may re-cast the entire transaction as a gift, which could require a substantial payment of gift tax.

• Observe the exceptions. If possible, try to keep loans below the $10,000 and $100,000 levels, as explained above. Avoid making loans of, say, $10,500 or $110,000.

Key: If you are lending your child between $10,000 and $100,000, keep the child's investment income down. The child might invest any surplus cash in growth stocks (many of which pay little or no dividends), rather than in bank CDs or bonds.

• Consider demand loans. A loan that is payable in full at any time, rather than after a certain number of years, is a demand loan. Such loans are considered short-term by the IRS so the interest rates may be lower.

In April 2005, for example, when the midterm AFR was 4.09%, the short-term rate was only 3.35%. On a $200,000 loan with no interest paid currently, the foregone interest imputed as income to the lender would be only $6,700 per year, instead of $8,180.

Source: Albert Ellentuck, Esq., CPA, of counsel to the law firm King & Nordlinger, LLP, 2111 Wilson Blvd., Arlington, VA 22201. Past chairman of the Tax Division of the American Institute of CPAs (AICPA), he writes a monthly tax column for the AICPA publication, *The Tax Adviser.*

"FAMILY SUPPORT" PAYMENTS QUALIFY AS DEDUCTIBLE ALIMONY

A state court required a divorcing husband to pay "family support" to his wife, and he deducted it as alimony.

IRS objection: The "family support" wasn't allocated between alimony and nondeductible child support, and no term required it to end on the wife's death, as alimony must. So it didn't qualify as alimony.

Court: Nobody else could step in to enforce continuation of the spousal payments after the wife's death, so they are deemed to end at her death, as alimony does. The fact that the husband might then still have to make some payments to support the children does not, by itself, disqualify payments as alimony today.

Source: Michael K. Berry, TC Memo 2005-91.

Chapter Eight

SHIFT INCOME FOR TAX SAVINGS

There is a considerable spread in the tax rates on individuals—from a low of 10% to a high of 35%. The rates on dividends and long-term capital gains for lower-bracket taxpayers is just 5%, compared with 15% on other taxpayers.

Strategy: Shift income to lower-income family members, such as children or retired parents, to drop the family's overall tax bill. Here are some ways you can do it...

Hire your kids

The best way to shift income is to hire your child or grandchild.

If you run your own business or professional practice, hire a low-bracket relative and pay prevailing wages.

Loophole: Money paid in wages is fully deductible at rates of up to 35%. Yet your child/grandchild can earn up to $5,150 in 2006 without owing a penny of income tax.

This number, equivalent to the standard deduction for single taxpayers, increases most years with inflation.

Even if the youngster is paid more than $5,150 in 2006, you'll still enjoy tax savings.

Key: A 10% tax bracket is in effect for up to $7,550 of taxable income in 2006 while the 15% bracket goes up to $30,650 of taxable income, for single filers. In contrast, your rate may be as high as 35%.

You'll save money by deducting compensation at a high tax rate, even if your youngsters pick up some income taxed at 10% or 15%.

Loophole: If your business is not incorporated, you won't have to pay payroll taxes (Social Security, Medicare, unemployment) for your child under age 18.

Bonus break: The "kiddie tax" (see next page) does not apply to earned income.

Roths for your kids

Your kids can contribute the amount they earn, up to $4,000 in 2006, to a Roth IRA. Assuming historic rates of return, a substantial sum can be accumulated over several decades.

Example: Your 15-year-old son contributes $4,000 to a Roth IRA, which earns 8% a year. By the time he's 60, that account will be worth about $96,000.

Payoff: Roth IRA withdrawals are tax free after five years and once you reach age 59½.

Hire your parents

Hiring your retired parents also may be a tax saver. The 15% tax bracket covers taxable income up to $61,350 in 2006 on a joint return.

Thus, you might be able to hire one or both of your parents, deduct their salaries, and shift income to their low brackets. This may be an ideal way to provide them with financial support, if that's necessary.

Example: If you own investment property, hire your parents for management or maintenance.

Required: In order for any compensation payments to be deductible, reasonable wages must be paid for work actually performed. Keep thorough records to support your write-offs.

College savings accounts

Some investment vehicles make taxable income disappear.

Examples: 529 college savings accounts...Coverdell Education Savings Accounts.

Rules vary but both accounts permit investment income to accumulate, tax free. Withdrawals are tax free as well, under current law, if the money is used for certain education-related expenses.

Investment income earned inside these two education-related accounts is not subject to the kiddie tax.

More about the kiddie tax

How it works: In 2006, the first $850 worth of unearned income received by a child under age 14 is untaxed while the next $850 is taxed at the child's low rate. Again, these $850 limits will increase gradually over the years, in sync with inflation.

Bottom line: Children under 14 can have only $1,700 in low-taxed investment income in 2006. Typically, they'll owe only $85 in tax—the second $850 will be taxed at the lowest federal rate, currently 10%.

Trap: Over the $1,700 mark, the kiddie tax takes effect. Excess unearned income is taxed at the parent's rate.

Strategy: For young children, you can place up to approximately $68,000 worth of investments, bank accounts, money market funds, etc., in their names. Assuming interest rates around 2.5%, they would earn $1,700 of low-taxed income each year, an amount that keeps you free of the kiddie tax.

Once your children reach age 14, they can earn more than $1,700 and even more income shifting is possible.

Caution: Money transferred to such custodial accounts will belong to the children when they come of age. If you're concerned that your children won't act responsibly, you may prefer other strategies.

Give away gains

Invest in your own name, emphasizing stocks for growth potential rather than current income.

• Children without earned income. When you want to sell appreciated stocks or funds that you've held for more than a year, first give the shares to your children, especially those age 14 and older.

Limits: In 2006, a married couple can give away $24,000 worth of assets per recipient per year, with no gift tax consequences. You can also make direct payments for tuition and medical expenses without eating into the $24,000 gift tax allowance.

Outcome: Your children can sell the shares they've been given and owe only 5% in tax on the gains, on up to $30,650 in taxable income in 2006. Such low-bracket taxpayers will owe 0% on gains in 2008!

Then, the children can use the after-tax proceeds to pay for college, buy a new computer, etc.

• Children with earned income. If your children or grandchildren earn $4,000 per year, give them appreciated securities worth just over $4,000. That way, they can sell the shares, pay 5% tax, and net around $4,000—the Roth IRA contribution limit—and put the money into their own Roth IRAs.

Results: You unload the capital gains tax obligation while your descendants can enjoy many years of tax-free growth.

Dividend-paying stocks

Some of the tactics mentioned above also will apply to your retired parents.

Example: If you're helping your parents to pay for home health aides or long-term-care insurance, give them appreciated stocks that they can sell, taking advantage of their low tax bracket.

The same gift tax rules apply, as explained above.

Moreover, the tax law provides another income-shifting opportunity between you and low-bracket parents.

Strategy: Give your parents dividend-paying stocks or stock funds. Your parents can pay tax at only 5% and use the other 95% for living expenses.

Loophole: At death, your parents can bequeath those stocks or funds to you. Under current law, you'll get a basis step-up to market value and owe no income tax on prior appreciation.

Required: At least one year must pass between you making a gift of the shares and the death of the person who leaves them to you. (This rule prevents deathbed transfers.)

Strategy: If you are concerned you'll face estate tax, the stocks you give away may be left by your parents to your children.

For more control over the securities' disposition, make gifts to a trust, rather than outright to your parents. The trustee has the discretion to make distributions to your parents, your children, and even to you or your spouse.

As long as dividends are paid to your parents or your children in a low bracket, distributions will be taxed at only 5%.

Source: Bernard S. Kent, Esq., CPA, personal financial services partner, PricewaterhouseCoopers LLP, 400 Renaissance Center, Detroit 48243. Coauthor of *PricewaterhouseCoopers Guide to the New Tax Rules* (Wiley), he is a former chairman of the personal financial planning committee of the Michigan Association of Certified Public Accountants.

Chapter Nine

GENEROUS TAX BREAKS THAT HELP YOU SUPPORT YOUR AGING PARENTS

As baby boomers age, so do their parents. In many cases, middle-aged children will help support parents or other elderly loved ones—and those costs can be extensive.

Opportunity: Tax credits and deductions help reduce the effective cost of supporting your parents. Also, making some minor adjustments in spending patterns or behavioral habits, such as switching investment and savings accounts, can bring you major tax savings.

Key: Some of the rules relating to supporting parents have recently changed with the Working Families Tax Relief Act of 2004.

Dependency exemptions

One possible tax break is being able to claim one or both of your parents as dependents.

Each dependency exemption you can claim provides a $3,300 deduction in 2006, up from $3,200 in 2005.

Limits: This break may not mean much for upper-income taxpayers. In 2006, couples filing jointly start losing the benefit of dependency exemptions (and deductions) when their income exceeds $225,750. They get no benefit at all if their income tops $348,250.

Required: Even if you are generally eligible for the dependency exemption, certain tests must be met for a parent to be a "qualifying relative," as defined under the new law...

- Income. Your parent's income can't exceed the dependency exemption amount, which is $3,300 in 2006.

This amount refers to the taxable amount. For low-income parents, Social Security benefits aren't taxable, so this won't be a problem.

Tax-exempt interest doesn't count, either, so you might want to switch your parent's bank accounts, taxable bonds, and bond funds to tax-exempt bonds or funds.

- Support. You must provide more than half of a parent's support during the year.

Key: If your parent lives with you, put a fair market rental value on the housing you provide, as well as food, medicine, transportation, etc., that you pay for.

If your parent does not live with you, money you pay toward rent or housing costs can be included in support along with other expenses, such as those mentioned above. Optional items—clothing, entertainment, etc.—also can be included.

Strategy: Keep track of this calculation throughout the year and make sure you wind up paying at least 51%. Urge your parent to defer year-end spending of personal funds if it's a close call.

- Other tests. In addition to meeting the above income and support tests, a dependent must be a US citizen or a resident of North America. He/she can't file a joint tax return, unless the return is filed only to receive a refund for taxes paid.

The person must be a relative (parent, stepparent, parent-in-law, grandparent, great-grandparent, aunt, uncle) or a full-time member of your household.

Multiple support agreements

If you have siblings, it's only natural that you share the burden of supporting, say, your widowed mother. In such situations, it's possible that all siblings together provide more than 50% of the parent's support, but no one sibling does alone.

Strategy: You and your siblings can agree to file Form 2120, Multiple Support Declaration, with your tax return.

Required: Each signer must contribute at least 10% of the parent's support for the year, and the total must exceed 50%.

The siblings can agree that one brother or sister will take the dependency exemption in a given year. For example, have the sibling who provides two-thirds of the support claim the exemption in two years out of three.

Wrinkle: A high-income sibling should not be included in the rotation because he will get little or no tax benefit, as explained earlier.

Note: Starting in 2006, the deduction cutback for high-income taxpayers starts to be phased out. The cutback will disappear entirely in 2010.

Dependent care credit

If you pay someone to care for your parent so you can work, you might be eligible for a dependent care tax credit. As much as $3,000 that you spend for such care is eligible for the credit.

What it's worth: Assuming your family income is more than $43,000, the credit rate is 20% (lower incomes get a credit rate as high as 35%).

What's covered: Home care as well as fees paid to an elder care day care center.

Example: You and your spouse both work and your joint income is more than $43,000. You spend more than $3,000 to have someone care for your widowed mother during the day.

Your tax credit would be worth $600 (20% of $3,000). If you hire someone to care for two people, that 20% credit can be applied to $6,000 in expenses, for $1,200 in tax savings.

Opportunity: Some employers offer a flexible savings account (FSA) that covers dependent care. Up to $5,000 can be contributed to the FSA and used for dependent care expenses, tax free.

If you're in such a plan and your parents are included as qualifying dependents, you probably will be better off using the FSA and forgoing the dependent care tax credit. If you use $5,000 in an FSA and you're caring for one parent, you can't also claim the $3,000-per-person credit. If you're caring for two parents, spending at least $6,000, use $5,000 from the FSA, then you can figure the credit on $1,000 worth of expenses.

Medical costs

If you pay some or all of an elderly relative's medical bills, they might be deductible as long as the relative is a dependent.

Loophole: Even if you can't claim a relative as a dependent, you still may be able to deduct medical payments made for that person. You need to be able to meet all the dependency tests except for the $3,300 income limit, mentioned earlier.

Adding medical bills paid for a parent may put you over the 7.5%-of-income requirement for medical deductions.

Example: Your income this year is $100,000, so you need to spend more than $7,500 on medical expenses to deduct any of them. However, the total of your own unreimbursed medical outlays is only $4,000, so no deduction would be allowed. (Your unreimbursed medical outlays equal the amount you would normally claim on your tax return, without counting outlays for a parent.)

Suppose you provide more than 50% of your widowed mother's support, including $10,000 you spend on her medical bills. That brings your total to $14,000, allowing you a $6,500 medical deduction ($14,000 – $7,500).

Don't forget to include any premiums you pay for a parent's Medigap or long-term-care insurance.

If you and your siblings file a multiple support declaration, the sibling that claims the exemption should pay all the medical expenses for that year. The other siblings can pay different expenses to even out the total support costs for a given year.

That will maximize deductible medical expenses for the year. The other siblings relinquish parent-related tax benefits for the year so any medical bills they pay won't be deductible.

Trap: Money you spend on dependent care also may qualify as a medical expense, but you can't take both the credit and the deduction for the same outlays.

Strategy: Do the math both ways to see which provides the greatest tax benefit. If you're able to deduct medical expenses and you're in a 25% tax bracket or higher, that's a better deal. If you can't take medical deductions because you're below the threshold, or if your tax bracket is 15%, you're better off with the 20% credit.

Head of household status

If you're not married and you help to support a parent, you may claim head of household filing status. The requirements here are less stringent than those for claiming a parent as a dependent.

Benefit: You'll owe less than you would as a single filer.

Required: To qualify, you must provide more than half of your parent's housing costs or nursing home costs. Alternatively, your parent can live with you for more than half the year.

Various other tax rules are much more favorable for head of household filers than for singles, so this can be a valuable tax break.

Source: Sandy Soltis, CPA, tax partner, Blackman Kallick Bartelstein, LLP, 10 S. Riverside Plaza, Chicago 60606. Ms. Soltis provides tax-consulting services to middle-market businesses and their owners.

Section 5: Family Loopholes

Chapter Ten
PROTECT AGAINST SPOUSAL LIABILITY

When one or both spouses is a professional or owns his/her own business, potential business liabilities could put the other at risk.

Example: A doctor marries a lawyer. Each spouse's assets could be jeopardized by a malpractice suit brought against the other.

Self-defense: Set up a limited liability company (LLC). This can provide the owner with protection against personal liability for business obligations as a corporation provides, while preserving the tax treatment of the business as a proprietorship or partnership. Adequate separate malpractice insurance could also protect against claims.

Also maintain separate ownership of personal assets, so one spouse's assets won't be subject to claims made against the other through joint ownership.

Assets may be further insulated against claims by placing them in trust for the benefit of children or other family members. Consider this especially if obligations exist to children or other family members through a prior marriage.

Also, be aware of innocent spouse relief. For information, see Form 8857, *Request for Innocent Spouse Relief.*

Source: Laurence I. Foster, CPA/PFS, consultant, and former partner at Eisner LLP, 750 Third Ave., New York City 10017. Mr. Foster was chairman of The Personal Financial Specialist Credential Committee at the American Institute of Certified Public Accountants.

Section 6: Real Estate and Investment Loopholes

Get the Most Tax-Free Gain When You Sell Your Home 309

Pros and Cons of Home Loans and Margin Loans 313

Protect Your Family for Generations with a Dynasty Trust 317

Deducting Worthless Enron Stock 321

Tax-Free Exchange Loopholes—Swapping for Bargains 322

Tricks to Avoid Taxes When Buying and Selling Mutual Funds 325

Tax-Sheltered Alternatives to Mutual Funds 328

Investors: Take Losses Now for Tax Benefits Tomorrow 333

Cut Your Taxes by Investing in Low-Income Housing Deals 337

Gigantic Tax Breaks for Real Estate Investors 341

Year-End Tax Moves for Investors 346

Investors: Get Big Deductions by Qualifying as a "Trader" 350

Section 6: Real Estate and Investment Loopholes

Chapter One

GET THE MOST TAX-FREE GAIN WHEN YOU SELL YOUR HOME

IRS rules for home sales now make it easier to sell a home for tax-free gain—even if you haven't owned and used it as your residence for two of the previous five years.

Even better, these rules apply retroactively to create tax refund opportunities for some who sold homes within the past three years. What you need to know now...

Background

The Tax Code's basic rule for home sales is that if a person both owns a home and uses it as a main residence for two of the five years before selling it, up to $500,000 of gain on the sale can be taken tax free on a joint return, or $250,000 on a single return. This is called the home sale exclusion.

Regulations implementing this provision are very pro-taxpayer. Among the new rules...

• It's now easier to meet the two years of ownership and use test. The two years in which you must own a home don't have to be the same two years that you use it as a residence to qualify for the exclusion.

Example: You rent a home that you live in for two years. Then you buy the home but move out of it and rent it to someone else for two years. At the end of that period, you have both owned and lived in the home for two of the five prior years, so you meet the "two year" test—even though you never owned and lived in the home at the same time.

• The exclusion is now available for a separate sale of land adjacent to a home, when you used the land as part of your residence, even if it is sold at a different time and to a different buyer than the home was. The sale of the land must take place within two years before or after the sale of the home. Only one maximum exclusion applies to the combined sale of the home and the land.

Example: You sold your former home on December 1, 2004, qualified for the exclusion and took a $300,000 tax-free gain while filing a joint return. If you retained ownership of land adjacent to the home that you used as part of your residence, you can sell that land as late as December 1, 2006, and take up to an additional $200,000 of tax-free gain—$500,000 total as a joint filer.

• The exclusion is available even for part of your home that was used for business—such as a home office. Under prior law, residential tax breaks were not available for any portion of a home that was used for business.

Example: You use 20% of your home as a business office for which you take a home-office deduction for costs such as depreciation, then sell the home for a $100,000 gain. Under old law, only $80,000 of the gain would qualify for "residential property" treatment, while the $20,000 (20%) of gain allocable to the office would not. But under the new rules, all the gain qualifies for the exclusion, provided that both the personal and business portion are within the same dwelling unit. Note that depreciation taken on a home office after May 6, 1997, is subject to 25% capital gains tax and the exclusion cannot offset this income.

• New rule for singles. When unmarried individuals each have an ownership interest in a home, upon its sale, each can take a gain of up to $250,000 tax free on their own returns—$500,000 total—provided they meet the other requirements for the exclusion.

Faster sales

The new rules also allow tax-free gain to be taken on the sale of a home even when it hasn't been owned and used as a principal residence for two of the prior five years. This exception is made for those forced to sell the home due to a job change, for medical reasons or as a result of other "unforeseen circumstances."

• Job change. You qualify for the exclusion if you sell your home due to a job change and your new place of work is at least 50 miles farther from the home you sold than the old workplace was from that home.

But even if you don't meet the 50-mile test, you can still qualify for the exclusion by showing you had to move to a new home to take the new job.

Example: The new job requires that you be on call at the work site on short notice, and your old home was located too far away for you to meet the requirement.

The person changing jobs does not have to be the taxpayer/home owner. It can be any "qualified individual," including the taxpayer, taxpayer's spouse, a co-owner of the residence or a person who lives in the home as a member of the taxpayer's household.

• Medical reasons. The exclusion is available if you sell your home for medical reasons relating to providing medical treatment or care for a "qualified individual"—which, for this purpose, includes the individuals mentioned above plus other family members. So if you move to be closer to an elderly parent who requires your care, but who was not a member of your household, the exclusion is available.

• Unforeseen circumstances. The new rules also allow the exclusion to be taken if a house is sold before the two-year rule is satisfied as a result of an unexpected event.

Examples: Death, divorce or legal separation, becoming eligible for unemployment compensation, a change in employment that leaves the taxpayer unable to pay the mortgage or reasonable basic living expenses, multiple births resulting from the same pregnancy, a casualty loss to the home, condemnation or other involuntary conversion of the property.

Note: In all these cases, the maximum exclusion is reduced to an amount equal to the percentage of the two years during which the ownership and residence requirements were met.

Example: You owned and lived in a home for 18 months—75% of two years—before being relocated and forced to sell. Your maximum exclusion on the home sale is $375,000 if you file jointly or $187,500 if you file a single return—75% of the normal maximum exclusion amounts.

Useful: See the new IRS Publication 523, *Selling Your Home,* available at *www.irs.gov* or call 800-829-3676.

Source: Barbara Weltman, Esq., small-business expert and author of *J.K. Lasser's Small Business Taxes* (Wiley). One of her books is *The Complete Idiot's Guide to Starting an eBay Business* (Penguin). *www.barbaraweltman.com.*

Chapter Two
PROS AND CONS OF HOME LOANS AND MARGIN LOANS

Borrowing against a home provides handsome tax benefits. And borrowing against a securities portfolio can offer even greater tax breaks.

Home loans

Under the mortgage interest rules, you can fully deduct the interest on home-acquisition loans for a first and second residence up to a total of $1 million.

To qualify as a home-acquisition loan, the money must be used to buy, build, or improve your first or second home and the debt must be secured by the same residence.

Trap: Debt secured by a primary residence to buy a second home doesn't pass the second test, so the interest isn't deductible, up to the $1 million limit.

Note: If you refinance home acquisition debt with a larger mortgage, only the amount of the original mortgage that is refinanced qualifies as home-acquisition debt.

What happens to debt secured by a home that is not home-acquisition debt? It's considered "home-equity debt."

Lower limit: You can deduct the interest on no more than $100,000 worth of home-equity debt.

Loophole: Even though less interest is deductible, you can take the deduction, no matter how the money is spent.

Example: Using a line of credit secured by your home, you borrow $150,000 to pay personal bills. Your total interest comes to $9,000 the first year.

Interest on the first $100,000 of home-equity debt ($6,000) is deductible but interest on the excess $50,000 ($3,000) is not deductible.

Loophole: You can elect to treat home-equity debt as debt not secured by your home. In some cases, this results in a larger deduction.

Example 1: If you borrow $150,000 on a home-equity line of credit and $50,000 of that is used for business-related expenses, then you can elect to treat that $50,000 as trade or business debt, which may be deductible.

Example 2: In another situation, you borrow $150,000 to buy a second home. You can elect to have the excess $50,000 treated as investment-related debt, stating that you're holding the second home for investment.

In that case, the interest on the excess $50,000 may be investment interest, deductible up to the amount of your net investment income.

Limit: Your net investment income will come from dividends and interest. You can count net capital gains, too, if that would work to your advantage, knowing that you may lose the benefit of the lower 15% long-term capital gains rate.

Margin Loans

As you can see, borrowing against your home poses some problems...

1. Home-acquisition debt can be used only for buying, building, or improving a home.

2. Home-equity debt is limited to the equity you have in your home.

3. Only $100,000 of home-equity debt provides deductible interest.

Strategy: Instead of borrowing against your home, borrow against your securities portfolio. Most brokerage firms extend so-called margin loans. Ground rules...

• "Purpose" loans are used to purchase other securities. Typically, you can borrow up to 50% of the value of your collateral with purpose loans (90% for government securities such as T-bills).

Example: With $500,000 worth of stocks, bonds, and funds in your portfolio, you might borrow $500,000 to buy other securities. You now hold $1 million worth of securities, securing your $500,000 loan.

- "Nonpurpose" loans can be used for anything else, other than buying securities.

- Interest rates. You'll pay less for a margin loan than you would for credit card debt or a personal loan from a bank.

Example: For margin loans, your brokerage firm might charge one point over the prime lending rate. If the prime rate is 4%, you would pay 5% on margin loans.

Tax treatment: Purpose loans produce investment interest, which is deductible up to the amount of net investment income.

Nonpurpose loans generally produce nondeductible personal interest. However, if the borrowed money is used in your trade or business, the interest may be deductible.

Spreading the risk

Borrowing against your securities may make sense if you have a large position of one highly appreciated stock.

Example: You own $1 million worth of ABC Co. stock, bought many years ago for $50,000.

Trap: If you sell the shares, you'll have a $950,000 capital gain and could owe nearly $200,000 in tax ($142,500 in federal, plus any state taxes).

If you hold the shares, though, an Enron-like disaster could wipe out a great deal of your net worth.

Strategy: Borrow against your ABC shares, and use the proceeds to invest in a diversified portfolio. The interest will be deductible, up to the amount of your net investment income, while you reduce your exposure to a single stock.

Savvy maneuvering can cut your exposure to your large stock position and your tax bill.

Example: You borrow $1 million against your ABC shares and invest $100,000 in each of 10 different stocks. Some of your new holdings go up, others go down.

Suppose you sell the losing positions and take losses that total $150,000.

You also sell enough of your ABC shares to take a $150,000 gain.

Your losses offset your gains so no taxes are due. All sales proceeds can be invested in other securities, further diversifying your portfolio.

Risk: This strategy still leaves you exposed to a steep drop in the price of ABC shares.

However, brokerage firms offer sophisticated techniques for limiting your losses. Often, this will involve the purchase and sale of listed stock options.

Caution: If you create too much protection for your appreciated shares, you may be subject to "constructive sale" rules that trigger gain recognition, for tax purposes. (If your options are structured in such a way as to eliminate virtually all of your risk, you have made a sale for tax purposes.)

Once you have the downside protected (limiting your risk of losses), you can borrow against the resulting position. Your interest payments will be deductible against your net investment income.

Margin loan risk

Margin loans pose risks. If the value of the securities used as collateral declines, you'll face a margin call. You'll have to come up with additional cash or securities to back the loan, or some collateral will be sold.

A forced sale of appreciated collateral, in turn, will trigger a capital gains tax.

Strategy: Keep your borrowing to only 20% to 30% of the value of the collateral to reduce your exposure to margin calls. At most firms, a drop of 28% will trigger a margin call. You'll still be able to enjoy tax and investment benefits.

Source: Jerry Lerman, CPA, managing director, American Express Tax and Business Services Inc., 1185 Avenue of the Americas, New York City 10036.

Chapter Three

PROTECT YOUR FAMILY FOR GENERATIONS WITH A DYNASTY TRUST

Properly structured trusts can provide several advantages, including tax savings and asset protection. However, those benefits may be lost when the trust terminates and the assets are distributed.

In recent years, nearly half the states have passed laws allowing trusts to last for hundreds of years, or even in perpetuity, something that was not allowed in the past. The benefits of such "dynasty" trusts may be extended over many future generations. Setting up a dynasty trust properly will eliminate gift and estate tax and shield the assets from creditors.

Caution: Highly publicized research indicates that $100 billion worth of assets has flowed into personal trusts in those states in the past two years. In response, the staff of the Congressional Joint Committee on Taxation has proposed limits on these long-lasting trusts.

Strategy: There is no certainty that any legislation will pass. However, if you are interested in a dynasty trust, you may want to act before any restrictions are put in place.

Tax tactics

A dynasty trust is an irrevocable trust, typically funded with a substantial amount of assets. Currently, each individual can transfer up to $1 million to such a trust (assuming no other taxable gifts have been made), without having to pay a gift tax.

Example: John and Mary Smith are married. Each may transfer $1 million to the Smith Family Trust without paying gift tax.

If John does not have the ability or the inclination to make a gift to the trust, Mary can make a $2 million gift. As long as John consents to a spousal gift, no tax will be owed.

Drawback: Any tax-free lifetime gifts will reduce the donor's eventual estate tax exemption, dollar-for-dollar. If Mary makes a $1 million gift and dies when the estate tax exemption is $3.5 million, her estate will have a $2.5 million exemption remaining.

Exclusions: By using the annual gift tax exclusion, both gift and estate tax consequences may be avoided. In 2006, anyone can give up to $12,000 worth of assets to any number of recipients.

In the case of gifts to a trust, the recipients are the trust beneficiaries. Special care is needed, though, if the gifts are to qualify for the annual gift tax exclusion.

Example: Suppose John and Mary Smith fund a trust, as described above. Their three children and six grandchildren are beneficiaries. John and Mary can give $216,000 worth of assets to the trust this year—$12,000 times two donors times nine beneficiaries—with no gift tax obligation.

Such tax-free gifts can be made each year. In fact, the number will increase as the annual gift tax exclusion is raised in order to keep pace with inflation.

Required: To qualify for the gift tax exclusion, each trust beneficiary must be notified of the gift. He/she must be given a time period in which the gifted assets can be withdrawn from the trust—$24,000 per beneficiary in this example.

Key: After the withdrawal window closes, the assets can remain in the trust and no gift tax will be assessed, provided the proper formalities have been followed.

Generation skipping

In the above example, grandchildren have been named as trust beneficiaries. That's often the case with a dynasty trust.

Trap: If grandchildren or great-grandchildren are trust beneficiaries, the generation-skipping transfer (GST) tax must be considered.

This is an extra level of transfer tax levied on bequests or gifts that "skip" at least one generation. In 2006, the GST tax rate is 46%!

Fortunately, each individual now gets a $2 million exemption from the GST tax.

Thus, if John and Mary Smith transfer $4 million to a trust, they can each designate $2 million worth of their GST tax exemption. No GST tax will be paid.

Transfers to such trusts that exceed the $2 million-per-person ceiling will incur the GST tax, though.

Seeking shelter

By following the above rules, substantial amounts can be transferred to a trust, with little or no tax obligation. If the trust is irrevocable, created in a state that allows long (or perpetual) trust terms, the assets can remain in trust for many years. Reasons for creating and funding such trusts...

• Eliminate estate tax. Once assets are properly transferred to a trust, they don't belong to any individual. Thus, they won't be taxed at anyone's death.

Example: John and Mary Smith fund a trust with $2 million, as above. At John's death, suppose the trust fund has grown to $4 million.

No estate tax will be due.

Key: The same is true at Mary's death, the deaths of their children, etc. Their original $2 million gift could grow to $20 million, even $200 million over the years, and never be reduced by gift, estate, or GST tax.

• Curbing creditors. Just as assets that don't belong to any individual will be out of the reach of transfer taxes, they also will be protected from the creditors of John, Mary, and the other trust beneficiaries.

Thus, the trust assets won't be exposed to divorce settlements, bankruptcy, judgments, etc.

A benevolent banker

Just because the assets are beyond the reach of creditors and tax collectors doesn't mean that John's family will get no benefit from the trust assets.

In dynasty trusts, the trustee typically has the discretion to distribute trust assets among the beneficiaries.

These assets might be available to help a child pay medical expenses, fund a grandchild's college education, purchase a home (to be retained in the trust) for a great-grandchild, and so on.

Motivating beneficiaries: One popular wrinkle is the "incentive trust." The trust can include language saying that trust beneficiaries will receive distributions based on certain achievements, such as educational degrees or reaching specified amounts of earned income.

Fine points

If dynasty trusts remain in existence for decades (even centuries), they may grow unmanageable, as future beneficiaries are added. If one trust has to provide for 50 beneficiaries in 22 states (just a hypothetical instance), that might be hard for one trustee to handle.

Solution: The original trust may be designed to divide into "subtrusts" at some future date, perhaps one for each of the grantor's children. Then those subtrusts can subdivide further, as more beneficiaries arrive on the scene.

State selection: You don't have to live in a state that offers long-term trusts in order to create one. Generally, all that's necessary is that you use an in-state trustee and keep some trust assets in the state.

Strategy: When choosing among states for a dynasty trust, you may want to consider the lack of a state income tax (Alaska, Delaware, Florida) or a long history of settled trust law (Delaware). (While these trusts are estate, gift, and GST tax free, they're subject to income tax on trust income.)

Eight states—Alaska, Delaware, Missouri, Nevada, Oklahoma, Rhode Island, South Dakota, and Utah—permit the grantor of a dynasty trust to be a beneficiary. Thus, assets may be returned in case of a financial setback. Such "self-settled trusts" might be affected by legislation now before Congress, though. The bill might extend the waiting period before assets placed in such trusts are protected from creditors.

In any case, be sure to consult with an attorney experienced in trusts and estate planning if you are considering a dynasty trust.

Source: Gideon Rothschild, Esq., CPA, partner in the law firm Moses & Singer LLP, 1301 Avenue of the Americas, New York City 10019. He is adjunct professor in estate planning and wealth preservation at New York Law School and University of Miami Law School. For additional articles on asset-protection strategies, go to *www.mosessinger.com.*

DEDUCTING WORTHLESS ENRON STOCK

Worthless Enron stock is deductible on 2004 tax returns. Few investors know that the stock officially became worthless as of December 31, 2004, making their losses deductible as capital losses. Claim the loss on an amended return for 2004.

Source: Sidney Kess, attorney and CPA, 10 Rockefeller Plaza, New York City 10020.

Chapter Four
TAX-FREE EXCHANGE LOOPHOLES—SWAPPING FOR BARGAINS

The swapping of goods and services by taxpayers generally is viewed by the IRS as barter and is treated as a taxable sale and then a purchase—income from a barter transaction is taxable. But the Tax Code clearly authorizes tax-free exchanges of some types of assets. Consider these tax-free swap opportunities...

• Real estate. When you exchange a piece of business or investment property for "like-kind" business or investment property, taxes are deferred.

Example: You pay no tax when you swap a motel in Virginia for an apartment building in Sacramento because this is considered a "like-kind" exchange. You can also exchange a warehouse for an office building tax free. These properties are alike because both are held for productive use in a trade or business or for investment.

Caution: You cannot swap property that isn't alike, tax free, such as a vacation house, which you use for personal purposes, for an office building.

Strategy: Tax-free transfers can take place even if the property is sold, as long as the funds are held in trust, the property to be received is identified as trade property within 45 days, and the exchange is completed within 180 days.

• Charity. When you transfer appreciated assets to a charitable remainder trust in exchange for lifetime income payments, the transfer is tax free. However, you may owe tax on any payments you subsequently receive from the trust.

Opportunity: You can deduct in the year you set up the trust the present value of the remainder interest the charity will get when you die.

322

• Life insurance. You can exchange one type of life insurance for another without owing tax.

Example: You can swap a whole life policy that requires large payments for another contract with the same insurer that requires lower payments.

Opportunity: If you surrender an insurance policy or an annuity contract of a financially troubled company (based on state insurance department regulations) and reinvest the entire cash proceeds within 60 days in another company's policy, the transaction is tax free.

• Private annuities. You can exchange assets tax free for a private annuity —a promise by someone not in the insurance business, such as a son or daughter, to make annual payments for the rest of your life in exchange for certain assets, such as shares in the family business.

Benefit: You remove the assets from your taxable estate, which lets you avoid both gift and estate tax, and you receive income for life. You do, however, have to pay income tax on a portion of the annual payments you receive.

Trap: If you outlive your life expectancy at the time of the transfer, you receive far more in annual payments than what the business or asset was worth when the annuity was established—and the payments are taxed as ordinary income.

• Divorce. Property transferred from one spouse to another because of a divorce settlement is tax free. There is no limit to the amount of property you can transfer tax free under these circumstances.

Opportunity: Limited partnership interests with accumulated losses that create "phantom income" can be transferred tax free to a spouse you are divorcing. Normally, you would owe tax on the phantom income.

Note: The spouse who gets the property picks up the liability.

• Stocks and bonds. Stock received as the result of a merger or spin-off— where one company's shares are received in exchange for another's—is generally tax free.

• Corporate recapitalizations. Your stock is exchanged for shares of preferred stock during a recapitalization. Preferred shares generally pay much bigger dividends than common shares.

When you sell preferred shares received in a corporate recapitalization before the company is sold or anytime during your lifetime, the gain is taxed at dividend tax rates not capital gains rates (under current law these are the same).

• Transfers to controlled corporations. Transfers of assets to controlled corporations in which the person transferring owns 80% or more of the corporation's stock immediately after the transfer are tax free.

Example: When you transfer almost fully depreciated equipment to a controlled corporation that you own, you don't have to pay tax on the difference between the market value of the equipment and its tax basis.

• ESOP Transfers. If at least 30% of a seller's stock in a corporation is sold to an Employee Stock Ownership Plan (ESOP), and the proceeds are reinvested within one year in qualified securities of publicly traded companies, the exchange is tax free—until the replacement securities are sold.

Source: Edward Mendlowitz, CPA, shareholder in the CPA firm WithumSmith+Brown, 120 Albany St., New Brunswick, NJ 08901. He is author of *Estate Planning* (Practical Programs).

Section 6: Real Estate and Investment Loopholes

Chapter Five

TRICKS TO AVOID TAXES WHEN BUYING AND SELLING MUTUAL FUNDS

Even if you lost money in the bear market, you may still owe hefty taxes on your mutual funds. Use these techniques to avoid or at least lessen them...

• Use specific identification accounting when selling shares. The IRS generally calculates gains and losses on fund shares with "first-in, first-out" (FIFO) accounting. That means using the price that you paid for the shares you have held the longest.

Specific identification accounting allows you to sell select shares to provide the best tax result.

Example: You bought shares of the same fund first for $10, then $30 and then $60. They are worth $40 now. If you sell a portion of the shares, under FIFO accounting rules you will be deemed to sell the $10 shares first—for a $30 taxable gain.

Specific identification rules let you select the shares you sell. You can sell the $60 shares to produce a deductible capital loss. If you want to report a gain, select the $10 or $30 shares.

This method of accounting can create a specific amount of gain that can be matched against an offsetting loss.

Specific identification accounting requires more paperwork than FIFO. You must keep records showing purchase prices and dates for all fund shares. Your sell order must specify the specific shares to be sold on the sale confirmations. Your broker or fund firm may not track these records—you must do it.

• Buy tax-efficient funds. Investors incur two types of tax on mutual funds—tax on the sale of fund shares and tax on gains earned inside the fund. Gains earned inside the fund are distributed to shareholders annually as taxable dividends.

Trap I: Tax bills from an actively managed fund often include more short-term capital gains, which are taxed at a higher rate than long-term capital gains. This lowers your total after-tax return.

Trap II: Actively managed funds have higher fees and expenses than most index funds, which are not actively managed. Compare fees on similar funds.

These factors can significantly reduce mutual fund returns. To protect yourself, look for index funds or actively managed mutual funds that are tax efficient. Funds state in their prospectuses if they manage trades to minimize taxes. You also can find this information on fund Web sites or at *www. morningstar.com*.

• Track reinvested dividends. When dividends from a fund are reinvested, those dividends are, in effect, the cost of new shares.

Add the dividends to the cost basis of your holdings when you sell your shares. If you don't, you risk over-stating your taxable gain or understating your loss.

Example: You buy fund shares for $5,000 and receive $100 in dividends, which you reinvest in additional shares. Your basis in the shares is now $5,100.

• Check a fund's capital gains exposure. Even tax-efficient funds can incur large capital gains when they sell to finance shareholder redemptions. That means you might owe gains tax even as the fund value declines. Go to *www.morning star.com* to find out how much of a fund's value is preexisting appreciation on investments. If you are comparing two similar funds and one's value is based more on appreciation, the other fund may be the better investment.

• Time purchases and sales around the dividend date. Every mutual fund has an annual dividend date on which it distributes internal gains—and the tax liability on them. If you buy a fund just before the dividend date, which typically is close to the end of the year, you will pay a price that already has been factored into the dividend—but you will owe tax on it. If you wait until after the distribution, you will pay the same price and avoid the tax.

The same principle is true for selling fund shares. Sell them just before the dividend distribution.

• Avoid wash sales. If your fund shares have declined in value but are still an attractive investment, you might want to sell them for a tax-deductible loss and repurchase them later.

Wait 31 days to repurchase shares. The wash-sale rule bars deductions for losses incurred on securities sold and repurchased within 30 days.

If you do not want to reduce your stock market investments at that time, use the money from the sale to purchase shares of a different fund that has a similar objective and track record or an index fund.

Source: Edward Mendlowitz, CPA, shareholder in the CPA firm WithumSmith+Brown, 120 Albany St., New Brunswick, NJ 08901. He is author of *Estate Planning* (Practical Programs).

Chapter Six

TAX-SHELTERED ALTERNATIVES TO MUTUAL FUNDS

Several major mutual fund families have been implicated in highly publicized scandals.

These families permitted selected investors to engage in improper trading and pocket no-risk, short-term profits. Such in-and-out moves may have diluted the earnings of long-term shareholders while increasing expenses that all must bear.

Going forward: There is no way to know whether more fund families will be named. However, you may want to seek other ways to invest besides (or in addition to) mutual funds.

Bonus: Some alternatives to mutual funds offer tax advantages to investors.

Individual securities

By buying individual stocks and bonds, you control your own tax position. Buying and holding winners, for example, can defer taxable gains. If you take gains, you can take offsetting losses to avoid owing tax.

What's more, you can determine your own investment strategy.

Example: You can emphasize funds with dividend-paying stocks to take advantage of the 15% tax rate on dividends.

Separate accounts

Also known as managed or "wrap" accounts, these programs are offered by many financial advisers.

How they work: After going over your goals, risk tolerance, etc., the adviser will suggest a lineup of money managers. Each money manager will pick the securities that you'll own in a given category.

Examples: One manager might focus on large-cap domestic growth stocks, another on stocks from developed foreign markets, etc.

Such an approach offers a number of advantages...

• Diversification. You'll own many different securities in multiple asset classes.

• Professional portfolio management. Your stocks and bonds will be chosen by people who have posted solid performance records.

• Access to elite managers. By investing through these programs, investors with moderate-sized portfolios may have access to money managers who usually are available only to the very wealthy.

• Congruence of interests. Typically, investors in these programs pay an asset-based fee rather than commissions. Your adviser is motivated to enlarge your account, not churn it.

• Less chance of trading improprieties. What about exposure to the improper trading practices of some mutual funds? With a separate accounts program you own your own securities. If another investor takes quick profits, it won't affect yours.

• Tax efficiency. Participating managers promise to customize trading to take investors' tax situations into account. They can hold on to winners, take losses, and refrain from selling until securities qualify for long-term gains, etc.

Exchange-traded funds

Exchange-traded funds (ETFs) trade like stocks but give you the diversification of mutual funds. Most ETFs are traded on the American Stock Exchange.

They track an index such as the S&P 500 and are listed under names such as iShares and SPDRs ("spiders").

Because prices change throughout the day, ETFs are unlikely to be affected by the late-trading and market-timing strategies that have tarnished some mutual funds.

Tax reduction: As index funds, ETFs don't trade very often. Thus, they seldom generate capital gains.

Moreover, ETFs are allowed to use certain techniques that further lessen the chances that investors will have to pay tax on capital gains distributions.

Variable annuities

These investments offer buyers the chance to choose among sub-accounts, many of which resemble stock or bond funds. Your contract value will grow or shrink, depending on how these subaccounts perform.

Caution: Many variable annuity subaccounts are managed by the same companies that run mutual funds. Check to see if you're comfortable with the people who'll be responsible for your investments.

Although mutual fund families manage money in variable annuities, improper trading practices are less likely due to higher fees and the lack of easy liquidity.

If you invest within a variable annuity, you can enjoy several tax benefits...

• Tax-free buildup. Investment earnings won't be taxed as long as they're held within the annuity.

• Tax-free switches. You can move money from one equity subaccount to another without paying any tax.

Outside of an annuity, on the other hand, switching among mutual funds is a taxable event. That's true even within the same fund family.

• Tax-free exchanges. You can replace one annuity contract with another without owing tax, under Section 1035 of the Tax Code.

• No capital gains distributions. As a mutual fund investor, you owe tax on the fund's realized net gains, even if you didn't sell your fund shares. Annuities don't pay out such gains.

• Tax-sheltered income. If you choose to annuitize a variable annuity and receive lifelong income, part of your payment stream will be a tax-free return of capital.

Trap: Variable annuities have tax disadvantages, too. Investment earnings are taxed at ordinary income rates when withdrawn. You don't enjoy the low tax on capital gains.

Strategy: If you keep money in a variable annuity for 10 years or longer, the value of tax deferral may outweigh the loss of the capital gains tax break. A long holding period also will reduce your exposure to surrender charges for liquidating the annuity before a certain minimum holding period.

Be sure to avoid withdrawals before age 59½. Such distributions are usually subject to a 10% penalty tax, in addition to income tax.

Other advantages: Some variable annuities now offer "living benefits" by offering you the chance to gradually withdraw the amount you put in, even if your chosen subaccounts lose money.

Other variable annuities promise to increase your account value by at least 5% per year. In order to cash in on this guarantee, you must annuitize the contract with the same insurance company.

Such guarantees enable you to invest in stock market subaccounts without worrying about losing money.

These guarantees come at a price. You'll pay higher expenses each year, so weigh the costs before buying.

Variable life insurance

If you have a need for life insurance, consider investing inside a variable life insurance policy. In some ways, these resemble variable annuities. You invest via mutual fund look-alikes. Current income taxes are avoided, and the chances of trading improprieties are reduced by higher fees.

The tax benefits of variable life insurance are even greater than they are for variable annuities...

• Death benefits. At your death, your beneficiaries receive insurance proceeds that exceed the policy's cash value. Typically, these proceeds will be free of income tax.

• Living benefits. You can take policy loans and withdrawals, and if handled carefully, these distributions can provide an ongoing stream of tax-free cash flow.

Trap: If you withdraw or borrow too heavily, the policy will lapse and deferred income tax will be due.

Again, you'll have to hold on to a variable life policy for a period of years before the tax benefits offset the up-front costs. But, if you have a need for life insurance, these vehicles can enable you to avoid mutual fund pitfalls and gain access to tax-free investment income.

Source: Marilyn Gunther, CFP, president, Center for Financial Planning, 26211 Central Park Blvd., Southfield, MI 48073. A past president of the Michigan International Association for Financial Planning, she has been named one of the nation's top financial advisers by *Worth* and *Medical Economics* magazines.

Chapter Seven

INVESTORS: TAKE LOSSES NOW FOR TAX BENEFITS TOMORROW

The stock market enjoyed impressive gains in 2003, and in 2004, it was rather flat. And 2005 showed only modest gains. Nevertheless, many investors have losses (realized and unrealized) after the three-year bear market that ended last year.

Strategy: Take capital losses now for tax savings you can claim this year and perhaps far into the future.

Trap: After you take losses, be careful how you reinvest. If you run afoul of the wash-sale rule, your losses will be disallowed.

Some investors find it difficult to accept that they've bought a loser. They feel that as long as they don't sell, it's "just a paper loss."

In reality, taking losses can help you to pay less tax for years.

The $3,000 limit

Despite a number of tax law changes in recent years, the rules on deducting capital losses have remained the same. Up to $3,000 worth of net capital losses may be deducted each year against salary and other income. Excess losses may be carried forward indefinitely.

Strategy: Sell enough losing investments to have at least $3,000 worth of net losses each year.

Example: Near the end of the year, you tally your trades and discover you have $15,000 worth of net gains. You should consider taking at least $18,000 worth of losses by year-end.

A $3,000 deduction on your tax return will save you $1,050 in tax in the 35% federal tax bracket.

Bonus break: A net capital loss reduces your adjusted gross income (AGI), which may provide other tax savings.

You may enjoy state and local tax savings, too.

Enjoy tax-free gains

If you've already banked losses during the 2000–2001–2002 stock market collapse, you have an opportunity to take tax-free gains now.

Example: You go into 2006 with $50,000 of accumulated capital losses carried forward. Then you take $10,000 in net capital gains.

Strategy: You can take another $40,000 worth of gains this year, tax free.

Loophole: Even short-term gains can be cashed in. Instead of owing tax at ordinary income rates of up to 35%, you'll owe no tax if those gains can be offset by capital losses.

Offset fund gains, too

Include capital gains distributions from mutual funds in your calculations. Mutual funds have to pass through any realized gains to investors each year.

Example: You have a $15,000 net gain from trading this year. Mutual funds you own in taxable accounts distribute $5,000 in capital gains.

Now you have a total of $20,000 worth of net gains for the year. You'll need to take $23,000 worth of losses for a $3,000 net loss, which you can deduct. This is true regardless of whether you reinvest the $5,000 in capital gains distributions from your mutual funds.

Distributions from mutual funds held in tax-deferred retirement accounts don't count when you tally your gains.

Trap: If you're reinvesting the money in mutual funds for a taxable account, don't acquire shares just before a capital gains distribution—you'll owe tax on that distribution. Wait to purchase the shares until after the capital gains distribution, when the share price will fall.

Be aware that many funds now have loss carryovers so they won't be distributing taxable gains for a while. If you're interested in such a fund, you don't have to wait.

To find a fund with carryover losses, decide on what type of fund you want, then check a specific fund through a service such as Morningstar. Or call the fund and ask. Be aware that you will be getting only an estimate—not a guarantee.

Other gains to offset

You might want to take losses in excess of $3,000.

Advantage: Excess losses can be used against other gains, now or in the future.

Example: You have $20,000 in net capital gains for the year, as above. Instead of taking $23,000 worth of losses by year-end, you liquidate all your loss positions, taking $70,000 worth of losses, and wind up with a $50,000 net loss for the year.

Result: In addition to a $3,000 deductible loss, you have $47,000 worth of excess losses.

That $47,000 worth of net losses can be used to offset capital gains from investments other than stocks and mutual funds, such as real estate or hedge funds.

Losses you can't use right away can be "banked" for the future. Later, you might be able to take $47,000 worth of capital gains, tax free, because of those offsetting losses.

If you own a business, having a bank of losses will make it easier when it's time to sell your company. With losses to help offset your gains, the tax bill won't be as steep.

Reinvesting the money

After taking losses, reinvest with care. If you sell a stock and buy it back within 30 days, you'll violate the wash-sale rule and the loss won't count.

If you take gains, you can reinvest any way you want—even in the same securities. The wash-sale rule doesn't apply.

To avoid the wash-sale rules, yet maintain your investment strategy...

• Wait. You can sell a security at a loss and hold the sales proceeds for 31 days. Then you can buy back the same stock, bond, or fund.

Key: Be sure to wait until the 31st day. A purchase on Day 30 will blow the tax loss.

Risk: With this method, the stock might shoot up while you're waiting on the sidelines.

• Switch. You can buy a similar but not identical security, hoping for minimal portfolio impact.

Example: You sell Qwest Communications, a telecommunications stock, at a loss and immediately buy competitor SBC Communications, expecting performance to be similar. After 31 days, you can go back to your position in Qwest, if you choose.

• Double up. Instead of waiting out the wash-sale period with no investment position, before you sell a security at a loss, buy an equivalent amount. On the 31st day, you can sell the original lot at a capital loss.

Key: To implement this strategy, you need sufficient cash to buy the additional securities or a willingness to use margin.

Deadline: Double-up tactics must be in place by November 30 to result in a calendar-year tax loss.

Source: Diahann W. Lassus, CPA, CFP, president of the wealth-management firm Lassus Wherley & Associates, 1 Academy St., New Providence, NJ 07974. A regular on CNBC, she has been named one of the nation's top financial advisers by *Robb Report*, *Worth* and *Medical Economics* magazines.

Chapter Eight

CUT YOUR TAXES BY INVESTING IN LOW-INCOME HOUSING DEALS

Despite recent reports of abusive tax shelters, some shelters have the explicit approval of the federal government. They not only permit you to cut your taxes, they also serve a purpose that Washington deems worthwhile.

Example: Federal low-income housing tax credits. While you reduce your taxes, the money you invest helps to finance living space for low- and moderate-income residents.

These credits help working people and retirees afford decent housing. The real estate you acquire through such investments may well maintain its value and even appreciate.

If so, profits might qualify for the favorable 15% rate on long-term capital gains.

How it works

If you invest in residential real estate that's rented to certain tenants, you can qualify for a tax credit—a direct reduction in your tax bill. You can earn this credit on your own, but you're probably better off in a limited partnership, relying upon the general partner to deal with all the requirements.

Time period: These tax credits are spread over 10 years. Often, the period will stretch to 11 or 12 years because it may take some time for a partnership to invest all its capital.

Tax credits are "pre-funded"—attached to a property for the full time period. Congress can't change the rules midstream and sink the tax benefits.

Payoff: Expect an annual tax credit of roughly 10%.

Example: You invest $10,000 in XYZ Affordable Housing Partnership. Once XYZ is fully invested, you'll get about $1,000 worth of tax credits per year. Altogether, expect $10,000 in tax savings from a $10,000 investment.

Thus, you'll probably break even from the tax savings these deals offer. Any other proceeds you receive, from property sales or refinancing, will turn the deal into a money maker.

Loophole: The returns may be greater if you control a C corporation and invest corporate dollars. C corporations may enjoy greater tax benefits by deducting "passive losses" that are not deductible for most individual investors.

For individuals, these tax credits may be especially appealing if they are collecting, or about to collect, Social Security benefits. Advantages…

• They are not considered earned income, so your benefits won't be reduced before age 65.

• They aren't considered income, so receiving them won't expose your benefits to income tax. By contrast, investing in "tax-exempt" municipal bonds may expose your Social Security benefits to income tax.

Learn the limits

In effect, investing in an affordable housing partnership can be a heads-you-win, tails-you-don't-lose venture. Therefore, there are limits on the amount you can invest.

Loophole: Unlike many tax breaks, these tax credits are available to all investors, even those with high incomes. In fact, higher-income investors may be able to use more of these credits.

Example: If you're in the top 35% federal tax bracket, you may be able to use up to $8,750 worth of these tax credits per year—based on a $25,000 maximum deduction equivalent (35% x $25,000 = $8,750). Thus, you might invest up to $87,500 in a partnership.

If your tax bracket is lower, you're restricted to fewer tax credits. In a 25%

bracket, you're probably limited to $6,250 worth of credits per year (25% x $25,000 = $6,250), so you probably shouldn't invest more than $62,500.

Minimum: Generally, the minimum investment for an affordable housing partnership is $5,000.

If you have passive income from other sources, perhaps from rental properties that generate taxable income, you probably can invest more in affordable housing than the limits described above. On the other hand, if you deduct losses from actively managed investment property, you'll be eligible for fewer credits.

Other limits on these investments may apply. In particular, low-income housing credits can't offset the alternative minimum tax (AMT). You might be able to invest less than the amounts mentioned above because you'll run into the AMT.

Example: Your regular tax bill is $20,000. But, working with your tax professional, you determine that the AMT would be triggered if you reduce your regular tax bill below $15,000.

Result: You can use up to $5,000 worth of these credits per year ($20,000 minus $15,000) before you hit the AMT so $50,000 might be the most you'd want to invest.

Loophole: Low-income housing tax credits you can't use in a given year can be carried back one year or forward up to 20 years.

Downside and dangers

Investors in these partnerships should be prepared to buy and hold for 15 years. Even though you may sell your partnership interest, if you need to cash out early, you may not receive full value for it.

Meanwhile, tax credits likely will provide your only returns from the partnership for 10 years or more. After they end, you are not likely to receive cash flow from rents, which are held below market levels for moderate-income tenants.

Key: The greatest risk in these deals is investing with an inept sponsor. You'll want a general partner who can verify tenant eligibility, handle all the paperwork, and provide investors with clear reports.

Check on a sponsor carefully before investing. Speak with other investors who have been in partnerships formed at least five years ago. See if the sponsor has lived up to its promises.

Read the sponsor's reports to investors in prior partnerships to see if they contain warnings about the properties or the tax consequences. Check that the sponsor will provide materials to help your tax preparer handle the necessary tax return schedules.

Profit potential

Investing with a proven sponsor may increase your chances of receiving additional returns from the properties in the partnership.

• Your partnership may be able to refinance its properties, paying out the borrowed funds as tax-free cash to investors.

• Your partnership may decide to sell its properties. Potential buyers include new investor groups as well as nonprofit housing groups eager to maintain affordable rent levels.

Key: If the buildings are maintained and the neighborhood holds up, the demand for these properties may exceed the supply so that resale or refinancing is possible.

Loophole: Low-income housing credits are not "recaptured" and taxed after 15 years so there is no payback to the IRS.

To find brokers or financial planners offering these programs, go to an Internet search engine and enter, "invest low-income housing tax credits." Make sure to check on the financial adviser as well as the partnership sponsor.

Source: Thomas P. Ochsenschlager, Esq., CPA, vice president, taxation, American Institute of Certified Public Accountants, 1455 Pennsylvania Ave. NW, Washington, DC 20004.

Section 6: Real Estate and Investment Loopholes

Chapter Nine
GIGANTIC TAX BREAKS FOR REAL ESTATE INVESTORS

Today's low interest rates and recent property appreciation may entice you to buy investment real estate. If you take such a step, focus first on the deal's profit possibilities.

But also factor in the following tax breaks, which can make a successful real estate venture even more rewarding.

Tax-free cash flow

Real estate investors may claim some noncash deductions, such as depreciation. So, if you receive net positive cash flow from your property, some or all of that cash may avoid immediate income taxation.

Example: You buy a small office building. This year, your net cash flow from rents, after paying all of your expenses, puts $10,000 in your pocket. For tax purposes, though, you wind up with an $8,000 loss, after taking depreciation deductions. Therefore, you owe no tax on the $10,000 you put in your pocket.

Trap: The depreciation deductions lower your basis in the property. A lower basis, in turn, will increase your capital gains tax on an eventual sale.

Loophole: Under current law, the tax on prior depreciation deductions is capped at 25%. Thus, you may defer income tax normally owed at rates up to 35% and pay those taxes years later at a 25% rate.

The ultimate loophole: Under current law, certain assets (including real estate) left to heirs get a basis step-up to market value. Thus, if you hold on to investment property until death, the tax-free cash flow you receive during your lifetime will remain untaxed.

Loss deductions

In the above example, you wound up with an $8,000 paper loss, after depreciation. Can you deduct such a loss? Perhaps.

Your ability to deduct such losses depends on several factors, especially your adjusted gross income (AGI).

Basic rule: Losses from rental properties are known as passive losses. For many taxpayers, such losses are deductible, up to $25,000 per year.

Required: For you to take the full $25,000 deduction, your modified AGI (MAGI) must be no more than $100,000. Over $100,000, this deduction is phased out, $1 for every $2 over the threshold.

Thus, you can take no deduction if your MAGI is $150,000 or greater.

Example: You own a rental property that turns in tax losses every year. This year, your MAGI is $95,000. You can deduct losses up to $25,000.

Next year, your MAGI goes up to $130,000. You're $30,000 over the threshold, so your maximum loss is cut by $15,000 ($30,000 ÷ 2). You can deduct up to $10,000 worth of losses from this rental property.

Say your MAGI reaches $160,000 the following year. Now you can deduct no losses, in most cases.

In our example, with an $8,000 paper loss, you can have MAGI up to $134,000 ($150,000 − $16,000) and take a full deduction right away. With MAGI of $136,000, for example, only $7,000 can be deducted currently.

Loophole: Any passive losses that you can't deduct right away may be carried over to future years, where they can offset any income from rental properties.

Eventually, when the property is sold, any unused losses will be deductible against your ordinary income in the year of sale. The sale proceeds, meanwhile, will be taxed at favorable capital gains rates.

Loophole: The laws are more favorable if you spend so much time as a landlord that you get to be treated as a real estate professional.

Required: If you spend more than half of your working time on real estate and at least 750 hours a year, you're entitled to deduct any losses right away, regardless of your AGI.

Learning to love leverage

You'll probably want to buy real estate with as small a down payment (and as much borrowed money) as possible, as long as you can borrow at an attractive fixed rate.

Strategy: When you borrow money to buy investment property, ask for the debt to be "qualified non-recourse." This means that only the property (not your other assets) secures the debt. Your downside is limited if things don't work out.

Today's interest rates on real estate loans are relatively low, by historical standards. That makes the use of leverage even more appealing.

Leverage, in turn, will magnify any gains on investment property.

Example: You buy investment property for $400,000, making an $80,000 (20%) down payment. A few years later, your property has grown in value to $500,000.

That's a $100,000 profit on an $80,000 outlay—a 125% gain on a 25% increase in the property's value.

Tax break: The interest you pay on this loan will be tax deductible against your income from the property.

What's more, refinancing an appreciated property can allow you to pull out tax-free cash.

Example: As above, you buy a property for $400,000, putting $80,000 down, and see it appreciate in value to $500,000.

Strategy: Instead of selling, triggering a tax, you refinance the property. With property valued at $500,000, you might be able to borrow $400,000 (an 80% loan-to-value ratio).

Result: You can use your new loan to pay off what's left of the original $320,000 loan and keep the excess $80,000 tax free. Borrowing money won't create a tax obligation.

Drawback: Now you're paying interest (perhaps at a higher rate) on a $400,000 loan, not a $320,000 loan, so your payments will be higher. However, the fact that your property has appreciated in value may indicate your rental income has gone up or could go up, so you'll be able to cover the higher debt service.

Endgames

As mentioned, rather than sell your property, triggering a tax bill, you can hold on until death. Your heirs may avoid paying income tax because of a basis step-up. Note: Estate tax might still apply.

Alternative: Enter into a like-kind exchange—usually referred to as a "Section 1031" exchange after a section of the Tax Code—for a different investment property. Such a maneuver may defer any taxable gains.

Example: You are ready to retire and move to Florida. You no longer wish to manage the office building you own up north, especially now that you would be a long-distance landlord.

Strategy: Sell your office building, and have the proceeds held by an unrelated intermediary. Then find a low-maintenance property, such as a self-storage center, selling for approximately the same price near your new home in Florida.

Instruct the intermediary to use the proceeds from the original sale to buy the replacement property on your behalf.

Caution: There are various deadlines you have to meet to guarantee that such an exchange will be tax free. Working with an experienced professional—an attorney or accountant—is recommended.

Alternatively, you can do an Internet search under "1031 exchanges" to find companies specializing in these transactions. And consult someone you trust in the real estate business for a referral.

As long as you enjoy neither cash from the transaction nor debt reduction, you can exchange properties in this manner tax free.

Caution: A tax-free exchange reduces the depreciable basis of the replacement property.

Variation: You can exchange commercial property for a home that you rent to tenants. If the rules are followed, no tax will be due.

Bonus: In the future, you can move into the house yourself without triggering any tax. After living in the house for two or more years, you can sell it and claim the $250,000 capital gains exclusion on sale of a primary residence, or $500,000 if you're married.

Source: William G. Brennan, CPA/PFS, CFP, Capital Management Group, LLC, 1730 Rhode Island Ave. NW, Washington, DC 20036. Mr. Brennan is a widely quoted expert who has written extensively on income tax and investment planning.

Chapter Ten

YEAR-END TAX MOVES FOR INVESTORS

Investors may have significant gains as well as losses for a seesaw year. This generates opportunities as well as pitfalls.

Key: Moves you make before year-end can pay off. Some of the moves are basic, others sophisticated.

The $3,000 question

Try to wind up 2006 with a net capital loss of at least $3,000.

Loophole: A net capital loss up to $3,000 can be deducted from your ordinary income. In a 35% federal tax bracket, for example, you can save $1,050 (35% of $3,000). Your total tax savings may be even greater, counting state and local income tax.

Trap: If you fail to offset all of your capital gains, you may wind up with short-term gains on positions sold after you've held them a year or less. Such gains will be taxed as ordinary income, at rates up to 35% on your federal tax return.

Excess losses: What if your net capital loss is greater than $3,000? Any excess loss can be carried forward to future years to offset future capital gains. If you have no gains to offset in a future year, loss carryforwards may be deducted, up to $3,000 per year.

Strategy: Tally realized gains and losses before year-end. Make trades that will give you a $3,000 net loss.

Example: Counting all your trades so far in 2006, you have a $10,000 net capital gain. You can sell securities by year-end, realizing $13,000 worth of losses, for a $3,000 net loss.

Key: Don't be reluctant to take additional capital losses. If you wind up the year with a net capital loss over $3,000, the overage is "banked" for use in the future.

Wash-sale rules

After you sell securities at a loss, you must be careful how you reinvest.

Trap: If you buy back the same securities right away, your loss won't be recognized, for tax purposes. To lock in the tax loss...

• Wait 31 days. After that, you can buy back the same stock or bond you sold. But, if you're out of the market for that long, you might miss a quick run-up in the price of that security.

• Double up. Another way to avert the wash-sale trap is to first buy a similar position to the one you already own and want to sell for a loss. Wait 31 days, then sell your original lot.

Example: You plan to take a tax loss on 500 shares of Mattel but you think the company's stock may bounce back shortly. So you buy another 500 shares of Mattel.

After waiting 31 days, you sell the first lot at a loss. You've maintained your position (from the second lot you purchased) yet you still have a deductible tax loss.

Caution: This strategy eliminates the risk that a stock will run up while you're not holding it, but creates the risk that the stock collapses while you're holding an enlarged position.

Key: A double-up strategy must be in place by late November to create a tax loss for 2006.

• Reinvest in something similar. As long as the replacement security is not substantially identical to the one you sold at a loss, that loss will be allowed on an immediate sale (including one made before 31 days are up).

Example: If you sold Pfizer at a loss, you can reinvest the proceeds in

Schering-Plough right away. The two drug stocks may move in sync with their industry, but the results won't be exactly the same.

Bond strategy: Rising interest rates have depressed bond prices. You can enter into a "bond swap," arranged by your broker, in which you take a tax loss on bonds you hold while replacing them with bonds that are similar but from a different issuer or with a different maturity.

Fund facts

When you calculate your 2006 gains and losses, don't forget to include capital gains distributions from mutual funds.

Trap: Mutual funds are required to distribute net realized gains to shareholders. If you hold a fund in a taxable account, such distributions are taxable income, even if you choose to reinvest them in the fund.

Hedge funds also may make taxable distributions of capital gains to investors.

Example: Above, it was assumed you had $10,000 worth of net realized capital gains from trading for the year. If you also receive $2,000 worth of capital gains distributions from funds, your net gain for the year goes up to $12,000.

Thus, you need to realize $15,000 worth of losses to wind up the year with a $3,000 net capital loss.

Strategy: Include capital gains distributions when you make your year-end calculations. Call your fund companies to find out if such distributions are planned for December.

Trap: Some fund distributions are short term. Again, net short-term gains are heavily taxed, at rates up to 35%, so you should try for offsetting capital losses.

Caution: Don't invest in a mutual fund just before a scheduled capital gains distribution. You'll get some of your own money back right away...and owe tax on that payout! Instead, check with the fund before investing around year-end. Wait to buy until after the record date of the distribution.

Tax-free gains

What if, instead of net gains for the year, you're sitting with a large realized loss instead?

Loophole: In this situation, you may be able to take capital gains, tax free.

Example: You have $10,000 worth of net capital losses so far this year. You can take $7,000 worth of capital gains by year-end (including fund distributions).

Result: You'll still wind up with a $3,000 net loss, which you can deduct. The proceeds from your year-end gains won't be taxed.

Loophole: If you wish, you can take gains and immediately reinvest in the same security you sold. The wash-sale rules don't apply to gains.

Why would you do this? The sale and repurchase raises your basis (price paid) in that security. A higher basis, in turn, probably will reduce the tax you'll owe on a future sale.

Key: Selling and immediately repurchasing the same security means that you'd rather have a higher basis on the appreciated holding than a capital loss you can carry forward. Also, keep any transaction costs in mind.

Lost causes

Did you buy stock in a business that failed? If so, you can take a capital loss in the year that your holding becomes worthless.

Key: To be considered worthless, a security you own must have absolutely no value. If it has scant value, you can't claim a capital loss.

Trap: Demonstrating worthlessness, for tax purposes, may be difficult.

Strategy: Realize your capital loss by selling your interest in the business to an unrelated party for a nominal amount.

Example: Sell a worthless security to your neighbor or the brokerage firm for $1. As long as you make the sale by December 31, you can claim a capital loss for 2005.

Source: Glenn Frank, CPA/PFS, CFP, vice president, Tanager Financial Services Inc., 800 South St., Waltham, MA 02453. He teaches postgraduate courses in portfolio construction at Bentley College, also in Waltham.

Chapter Eleven
INVESTORS: GET BIG DEDUCTIONS BY QUALIFYING AS A "TRADER"

If you frequently buy and sell stocks or other investments to profit from short-term gains, you may qualify as a "trader"—and receive valuable tax breaks not available to other investors.

Payoff: Larger deductions for investment expenses and investment losses than provided under normal rules...a possible home-office deduction...smaller AMT liability...possible tax refunds for past years.

A trader invests in stocks or other readily tradable investments (such as commodities) with the goal of profiting from short-term swings in price, rather than from long-term appreciation.

Traders qualify for either (or both) of two big tax breaks not available to other investors...

Business deductions for investment expenses

The IRS treats traders as being in the business of trading. Thus, while income from trading is reported on the Schedule D filed by all investors, trading expenses are reported on Schedule C as self-employment expenses —and escape the normal limitations that apply to investment expenses. This makes larger deductions available. Examples...

• Investment expenses are fully deductible. In contrast, under normal rules, investment expenses are reported among miscellaneous deductions, the total of which is deductible only to the extent it exceeds 2% of adjusted gross income

(AGI). So if AGI is $100,000, no deduction is allowed for the first $2,000.

Moreover, under normal rules, the deduction is further reduced by the general reduction of itemized deductions that applies if AGI is more than $150,150 in 2006 on a joint or single return. To the extent that AGI exceeds that amount, deductions are reduced by 3% of the excess. This does not apply if you're a trader.

• No AMT effect. Trading expenses are deductible above the line, whereas investment expenses treated as miscellaneous deductions are eliminated for purposes of calculating the alternative minimum tax (AMT). Since many taxpayers are finding themselves subject to the AMT, they would lose any benefits from miscellaneous itemized deductions. However, above-the-line trading expenses remain fully deductible under the AMT rules.

• A home-office deduction becomes available. Because trading is treated as a business, it can qualify you to claim a home-office deduction. This can enable you to deduct items such as...

☐ A portion of home ownership costs attributable to the office that otherwise wouldn't be deductible—such as insurance, maintenance, and utilities.

☐ Equipment used in the office, such as furniture, computing equipment, and a phone line. It is deductible without burdensome record keeping of the amount of business use.

Requirement: To be deductible, the office must be a portion of your home used exclusively for business—though it need not be a full room.

Normal investing does not qualify one to deduct a home office.

Who is a trader?

The first issue for any investor who wishes to qualify as a trader is that the term "trader" is not defined anywhere in the Tax Code, nor has it been by the IRS or courts.

The IRS and courts have limited themselves to stating that traders buy and sell "frequently" for short-term gains, do so "continuously" throughout the year, and spend "a significant amount of time" managing their trades.

But no specific number of trades has ever been stated to be a minimum amount required to qualify as a trader.

To be on the safe side, one seeking to qualify as a trader should hold some short-term positions at all times during the year, manage them actively, and keep full records of doing so.

Bigger loss deductions

Trading income—gain and loss—generally is taxable under the normal rules for investment income.

But traders, unlike other investors, have the option to make a "Section 475(f) election" to report their gains and losses under "mark-to-market" rules.

Important: A trader does not have to make a 475(f) election to get the other benefits discussed previously.

Under the 475(f) rules, all gains are treated as ordinary income and all losses are treated as business losses—instead of being treated as capital gains and losses. In addition, all unrealized gains and losses in a portfolio are taxed at current value at year-end. Benefits of the Section 475(f) election...

• A current deduction for losses can become much larger. Under normal rules, only $3,000 of net capital losses can be deducted against ordinary income in any one year. However, traders who make this election can deduct any amount of losses against ordinary income.

• "Wash-sale rules" do not apply to those who make the election. Normally, these rules prevent a loss on securities from being currently deductible if they are repurchased within 30 days. This can be an onerous limitation on active investors—but traders who make the 475(f) election are not subject to it.

• Protecting long-term gains. Individuals who qualify as traders can also invest to benefit from tax-favored long-term capital gains and the top 15% tax rate on qualified dividends.

Source: Janice M. Johnson, CPA, JD, A.B. Watley Group, 90 Park Ave., New York City 10016.

Section 7: Deductions, Deductions, Deductions

The Overlooked Trillion Dollar+ Income Tax Deduction 355

Best Way to Lower Your Property Tax 359

Best Tax Return Filing Strategies for a Bigger Refund 360

Loopholes in Tax Return Preparation 365

Biggest Tax Preparation Mistakes to Avoid 368

Special Purpose Trust Loopholes 373

Giving Stock vs. Collectibles 376

How to Shelter Your Income from the IRS 377

Mutual Fund Tax Saver 381

Nine Ways You Can Save Money Under the New Tax Law 382

Frequently Overlooked Deductions for Legal Fees 385

Lock in Business Expense Deductions with an Accountable Plan 386

Deduct Fun from Your Taxes 391

Smartest Ways to Deduct Business Start-up Costs 395

Protect Small-Business Deductions...that the IRS Looks at Every Time 400

Section 7: Deductions, Deductions, Deductions

Chapter One

THE OVERLOOKED TRILLION DOLLAR+ INCOME TAX DEDUCTION

The least understood and most complicated of income tax deductions is also the one that is most often missed—even though it could be worth a trillion dollars or more to taxpayers who are failing to claim it.

If you have deferred-income–type assets in your taxable estate—or inherit them from one—you must learn about this. Here's the story...

Double danger

When deferred-income–type assets are in your taxable estate, they can be subject to taxation at near confiscatory rates—80% or more. Assets that face this danger include...

- Balances in IRAs, 401(k)s, and other tax-deferred retirement accounts.
- Pension payments owed to designated beneficiaries.
- Survivor annuities issued by insurance companies.
- Proceeds due on installment sales.
- Royalty rights.
- Untaxed deferred interest on Series E, EE, and I savings bonds.
- Deferred compensation from employers.
- Damage awards from lawsuits.
- Other income-producing items.

IRD: The income from such items, when later paid to heirs, is called income in respect of a decedent (IRD).

Trap if you don't know the rules: The income-producing item's value is first subject to estate tax at rates up to 47%. Then the income later paid by the item—the IRD—is subject to income tax at rates up to 35%. The total tax due from adding these tax rates can be as much as 82%—leaving as little as 18% for heirs!

Example: An individual leaves $1 million in an IRA that is subject to 44% federal estate tax (this article does not consider state estate tax). The IRA's beneficiary is in the 35% tax bracket. The estate must first pay $440,000 tax on the IRA (his estate provides funds to pay this tax). Then the beneficiary must pay $350,000 of income tax payable on the distribution of the IRA balance—if he doesn't know the IRD rules. The total tax bill comes to $790,000 for the IRS.

Tax relief from Congress

Congress believed this full double taxation to be unfair. As a remedy, it created partial relief in the form of an income tax deduction for federal estate tax (but not for state estate tax) previously paid on an asset that creates IRD. This is often called the "deduction for IRD." It can be claimed as the IRD is paid out.

Example: An individual dies leaving $1 million in an IRA subject to 44% federal estate tax. The tax of $440,000 is paid as in the example above. The IRA's beneficiary is in the 35% tax bracket. If he...

• Takes a full distribution of the $1 million, the deduction for IRD lets him deduct $440,000 against it. As a result, he pays income tax on only $560,000—and the deduction for IRD saves him $154,000—plus state income tax savings on the deduction.

• Takes distributions from the IRA over time, the deduction for IRD is taken proportionately. If the IRA is distributed at a rate of $100,000 per year, the deduction for IRD is $44,000 per year until the entire $440,000 is consumed. This saves $15,400 of income tax per year plus state income tax savings on the $44,000 deduction. Any additional distributions from the IRA in excess of $1 million (due to investment returns) would be fully taxed.

Overlooked deduction

The biggest mistake made with the deduction for IRD is that many people—perhaps most—do not claim it at all. It is the most overlooked of all income tax deductions. Reasons why...

• Most individual taxpayers do not even know it exists.

• Professionals who deal with an estate often don't talk to each other about it, so it falls through the cracks.

Example: Neither the executor nor the adviser who prepares an estate's tax return has responsibility for the personal returns of heirs who would claim the IRD deduction, and doesn't even think about it—unless there is a formal agreement stipulating that he will take responsibility. At the same time, the tax advisers of those heirs do not know if any estate tax was paid. Or the heirs prepare their own returns and are ignorant of the whole issue. So the deduction is simply missed.

• There is no "information reporting" for the deduction. No form, such as a W-2, 1099, or K-1, is filed by anyone to report the deductible amount to a taxpayer who doesn't know about it.

• Records for past years are lost. The IRD deduction may be spread out over many years—in the case of an IRA distributed over the beneficiary's life expectancy, 20 years or more. And a balance of the available deduction must be carried forward from year to year—if past records weren't prepared or were lost, the deduction is lost.

• It's very hard to learn about the deduction. There is no single IRS publication dedicated to explaining its application in detail—information about it is spread around different IRS publications and rulings.

Result: The deduction is routinely missed by taxpayers, often year after year.

Trillion-dollar error

The dollar volume of overlooked deductions for IRD already missed as well as what might be missed in the future stands to be huge—perhaps a trillion dollars or more.

Government data show tax-deferred retirement accounts that can produce IRD now hold $11 trillion dollars. Of this, $3 trillion is owned by persons in the highest tax brackets who are expected to owe estate tax—and both of these numbers are growing rapidly.

Not all of these assets will be subject to estate tax. But, if out of this more than $11 trillion, only a little more than $2 trillion eventually becomes subject to estate tax, the total deduction for IRD will be $1 trillion.

What to do

To save the deduction for IRD, it's essential that the tax professional who prepares an estate's tax return works together with the tax advisers of the heirs of the estate and beneficiaries of assets included in the estate, such as IRAs.

The estate's tax professional should inform each heir in writing of the amount of estate tax that was paid on each item of IRD and should spell out how the rules work. Then each heir's tax adviser must use this information to create a schedule of available deductions that may be claimed against IRD in the future.

Important: The information and schedule may have to be used for many years, long after the professionals who prepared it are gone from the scene. So it must be fully self-explanatory to be able to survive a future IRS audit and be safely stored with other vital "permanent" documents.

• If your estate is large enough to be subject to estate tax, discuss planning for IRD with your advisers now.

• If you inherit an IRA or other item of IRD, contact the executor of the deceased to learn if any estate tax was paid and obtain needed information to manage the deduction for IRD.

Technical rules for deductions for IRD are complex, so be sure you are advised by a tax professional who is experienced in dealing with them.

Source: Seymour Goldberg, Esq., CPA, Goldberg & Goldberg, PC, 1 Huntington Quadrangle, Melville, NY 11747, *www.goldbergira.com*. One of the nation's leading authorities on IRA distributions, Mr. Goldberg is author of *What the Professional Advisor Should Know About the Income in Respect of a Decedent Rules*. (IRG Publications, *www.goldbergreports.com*).

Chapter Two
BEST WAY TO LOWER YOUR PROPERTY TAX

About 60% of residential homes are overassessed, yet only one in 50 home owners challenges their property tax assessments. What's more, many Americans don't realize that they may be entitled to exemptions that could result in a reduction of 5% to 20% of their bills. Unfair or inaccurate assessments happen for many reasons.

Here's how to appeal your property tax assessment—and win...

• Obtain your detailed property tax assessment record card from your local government's tax assessor's office, and review your property description. Look for defects that were omitted—such as proximity to noisy streets or traffic—and inaccuracies in the number of rooms and square footage.

• Ask the assessor's office to provide comparable property prices (and assessed values) in your community so that you can be sure your home is not being overtaxed. The *Freedom of Information Act* and "right-to-know" laws entitle you to any and all information relating to your property—property assessment lists...zoning maps...property tax exemptions, such as those for veterans, the elderly and disabled and low-income home owners...etc.

• If you believe your assessment is inaccurate, ask the assessor's office, in writing, to lower it. If the request is denied, you will need to go through a formal appeal. Ask for a list of procedures and deadlines. In cases of higher-value homes, you might want to hire an attorney if it becomes necessary to go to court.

Source: Richard Roll, president of American Homeowners Association (AHA), 3001 Summer St., Stamford, CT 06905, *www.homeownertaxcut.com*.

Chapter Three

BEST TAX RETURN FILING STRATEGIES FOR A BIGGER REFUND

You can still reduce your 2005 tax bill. To get as large a refund as you can, use these smart tax-saving filing ideas...

Home sales

The general rule is that if you used a home as your primary residence for two of five years before selling it, up to $250,000 of gain is tax free ($500,000 on a joint return).

Exception: Even if you didn't live in the home for two years, part of the gain can be tax free if the sale was compelled by "unforeseen circumstances."

Examples: Health problems, divorce or separation, unemployment, damage to the home due to a casualty or disaster, and other reasons.

Another new exception: The new rules say a home office is residential property that qualifies for tax-free gain. Many people formerly treated these offices as business property (which doesn't qualify)—and thus didn't claim tax-free treatment for the part of a home's sale price attributable to a home office.

The new rules are retroactive. So if you sold a home any time within the last three years and paid tax on gain that now qualifies as tax free, you can file an amended tax return to claim a refund.

Details: For more information, see IRS Publication 523, *Selling Your Home* (800-829-3676 or *www.irs.gov*).

Investments

If in 2004 you suffered investment losses you couldn't fully use on that year's return, you can carry them forward to offset gains on the 2005 return—with a net loss of up to $3,000 deductible against ordinary income. Don't overlook them. Also be aware of these opportunities...

• Capital gains and dividends. The top tax rate on these is 15%, and only 5% for taxpayers in the 10% or 15% bracket. Before you fill out your tax return, collect the records needed to show when dividends and gains were received.

Caution: Not all dividends issued by some entities, such as mutual funds and real estate investment trusts (REITs), qualify for the lower rate, so read the 1099-DIV, and any accompanying literature, that is sent to you.

• Bad debts and worthless securities. These are deductible in the year they become worthless.

Opportunity: The statute of limitations on deducting these is seven years instead of the normal three years. So you can file amended returns to claim tax refunds for these up to seven years back. Examine your portfolio to find any you may have overlooked.

• Installment sales. If you sold property at a gain for payments to be received over more than one year, defer tax so it comes due only as payments are received by reporting the gain on the installment basis.

• Savings bonds. If a child age 14 or over or other low-tax-bracket individual owns Series EE or I savings bonds, consider electing to have the interest received on the bonds taxed annually—then little or no tax will be owed on it. Otherwise, all the interest will be taxable when the bonds mature, when the individual may be in a higher tax bracket.

Charity deductions

Don't lose deductions for legitimate donations to charity by failing to meet IRS documentation rules...

• You must obtain an acknowledgment letter from the charitable recipient for every contribution of $250 or more, even if you have a canceled check proving it—and do so by the due date of your tax return.

• Contributions of property valued at more than $5,000 must be supported by an appraisal.

Details: For more about important documentation rules, see IRS Publication 526, *Charitable Contributions*.

Filing status

Changes in the Tax Code enacted this year reduce the "marriage penalty" that couples pay and can affect the choice of filing joint or separate returns. If you filed separately in the past or are considering doing so this year, run the numbers both ways to see which is better now.

If you aren't married, but maintain a household for a child or other dependent, you may qualify to lower your tax rates by filing using "head of household" status.

Dependents

Claim every exemption for dependents...

• If a group of people support an individual (such as a retired parent), but no one person provides more than half the individual's support, the group may be able to obtain a dependency exemption nonetheless by filing IRS Form 2120, *Multiple Support Declaration*, and assign it to one of its members.

• Parents who do not live with you may qualify as dependents.

• Medical deductions are available for medical expenses paid on behalf of a person who would qualify as your dependent except for the fact that he/she had too much income (more than $3,200 in 2005). This could include a parent in a nursing home.

• A divorced or separated parent who intends to claim a child who lives with the other parent as a dependent must obtain a signed IRS Form 8332, *Release of Claim to Exemption for Child of Divorced or Separated Parents*, or equivalent form, from the custodial parent. This is required regardless of the terms of a divorce decree or separation agreement.

State tax refunds

The following are very common filing errors...

• Receiving a 1099 from a state reporting a tax refund paid to you does not mean the refund is taxable on your federal return. It is taxable only if the original payment of the state tax was deducted on an itemized return. So check your past year's return to see what the proper treatment should be.

• You can deduct on your 2005 federal tax return only state taxes paid in calendar year 2005, not for 2005.

Example: Your fourth installment of 2005 state estimated tax payments paid in January 2006 isn't deductible on your 2005 return. You can deduct it on your 2006 return.

IRAs and retirement plans

Rules for these recently have been liberalized by both Congress and the IRS...

• The IRA contribution limit has been increased from $4,000 to $4,500 in 2005 for persons age 50 or older.

• A full contribution can be made for a nonworking spouse when the couple's income is within certain limits.

• Roth IRAs can provide totally tax-free distributions at retirement, though contributions to them are not deductible.

Children: Make Roth IRA contributions for children who had earned income during the year—even if only from a paper route or summer job. The contributed amount can be as large as the child's income, up to $4,000.

IRA contributions for 2005 can be made as late as April 17, 2006.

Best: If you intend to make an IRA contribution for 2005, do so as early in the year as possible to maximize tax-favored returns in the IRA account. If it later turns out that for some reason you are ineligible to fund an IRA during the year, you will be able to withdraw the funds without penalty by April 16, 2007. But make contributions for 2005 and 2006 by separate checks to keep them distinct.

Persons with self-employment income during 2005 can make a Keogh plan contribution for the year as late as the extended due date of the tax return. But the Keogh plan must have been opened by December 31, 2005.

If you didn't open a Keogh by then, you can still open a simplified employee pension (SEP) plan for 2005 by the extended due date of the return, and make a deductible contribution of self-employment income to it.

Source: Sidney Kess, attorney and CPA, 10 Rockefeller Plaza, New York City 10020. He is coauthor/consulting editor of *Financial and Estate Planning* and coauthor of *1040 Preparation and Planning Guide, 2006 Edition*. (CCH). Over the years, he has taught tax law to more than 710,000 tax professionals.

Section 7: Deductions, Deductions, Deductions

Chapter Four
LOOPHOLES IN TAX RETURN PREPARATION

To save money and reduce the odds of an audit, use these strategies to prepare and file your 2005 return.

Loophole: Report incorrect or missing 1099 information on your return. Banks, brokerages, and other payers of income file directly with the IRS, which crosschecks the information with the Forms 1099 that individuals report on their returns. Discrepancies automatically trigger written inquiries from the IRS...and can lead to an audit.

Example: Your bank sent you a 1099 reporting an incorrect amount of interest earned on your account in 2005.

What to do: Enter on your return the actual amount of taxable interest income you received or were credited with. On another line, show the amount reported on the 1099. Beneath that, show the 1099 amount as a negative number and write the following explanation beside the figure—"The interest amount reported by my bank is incorrect. A corrected 1099 was requested but not yet issued. The correct amount is reflected on my tax return."

Loophole: Reconstruct missing W-2s. If a company you worked for went out of business or your employer hasn't yet given you a Form W-2, *Wage and Tax Statement*, you can reconstruct your salary and withholding records on Form 4852, *Substitute for Form W-2, Wage and Tax Statement*, or Form 1099-R, *Distributions From Pensions, Annuities, Retirement or Profit-Sharing Plans, IRAs, Insurance Contracts, etc.*

On the form, estimate your salary and withholding, explaining how you arrived at the figures, and send it in with your tax return.

Loophole: If one spouse owes back taxes and the other expects a refund, file separate returns. While this may increase the overall tax rate for the couple, filing separate returns protects the refund. Otherwise, the IRS may apply the refund to the other spouse's tax bill.

If the back tax bill is paid within three years, you can file an amended return claiming the joint filing status for that year. This lowers the tax rate, and you can file for another refund. However, if you filed a joint return originally, you cannot later refile separate returns.

Loophole: Carefully consider the business code number you enter on the company's tax return. The IRS targets certain types of businesses for audit, such as cash businesses (small retail stores, restaurants, auto repair shops). Or check the audit guides at *www.irs.gov*. When your business could fit into more than one category, choose the business code number that's not on the IRS's hit list.

Loophole: File all the required supporting documents. You'll reduce your audit risk and secure your deductions. Examples...

• When claiming a home-office deduction, file Form 8829, Expenses for Business Use of Your Home.

• For charitable gifts of property valued at more than $500, you must file Form 8283, *Noncash Charitable Contributions*. You also need a professional appraisal for donated property worth more than $5,000.

Loophole: Disagreeing with the IRS. When you take a position contrary to an IRS rule, you are required to disclose your position. You can file Form 8275, Disclosure Statement, which explains the reasoning supporting the position you took or attach a sheet to your tax return with the same information.

Best: Attach a written explanation to your return instead of filing the official IRS form.

Reason: All the Forms 8275 are automatically reviewed, raising your chances of being selected for an audit.

Loophole: Ask for an automatic extension to file your return. Returns for 2005 are due on April 17, 2006, but you can extend the due date for filing to

366

October 15 by getting two extensions from the IRS.

The first extension gives you four months and is granted automatically.

The second is given at the discretion of the IRS when you provide adequate reasons.

Example: You may not have all your information and need the additional time to collect it.

Bonus: An extension also extends the amount of time that you can contribute funds to a self-employed income Keogh or SEP plan.

Loophole: Estimated taxes. When you are required to pay estimated taxes and if you are requesting an extension, include the first quarter 2006 installments as part of the tax due for year 2005 with the extension.

This covers any shortfall in your projection of the amount you will owe when you file your 2005 return. The cushion is important because the penalties and interest for failure to pay taxes owed are higher than the penalty for underestimating year 2006 taxes.

Source: Edward Mendlowitz, CPA, shareholder in the CPA firm WithumSmith+Brown, 120 Albany St., New Brunswick, NJ 08901. He is author of *Estate Planning* (Practical Programs).

Chapter Five
BIGGEST TAX PREPARATION MISTAKES TO AVOID

If you don't take every legitimate deduction and credit on your tax return, you'll pay more tax than necessary.

At the same time, you must be careful not to make common errors. Certain mistakes will draw unwanted attention from the IRS and may lead to an audit. Here's a list of pitfalls to avoid...

Of interest to investors

Mistake: Discarding carryforwards. If you were unable to deduct all your capital losses in a previous year, don't forget to use the losses you carried forward to offset any net capital gains from 2006.

Moreover, up to $3,000 worth of excess capital losses (including unused losses from prior years) can be deducted against ordinary income.

Other types of carryforwards from investments may be valuable now.

Examples: You were in an old tax shelter that wound up last year or you sold rental property. Suspended losses you were unable to deduct in the past now can be deducted against gains from that venture.

Similarly, if you rent out investment property, including a vacation home, you may have suspended losses you had not been able to deduct. If that property generated taxable income last year, old losses may wipe out that income and eliminate any tax on the profits.

Mistake: Incorrectly calculating basis in mutual funds. If you neglect re-invested dividends and capital gains distributions from your funds, you pay taxes twice. Instead, add the amount of the reinvestments to your tax basis.

Example: You bought a mutual fund for $10,000 a few years ago and reinvested $1,000 worth of distributions. Your tax basis is $11,000. If you sold all your shares in that fund last year for $14,000, your taxable gain is $3,000, not $4,000.

Mistake: Misreporting mutual fund sales. Many people do not realize that any mutual fund transaction is a reportable sale. That's true even if you move money between funds in the same "family."

Exception: Such transactions are not taxable inside of a tax-deferred retirement plan.

Key: Most mutual fund companies provide cost (basis) information, but many investors discard those schedules before they file their tax returns.

Without these records, investors may have a hard time putting together the information needed. Often, they file their returns without reporting the mutual fund transactions.

Trap: If you don't report mutual fund trades, the IRS will send you a letter, asking for information. Then your entire return may be examined.

Making charity count

Mistake: Confining charitable deductions to cash or check. Millions of taxpayers donate items to charity each year but many underestimate the value of the donated items.

Loophole: You can deduct the fair market value of all the items you donate—and it's up to you to establish a fair market value. Donations of tangible goods under $500 don't require explanations on a tax return.

Often forgotten: The driving you did as a volunteer for a charitable organization is deductible as a charitable contribution at 14 cents a mile. Keep a log of this mileage in case the IRS asks for proof.

Mistake: Cutting corners on car contributions. Recently, many people have been donating autos and other vehicles to charity. Too often, they don't follow through with the necessary paperwork.

Required: When the value of a charitable contribution exceeds $5,000, you must get an independent appraisal and attach the signed document to your tax return.

Trap: A documentation letter from the charity is not enough. Without an attached appraisal, the IRS can disallow the deduction entirely.

Strategy: To avoid having to get an appraisal, it may be better to claim a deduction of $5,000 or less even though a price guide reports a larger value.

Missed deductions

Mistake: Not taking mortgage deductions. If you refinanced your mortgage last year, as many people did, go over your settlement papers.

Any points you paid to refinance a mortgage can be deducted over the life of the loan. Points paid on a loan used for home improvements may be deducted right away.

Example: In 2005, you refinanced an outstanding $300,000 loan with a new, $400,000, 15-year loan, paying $8,000 in points. The extra $100,000 was used for kitchen remodeling.

Because 25% of the loan was used for home improvements, 25% of the points you paid ($2,000) can be deducted. The other $6,000 can be deducted over the 180-month term of the loan.

Mistake: Stumbling over travel deductions. Generally, unreimbursed employee business expenses (including auto-related costs) are included as miscellaneous itemized deductions. Those deductions, reported on Schedule A, are deductible to the extent that they exceed 2% of adjusted gross income (AGI).

Trap: Taxpayers with a lofty AGI may find that 2% exceeds the expenses, resulting in no deduction.

Loophole: Some people can qualify as "statutory employees." Such taxpayers can deduct all business expenses in full, on Schedule C, even if their compensation is reported on a W-2 form.

Examples: Statutory employees might be traveling salespeople, life insurance salespeople who work primarily for one insurer, commission-paid delivery people, commissioned salespeople dealing with retailers or wholesalers, and people who work at home under contract doing tasks such as word processing.

Mistake: Not including employment efforts. Job-hunting expenses are miscellaneous deductions, even if you didn't change jobs. When added to unreimbursed employee business expenses, tax preparation fees, and subscriptions to investment publications, the total may move you into tax-deductible territory—more than 2% of your AGI.

Paperwork problems

Mistake: Overpaying Social Security taxes. If you received paychecks from two or more employers last year and earned more than $90,000, you may be able to file a claim on your return for the excess Social Security withholding. For 2005, wages over $90,000 are not subject to Social Security tax.

Trap: There is no limit on withholding for Medicare.

Mistake: Disregarding the alternative minimum tax (AMT). The AMT, designed to make sure upper-income individuals pay some tax, now snares many with moderate incomes ($58,000 and over for joint returns, $40,250 for single 2005 returns). Taxpayers with many dependents, high miscellaneous itemized deductions, or substantial state income tax payments are vulnerable.

Required by the vulnerable: Calculate your taxes by regular rules and by AMT regulations. If your AMT is higher, you'll have to pay it in order to avert the wrath of the IRS.

Mistake: Losing the matching game. The IRS devotes a tremendous amount of effort to document matching. Make sure that whatever income is reflected on all the W-2 and 1099 statements you receive for 2005 is reflected on your tax return.

That includes any reinvested dividends. Discrepancies are likely to draw the attention of the IRS.

Strategy: Rather than group 1099 income, report each Form 1099 separately. The IRS computer matches individual Forms 1099 to individual amounts on your tax return. If there is no match, you'll get a letter from the IRS, requesting an explanation.

Bottom line: Do everything possible to get your tax return processed without human IRS inspection. If the IRS computers are satisfied that the data are complete, inquiries can be avoided. Once your return gets into the hands of an IRS employee, the chances of a detailed audit increase dramatically.

Source: Alan S. Zipp, Esq., CPA, 932 Hungerford Dr., Rockville, MD 20850. Mr. Zipp is an instructor of income tax courses for the American Institute of Certified Public Accountants. He specializes in the income tax problems of individuals and small businesses.

Chapter Six
SPECIAL PURPOSE TRUST LOOPHOLES

Here are some trusts for special purposes...

Loophole: A special-needs trust will provide for a child with a physical or mental handicap or illness, during your lifetime and after your death.

Typically, the income and assets of special-needs trusts are distributed at the discretion of the trustee. Undistributed income will be taxed to the trust.

Key: Payments should be made directly to providers of special programs, such as music or swimming lessons, birthday parties, etc., if the child is receiving Medicaid or Social Security supplemental income.

Reason: Direct distributions to the child are considered income and will reduce government benefits.

Loophole: An alimony trust set up under Tax Code Section 682 will minimize taxes payable on account of divorce. The Code rules apply to people who are divorced or legally separated under a decree of divorce or a written separation agreement.

How it works: Alimony trusts are treated as non-grantor trusts for tax purposes. This means that the spouse receiving the income is taxed on distributions and undistributed income is taxed to the grantor spouse.

Exception: Receiving spouses are not taxed on any trust income designated as child support in the divorce decree or separation agreement. Instead, that income is included in the taxable income of the paying spouse.

Additional benefit: In a properly structured alimony trust that owns life insurance policies, the proceeds pass estate tax free.

Loophole: A spendthrift trust will protect trust assets from a beneficiary's irresponsibility. Typically, state laws let creditors reach all assets available to a debtor. So-called spendthrift trusts are a type of asset protection trust, designed to prevent creditors from taking trust assets before they are distributed to the beneficiary. How they are commonly used...

• In the wills created by older generations that have concerns about the financial responsibility of one or more heirs.

• By parents transferring assets to a trust for a minor who want to extend the protection period past the age of majority.

Strategy: When distributions are made at the sole discretion of the trustee, creditors have nothing to attach and may be more willing to settle their claims on favorable terms.

Caution: Spendthrift provisions offer no protection when a beneficiary has the power to direct (appoint) trust property for his/her own benefit.

Loophole: A living trust can avoid or eliminate much of the probate process. Living trusts are revocable by the grantor and ignored for income and estate tax purposes. Upon death, the trust becomes irrevocable and the alternate trustee assumes complete control.

How to fund it: Consider funding living trusts with a business, partnership units, or certain types of investment property. This transfers control immediately upon the grantor's death—especially important when sales negotiations are in progress.

Loophole: A total return trust (TRT) will balance the concerns of a trust's income and principal beneficiaries. Typically, income beneficiaries want to maximize their income while principal beneficiaries want to minimize current income distributions so they can maximize their eventual inheritance.

How they work: These trusts provide a guaranteed return of income for beneficiaries based on the value of trust assets, regardless of actual income. This frees the investment manager to maximize total return and protect against inflation.

Income beneficiaries can receive fixed annual (or monthly or quarterly) distributions that might exceed actual current income. Trust assets must be revalued each year to determine the amount against which the TRT percentage will be applied.

Note: State law differs in detail but the concept is generally applicable in most states.

Asset protection: Almost any trust can provide asset protection, keeping assets out of the reach of creditors, future ex-spouses, or someone with a power of attorney. If this is your primary reason for setting up a trust, you should consult with an attorney specializing in asset protection methods.

With an irrevocable trust with an independent trustee, the grantor/beneficiary would have no control over the assets, making the assets unavailable to settle claims against the beneficiary.

The income and estate tax consequences depend upon the type of trust that is established.

Note: The degree of protection from claims of creditors varies from state to state.

Source: Edward Mendlowitz, CPA, shareholder in the CPA firm WithumSmith+Brown, 120 Albany St., New Brunswick, NJ 08901. He is author of *Estate Planning* (Practical Programs).

GIVING STOCK VS. COLLECTIBLES

The best charitable gifts are of appreciated long-term capital gains property, such as stock shares or collectibles. That's because you get a deduction for their full value while avoiding ever paying capital gains tax on their appreciation (such as if you sold them and then donated the cash proceeds).

The most tax can be saved on collectibles, because the long-term gains rate on them is 28% rather than the 15% top rate as on stock shares and other investments. Talk to your tax adviser about special rules that may apply to donations of your collectibles.

Source: Bob Carlson, editor, *Bob Carlson's Retirement Watch*, 3700 Annandale Rd., Annandale, VA 22003.

Chapter Seven
HOW TO SHELTER YOUR INCOME FROM THE IRS

In tax planning, even just a few dollars in the wrong place can cost you thousands.

How to preserve tax breaks, including those made more generous by recent tax legislation...

Shelter personal income

Ways to reduce AGI if you don't own your own business...

• Defined-contribution plans. If your employer sponsors a 401(k) or similar salary-deferral plan, contribute the maximum—$18,000 in 2006...$20,000 if you're age 50 or older.

Even if your employer doesn't match your contributions, putting the maximum allowable amount in a 401(k) reduces your AGI and expands your eligibility for other tax benefits.

• Deductible IRAs. If your employer does not sponsor a retirement plan, you can deduct a $4,000 contribution to a traditional IRA in 2005—$5,000 if you're age 50 or older.

If you participate in your employer's retirement plan, you can make a fully deductible IRA contribution if your 2006 AGI is $75,000 or less on a joint return ($50,000 single). Smaller deductible contributions are allowed for AGIs of up to $85,000 ($60,000 single).

• Capital losses. Up to $3,000 of net capital losses can be deducted each year. Additional losses can be carried forward indefinitely.

Example: Near year-end, you tally your investment trades for the year and discover a $2,700 gain. Sell enough holdings to generate $5,700 worth of losses for a deductible $3,000 net loss.

• Tax-free income. If you are in a high tax bracket, choose municipal bonds, tax-managed mutual funds and growth stocks—which don't pay dividends—instead of investments that raise your AGI with large amounts of interest and dividends.

Helpful: Keep only emergency funds in bank accounts and money market funds to reduce taxable income and monthly interest payments. Use any surplus to pay down credit card balances.

Shelter social security income

Even moderate-income seniors may find some or all of their Social Security subject to income tax—but there are ways to reduce it.

Whether benefits are taxable depends on your "provisional income." To calculate it, total...

• Your AGI

• Tax-exempt interest income from municipal bonds and bond funds

• One-half of annual Social Security benefits.

Example: With AGI of $20,000, tax-exempt income of $5,000 and annual Social Security benefits of $12,000, provisional income is $31,000 ($20,000 + $5,000 + $6,000).

No Social Security benefits are counted as taxable income if provisional income is up to $32,000 married, filing jointly ($25,000 single).

Up to 50% of benefits are included if provisional income is more than $32,000 ($25,000 single).

Up to 85% of benefits are included if provisional income is greater than $44,000 ($34,000 single).

Use these tools to safeguard Social Security benefits from Uncle Sam...

• Tax-deferred annuities. Even with the recent tax-law change, these provide a shelter that is not subject to income limits. They make sense for people who have maxed out retirement plan contributions and want to build more savings for retirement.

Two types of annuities...

• Fixed. An insurance company provides a guaranteed rate of return for a certain period. You might invest $50,000 and get a 5% guarantee for one year. After a year, your account balance will be $52,500 and a new—usually lower—interest rate will be set.

• Variable. These don't offer a guaranteed return. Instead, they allow you to invest in mutual fund–like accounts with higher potential returns and risks. Look for low commissions and no surrender fees (payments to the annuity issuer if you sell before a certain period).

• Loans. Borrowing allows you to generate cash flow without boosting taxable income. Consider these options...

Tap a home-equity line of credit or a margin account.

Take out a reverse mortgage.

Refinance your home or investment property.

Borrow against your home or cash-value life insurance, such as whole life or variable universal life. Make sure tax savings offset your interest payments.

Shelter business income (even a sideline business!)

Opportunities to trim your AGI are greatest if you or your spouse is a business owner. Deductions...

• Health insurance. All premiums paid by self-employed individuals (as well as by owners of S corporations and limited liability companies) are fully deductible.

• Retirement plans. Many plans offer rich writeoffs for those with business income.

Simplified employee pension (SEP-IRA) plans. You can deposit up to $44,000 in 2006, pretax, with these small-business IRAs. To set one up, fill out a simple form at a mutual fund firm or other institution.

• Defined-benefit pension plans. These types of plans can provide even higher deductions than a SEP if you're in your late 40s or older. Rules are complex. Consult a professional adviser.

• Children on the payroll. You can deduct the salaries of your children and grandchildren on your Schedule C, and they will owe no tax on up to $5,150 in earned income in 2006.

• Equipment. Up to $108,000 worth of expenses for business equipment may be written off in the year it is purchased, subject to income limitations.

Tax breaks for everyone

These strategies provide generous tax breaks regardless of income...

• Tax-deferred annuities. Again, you are taxed when you withdraw the money—but at that point, you are likely to be retired and in a lower income tax bracket. There is a 10% penalty on withdrawals made before age 59½.

• Permanent life insurance. These policies have high premiums, so they make sense only if you need life insurance for many years—for instance, if you are the sole breadwinner in a family with a disabled child. Cash value grows tax-free. After a buildup period, you or your beneficiaries can tap it via tax-free withdrawals and loans against the cash value of your policy.

• College savings plans. Consider these options...

☐ Section 529 college savings plans. In most states, you can set up plans for yourself, your child, grandchild, other relatives and friends. Some states, including New York and Missouri, allow you to deduct contributions from state taxes. There's no federal income tax deduction for contributions, but investment income is tax-free if used for education expenses.

If the money is withdrawn to pay higher-education expenses, no tax will be due. For more information, visit *Savingforcollege.com,* or check with your state's department of education.

☐ Coverdell education savings accounts (ESAs). Officially, married couples with AGIs of more than $190,000 ($95,000 single) can't make a full contribution.

Loophole: If you're over the limit, give money to relatives in a lower bracket or even to your children, who then can use it to contribute up to $2,000 per year to Coverdell ESAs. There are no deductions, but the investment grows tax-free.

Source: Sidney Kess, attorney and CPA, 10 Rockefeller Plaza, New York City 10020. He is coauthor/consulting editor of *Financial and Estate Planning* and coauthor of *1040 Preparation and Planning Guide, 2006 Edition.* (CCH). Over the years, he has taught tax law to more than 710,000 tax professionals.

MUTUAL FUND TAX SAVER

Many funds have tax loss carry-forwards that can be used to offset their future capital gains, reports fund tracker Don Philips. Ordinarily, investors must pay tax on these gains each year, even if they don't sell their shares. If your fund has losses carried forward, you might not have to pay tax on net gains for years. To check a fund's tax losses, go to *www.morningstar.com*, search for the fund by the ticker symbol, then click "Tax Analysis." A minus symbol denotes a loss.

Source: Don Philips is managing director of fund tracker Morningstar, Inc., Chicago. *www.morningstar.com.*

Chapter Eight

NINE WAYS YOU CAN SAVE MONEY UNDER THE NEW TAX LAW

Tax changes under President Bush's plan already are in effect. How individuals can get the most from them...

Investing

The top tax rate on common-stock dividends and long-term capital gains is reduced to 15%. You must hold a stock for more than 60 days to get the 15% tax rate on dividends...and for more than one year to get the 15% rate on capital gains. Previously, dividends were taxed at ordinary income rates (up to 38.6%) and long-term gains at up to 20%.

The tax rate on dividends and long-term gains is cut to only 5% for those in the 10% and 15% tax brackets.

Trap 1: Not all dividends qualify for the 15% rate. Among those that are excluded...

☐ Most dividends paid on preferred stock and by real estate investment trusts (REITs).

☐ Some distributions from mutual funds. Interest and short-term capital gains earned by a mutual fund will be taxable at ordinary income tax rates. Long-term gains and dividends received by a fund and "passed through" to investors will be taxable at the lower rate.

Trap 2: All distributions from IRAs and 401(k) plans will continue to be taxed at ordinary income tax rates. Holding high-dividend stocks in these plans may no longer make sense because your tax rate in retirement might be as high as 35%—versus a top rate of 15% on dividends and long-term gains outside of retirement accounts. Consult your financial planner.

What to do...

• For retirement accounts, favor interest-paying assets, such as taxable bonds and bond funds, money market accounts, CDs, REITs and mutual funds with high turnover—meaning that they trade frequently and generate substantial short-term capital gains. Make sure that you have enough in stocks across both taxable and retirement accounts to fund your retirement goals.

To find out a fund's turnover, check its prospectus or *www.morningstar.com.*

Important: Don't stop contributing to a 401(k) plan because of the new law—especially if you get a matching contribution from your employer.

• For taxable accounts, consider moving some income-producing assets from bonds to dividend-paying stocks. Remember, of course, that stocks are riskier than interest-bearing investments. Also consider...

☐ Tax-managed mutual funds, which strive to minimize capital gains taxes.

☐ Index funds, which generally are tax-efficient because they have low turnover.

☐ High-dividend stock funds with low turnover.

☐ Municipal bonds/funds. Because interest is tax-free, they still can make sense if you live in a high-tax state and your tax bracket has not dropped too much. Make sure the after-tax yield is higher than what you would get on a taxable bond or fund. Bonds from your own state are generally free of state tax as well.

Example: If you are in the 35% bracket, a corporate bond paying 6% would have an after-tax yield of 3.9%. Any municipal bond paying higher than 3.9% would be attractive.

Gifting

Dependent children over age 13 can pay tax on dividends and capital gains at only a 5% rate even when they have as much as $30,650 of taxable income. Previously, a child over the age of 13 would have paid as much as 10% tax on capital gains.

As with the old law, you can use the annual gift tax exclusion to make direct gifts of up to $12,000 per recipient free of gift tax—doubled to $24,000 when gifts are made jointly by a married couple.

What to do...

• Make gifts of appreciated stock to children or grandchildren to shift income into low tax brackets. It is more advantageous than ever to do so.

Important: Capital gains for children under age 14 still are taxed at their parents' rate. Avoid this tax when making gifts to children under age 14 by making sure they hold the stock until after they reach age 14, when their tax rate may be lower.

• Pay a child's or grandchild's college tuition with a gift of appreciated securities instead of cash. The child sells the stock, paying only the 5% tax rate. You can use the same strategy to pay for a retired parent's medical bills if he/she is in the 5% tax bracket.

Example: You want to sell $10,000 of stock to pay a grandchild's tuition. Tax on the sale would be $1,500 at your top 15% rate. Instead of selling the stock, give it to the child. A child paying the 5% rate would owe only $500, cutting the tax bill by two-thirds and giving him $1,000 more to use for tuition.

Many executives participate in deferred-compensation plans that delay receipt of part of their salary until a later date, when they expect to be in a lower tax bracket, such as after retiring. These executives may be better off taking their money now.

Caution: Under new law, the election to defer income must be made before the year in which the compensation is earned begins.

• Claim the generous child tax credit on your 2006 return if you have a child in 2006.

• You and your spouse each can take the standard deduction of a single person under the plan's marriage penalty relief. The law retains the 15% bracket for joint returns to cover taxable income in 2006 up to $61,300—which is double the size of the 15% bracket for singles.

Source: Laurence I. Foster, CPA, PFS, consultant and former partner, Eisner LLP, 750 Third Ave., New York City 10017. He is former chairman, estate planning committee, New York State Society of Certified Public Accountants.

FREQUENTLY OVERLOOKED DEDUCTIONS FOR LEGAL FEES

Few serious personal or business transactions can be pursued without a lawyer. Whether you're buying or selling property or a business, dissolving your marriage, or suing for a wrong that was done you, typically you use an attorney to represent you. Can you deduct the lawyer's fees? Sometimes you can and sometimes you can't.

Problem: With so many law changes and court decisions every year, it's hard to keep deductibility rules straight. Example...

Personal injury actions

• Physical personal injuries. If injured through someone's negligence, you may bring a personal injury suit to recover damages. Because compensatory damages for personal injury or illness are tax free, related attorney's fees are not deductible.

However, to the extent you recover punitive damages, which are fully taxable, you can deduct the portion of attorney's fees related to this amount. Such fees are deductible as miscellaneous itemized deductions to the extent they exceed 2% of your adjusted gross income (AGI).

Source: Joseph W. Walloch, CPA, president, Walloch Accountancy Corporation in San Bernardino and Redlands, CA. He is professor of advanced accounting and taxation at the University of California, Riverside.

Chapter Nine
LOCK IN BUSINESS EXPENSE DEDUCTIONS WITH AN ACCOUNTABLE PLAN

When you (or other employees) incur legitimate business expenses, reimbursement from your company may be expected. Properly structured, reimbursement under an "accountable plan" offers major tax advantages.

With an accountable plan...

• Your company need not withhold payroll taxes from the amounts disbursed.

• Your company can deduct the amounts paid, up to the amounts allowed by the Tax Code.

• Employees need not include the payments as taxable income.

Trap: Without an accountable plan, reimbursements will be treated as taxable income, subject to income and payroll taxes.

What's more, unreimbursed outlays by employees will be treated as miscellaneous itemized deductions. As such, they're deductible only to the extent that they exceed 2% of adjusted gross income (AGI).

The "accountable plan"

An accountable plan does not need to be in writing. Nor does it have to cover a particular class of employee.

Required: An understanding (implicit or explicit) between the company and certain employees that expenses will be reimbursed, under given conditions.

An accountable plan must...

• Reimburse employees for actual business expenses.

- Require substantiation of those expenses.

- Insist upon the return of any excess cash advances or reimbursements.

Although such a plan need not be in writing, your company should keep thorough records of all advances, expense reports, reimbursements, and returns from employees.

Wrong ways

Attempts to shortcut a reimbursement routine can lead to tax trouble.

Example: You receive $2,000 per week from your company but only $1,800 is treated as your salary. The other $200 is deemed to reflect estimated business expenses and is treated as an untaxed reimbursement.

The Tax Court has ruled that such a scheme is not an accountable plan. If you're not required to provide the company with any information regarding actual business expenses, the entire $2,000 will be subject to income and payroll taxes.

Trap: Payments made to employees for travel expenses, whether or not the employees are expected to travel, won't qualify as reimbursements under an accountable plan.

What about miles driven? If those miles are substantiated, reimbursements may be made up to the federal standard mileage allowance, which in 2005 is 40.5 cents per mile for the first eight months of the year and 48.5 cents per mile for the final four months.

Employee business expenses reasonably expected to be incurred can be excluded from an employee's gross income as well as from employment tax, as long as they're eventually substantiated.

Example: You use your personal car for 1,000 miles per month of business travel and substantiate this use. Your company reimburses you $5,600 (3,600 + $2,000) at 45 cents per mile for the first eight months and 50 cents per mile for the final four months.

Result: The first $5,180 (40.5 cents x 1,000 miles x 8 + 48.5 cents x 1,000 miles x 4) is considered to be tax free this year, under an accountable plan. The excess $45 is from a nonaccountable plan, so it is subject to income and payroll taxes.

Strategy: You may be better off with a company-provided car. However, you will be taxed on your personal use of the car.

Either way, a log can substantiate business versus personal use of the vehicle.

Sampling may take the place of a year-long log. A trip-by-trip log kept for part of a year can be extrapolated for the entire year if the sample period is representative of the whole year [see Treasury Department Temporary Reg. Sec. 1.274-5T(c)(3)(ii)]. Sampling also can be used for establishing the business versus personal use of a car or other listed property, such as cell phones and computers.

On the record

While sampling may be used for certain expenses, complete substantiation is necessary for other business reimbursements.

Loophole: Except for lodging, receipts are not required for expenditures of less than $75.

Otherwise, receipts are required in order for reimbursements to receive favorable tax treatment.

Strategy: The IRS has ruled that electronic records taken directly from a credit card company can be used to substantiate travel and entertainment expenses in an accountable plan.

Therefore, you (and perhaps selected employees) should have credit cards used solely for business expenses, which can be reimbursed.

Many happy returns

Many companies provide cash advances to employees, often before business trips.

Required: For favorable tax treatment, excess cash advances must be returned.

Example: You draw $1,000 from your company before leaving on a business trip. You spend only $800 on business-related items, of which $700 is substantiated.

All money not substantiated must be returned to the company. If $800 was spent but only $700 was substantiated, an accountable plan would require the return of $300. Any plan that did not require a $300 return is not an accountable plan.

Trap: If returns of excess cash advances aren't required and implemented, the plan automatically becomes nonaccountable. The tax benefits will be lost.

How soon must excess cash advances be returned?

Loophole: The IRS provides two safe harbor methods for sustaining the tax advantages of an accountable plan...

• Fixed-date method. Cash advances must be made no more than 30 days before an expense is incurred. After the expense has been incurred, substantiation must take place within 60 days and excess advances must be returned within 120 days.

• Periodic-statement method. Employers must provide statements to employees at least once a quarter, showing advances and substantiated expenses. Employees then have 120 days to substantiate more expenses or return excess advances.

Trap: These safe harbors may make it seem that you can withdraw and then return substantial amounts of company cash, tax free. However, the IRS won't recognize the safe harbors if it detects a pattern of excess advances and delayed returns.

Do you need to somehow return frequent-flier points to your company? Probably not.

The IRS won't tax employees on personal use of frequent-flier miles from business travel, unless those miles are converted to cash or other compensation. Thus, keeping your frequent-flier miles is not likely to jeopardize an accountable plan.

Day by day

Per diem arrangements can reduce record-keeping requirements for accountable plans. Several methods are acceptable.

Example: In the "federal high-low" method, employers use two per diem rates to reimburse employee travel expenses. One is for high-cost locations and one for low-cost locations.

The US government publishes a list of locations within the continental US deemed to be high-cost localities—all others are low-cost. From October 1, 2005, through September 30, 2006, the per diem rate for high-cost localities is $226, including meals, while the per diem rate for all other localities is $141 (Revenue Procedure 2005-67).

Required: If this method is adopted, it must be used for all localities in the continental US.

Advantages: This method simplifies record keeping because only two rates are applied. It provides a constant standard for reimbursing employees and reduces the need for receipts.

On the downside, $204 might not be enough for a day's expenses in New York, say, or San Francisco. If you and other employees want to avoid being out-of-pocket, you may be better off documenting your actual expenses.

Source: William J. Kenny, Esq., CPA, professor of business administration, Portland State University, Box 751, Portland, OR 97207. He is director of the University's master of taxation program.

Chapter Ten
DEDUCT FUN FROM YOUR TAXES

What's even better than spending wonderful weekends and evenings out on the town? Legitimately deducting the costs from your business taxes. You can do this if you have your own business—even if it is only a sideline...and it shouldn't increase your risk of an audit.

Meals and entertainment

You can deduct half the cost of meals and other entertainment that has a business purpose. There is no limit on the amount that can be deducted, and receipts are not necessary for expenses of $75 or less.

IRS requirements...

• A business purpose. It may be as simple as soliciting business from a prospect. Depending on your industry, anybody could be a prospect.

• Surroundings conducive to discussing business. The IRS won't believe you talked business at the theater or while playing golf. You must set aside some time to talk undisturbed within 24 hours of incurring the expense. Even a telephone conversation will do.

Example: You take business prospects out for dinner, then to a play and for drinks afterward. You don't have to mention business during the fun, so long as you discuss it at some other point within 24 hours.

• Adequate records. These must include who was entertained...when... where...the specific business purpose of the entertainment...its cost...and a receipt (if the cost was more than $75). Record the amount in a business diary or ledger on the same day.

Caution: All five items must be recorded in a "timely" manner—near the date on which the entertainment occurs—in order for the deduction to be allowed.

Home entertainment

Expenses incurred while entertaining at home are among the most overlooked deductions. The IRS considers your home conducive to business... and costs often are less than the $75 minimum for receipts.

Regulations don't require you to spend a specific amount of time discussing business, so it is easy to qualify everyone attending an event as a business guest.

Example: You invite a guest and his/her spouse to your home for a dinner party, during which you have a one-minute discussion with the guest about obtaining referrals for your business. This lets you deduct half the cost of entertaining both the guest and spouse. You can repeat the process with other guests.

Large parties can make it difficult to talk business with every guest and record each conversation in your diary.

Better: Demonstrate a business purpose for the party by announcing it in the invitation and having some form of display showing a business intent or discussion.

Example: Celebrate your business's anniversary, and put up a business-related display. For proof, take pictures of it with the guests milling around. Also save the invitation.

Follow the rules

• Spouses and guests. If your business guest brings his spouse or another guest, you also can bring a spouse or guest and deduct half the costs for all four people.

• Season tickets. When you purchase season tickets to sporting or cultural events, you must deduct each event separately.

Example: You have season tickets to eight football games a year. If you invite business guests six times, you can deduct half the cost of the tickets to those six games only.

• "Dutch-treat" meals and those you buy for yourself. If you split the cost of a business meal with another person or pay for your own meal, you can deduct half your expense to the extent that it exceeds your average meal cost.

Useful: My experience is that IRS auditors typically determine average meal costs by using a "50%/30%/20% rule." Total your food receipts for one month, and the IRS will deem 50% of the total to be for dinner...30% for lunch...and 20% for breakfast.

Example: If your food bills average $140 per week, $70 would be for dinner. The average cost over seven days would be $10 per dinner. Under the "Dutch treat" rule, your business dinners would be deductible to the extent that their costs exceed $10. Thus, if you and a business associate spend $200 on a fancy business dinner and split the cost, you could deduct half of $90.

Special 100% deductions

You can deduct the full cost of some business expenses...

• Entertaining employees. If you host an event to entertain your employees, you must invite an entire group or department—not just your friends.

Example: You own a small business. You invite all of your employees and their spouses for a night on the town as a business celebration. You can deduct 100% of the costs for everyone.

• Sales promotions. You can deduct the cost of food and beverages provided during a presentation at your home, office or an off-site location—not afterward.

Gifts

• Business gifts of up to $25 per recipient annually. There is no limit to the size of a gift and no dollar limit to the deduction if you give a gift to a company or a department without naming a specific person.

The pig rule

All of these deductions are subject to what CPAs call the pig rule—the deduction amounts must be reasonable.

Example: A doctor who deducted $35,000 for meals said that he "ate only for business reasons." He lost all of those deductions.

Source: Sandy Botkin, CPA, Esq., president, Tax Reduction Institute, 13200 Executive Park Terrace, Germantown, MD 20874, *www.taxreductioninstitute.com*. He is a former IRS attorney as well as a senior tax law specialist and author of the best-selling *Lower Your Taxes Big Time*. (McGraw-Hill).

Chapter Eleven
SMARTEST WAYS TO DEDUCT BUSINESS START-UP COSTS

Before your business is operating, your expenses aren't deductible. Therefore, when you start a new business, don't hesitate. Go into operation as quickly as possible.

The "best case" for expenses incurred before you're in business is a deduction up to $5,000. If costs exceed $5,000, they can be amortized over 180 months.

Note: If start-up costs exceed $55,000, all costs must be amortized.

Worst case? Certain expenses can't be written off. And failure to make a timely election erases the amortization opportunity.

As a result, business start-up costs that you can't amortize must be capitalized, in which case such costs might not be deducted until you sell or abandon the business.

Beginner's course

Start-up costs, according to the Tax Code, include expenses you incur before your business actually begins.

Money spent on the following activities might be considered start-up costs...

- The investigation into creating a business or buying one.
- Preliminary market research.
- Search for office space.
- Rental expenses.
- Supplies purchased before operations begin.

- Advertising and promotional expenses.

- Salaries and wages paid before the business starts.

- Other expenses that would be deductible if the business were operating.

Flip side: Expenses incurred while you're still trying to decide what business to go into are personal and nondeductible.

Example: Outlays for trips to evaluate potential investments or businesses won't qualify as start-up costs, so no tax recovery is available.

Up and running

Once your company is open for business, outlays aren't considered start-up costs. Instead, they are operating costs, which might be deductible expenses.

Opportunity: You can be in business before you have any revenues. Take action so that your company is in business as soon as possible. Don't wait until you have paying customers.

Example: You decide to create a system that makes it easier for doctors to track patient histories. Chances are, you won't receive any revenues for years.

Fortunately, you can be in business long before you sell your system to hospitals or medical groups.

How to do it: Advertise in industry publications and send out press releases. Have business cards printed. Actively solicit future sales. Hire employees.

These and other steps will show that you are truly operating a business.

Example: You develop a waterproof "thigh holster" for campers' snacks, to be sold through sporting-goods stores. When you have displays prepared and visit sporting-goods stores asking them to carry your displays, you're in business. That's true even though it may take months before sales start coming in.

Strategy: If you incorporate your business, hold a directors' meeting right away and keep minutes. Those minutes should state for the record that you're in business and list all the steps already taken to generate revenues.

Similarly, if you form an LLC, hold a meeting of the members or elected managers.

Key: For all business structures, keep careful records of all your efforts to bring a product or service to market. Such records may be vital in showing that you actually were in business as of the date certain expenses were incurred.

Rapid write-offs

When your company is in business, many of your outlays will be fully deductible.

Moreover, the purchase of otherwise depreciable business equipment can be deducted ("expensed") under Section 179 of the Tax Code up to $108,000 in 2006. This break applies if your total purchases for the year don't exceed $430,000 in 2006. It phases out, dollar-for-dollar, above the $430,000 threshold.

Strategy: A Section 179 election can be made only for the year equipment is placed in service, not necessarily when payments are made.

Thus, you can buy equipment at year-end on a credit card or installment sales agreement and take a full deduction, with no cash outlay.

Opportunity: These expensing deductions can't exceed your taxable income from business.

However, you can deduct these expenses against taxable income from the active conduct of any trade or business, including wages. If you're married, you can deduct them against income reported on a joint return, including your spouse's earnings.

Strategy: Many new businesses are short on capital. In this situation, you can lease equipment and deduct the leasing costs.

You may be able to lease with the option to buy at the end of the lease. This option often makes sense, but only if the equipment has a useful life significantly longer than the lease term.

Strategy: Lease your business car rather than buy it. The deduction of the lease cost will generally exceed the depreciation allowance that could be claimed if the car were purchased. The more expensive the car, the greater the tax advantage of leasing.

Loss leaders

In the first year of your new business, deductible expenses might exceed taxable revenues. With some business structures, you can report a loss and deduct it against other income.

Example: You went into a Web site design business in 2006, taking in $25,000 in revenues. However, you spent $60,000 on utilities, rent, etc. Thus, your business, which you run as a sole proprietorship, reports a loss of $35,000 for the year.

Key: You were ready to design Web sites for customers the first day you moved into your office and placed your equipment into service. As a result, your outlays were largely deductible in 2006.

Caution: The IRS will look hard at such losses, especially if (1) they go on for several years, and (2) the activity involved is one that might be an enjoyable hobby, such as travel photography.

Strategy: Keep records showing that you acted in a businesslike manner and had the goal of making a profit.

Cutting your losses

What can you do if your start-up business fails?

Loophole: If you put money into a specific business (not a mere search for a business opportunity), you can deduct the expenses incurred as a capital loss or an ordinary loss, depending upon the facts and circumstances of your investment.

Trap I: Expenses incurred to generally investigate the possibilities of going into business or to purchase a nonspecific existing business are considered personal costs and are not deductible.

Examples: Costs included as a capital loss might include professional fees incurred to establish a corporation as well as ordinary operating expenses of the corporation.

Trap II: While capital losses can be used to offset capital gains, only $3,000 worth of net capital losses may be deducted each year. Any unused losses can be carried forward to future years.

However, the costs of equipment purchased for a failed business cannot be used to figure your capital loss. Instead, your taxable gain or loss on such assets will be determined when you sell or otherwise dispose of them.

Keeping thorough records will help you maximize your tax benefits, as always.

Source: Sandy Soltis, CPA, tax partner, Blackman Kallick Bartelstein, LLP, 10 S. Riverside Plaza, Chicago 60606. Ms. Soltis provides tax-consulting services to middle-market businesses and their owners.

Chapter Twelve

PROTECT SMALL-BUSINESS DEDUCTIONS...THAT THE IRS LOOKS AT EVERY TIME

Deductions that straddle the border between business and personal pose the highest audit risk for small-business owners.

Examples: Travel, meals and entertainment, driving, home offices, insurance, phone costs.

These are examined by the IRS on every audit, since it always suspects that business owners are deducting personal costs.

Turnabout

The key to protecting these deductions is to look at special record-keeping requirements as an opportunity for making your return audit proof—even for items well into the gray area between business and personal.

When the Tax Code or IRS rules set specific paperwork requirements for a deduction and you meet them, an IRS auditor normally has little incentive to inquire further—and a real incentive not to, since auditors are under increasing pressure to close cases.

Example: If your records for meal deductions show, as required, who you entertained, when, where, the business purpose, and the amount, an auditor is very unlikely to insist on verification that you really discussed business at the meal. To do so would not be cost-effective and would add to the backlog of cases, so you can expect the deduction to be allowed—virtually audit proof.

Moreover, there's a carryover benefit when the auditor moves on to items that are less well documented. If an auditor starts by examining records that are full and complete, then moves on to records for another item that are less than perfect but still professionally presented, he/she is likely to view the latter in a manner that still leads to a satisfactory audit result. Reasons...

- The overall quality of the records indicates that you aren't trying to "get away with something," so suspicions are not aroused.

- High-quality records increase your chance of success at IRS Appeals or in the small case division of Tax Court, should you go there. The auditor knows it and so has a practical reason to give enough to avoid an appeal.

- When you present records in good order, you are being considerate, helping the auditor do his job—and it is human nature for consideration to be returned.

Pitfalls

Two easy ways to lose the audit-proofing benefit that good records can give to gray area deductions...

- The "pig rule." The courts know that they often approve business deductions for items that are really of a personal nature when required legal forms are followed—but also warn what happens when people push the rules too far. As one Court of Appeals has stated...

"Perhaps in recognition of human nature, the courts have been liberal in cases of shareholder[s]...channeling particular types of personal transactions through corporations. They have even approved payment of personal living expenses...but there is a principle of too much; phrased colloquially, when a pig becomes a hog it is slaughtered." [Dolese, CA-10, 605 F.2d 1146, 1154.]

Real-life examples of the "pig rule" from my practice...

☐ A professional deducted six personal phone lines. That piqued the IRS auditor's interest, so he looked up the phone numbers—and found that most were those of the professional's relatives. The professional not only lost a deduction for one or two business lines he could easily have had, but had his entire return scrutinized.

☐ A consultant took deductions for multiple trips to distant cities that offset almost all her income. She had records for the trips—but the auditor asked why the trips hadn't produced any consulting income. She said she had been seeking jobs that she didn't get—but couldn't produce any evidence, such as "turndown" letters from prospective clients, to support her claim.

The auditor might have believed she took one such trip—but not that she had spent all her income on such trips. She lost her deductions.

Similar: In other cases people have deducted three meals a day, business driving costs for seven days a week, and work expenses for 52 weeks a year.

But no matter how "complete" records are, an IRS auditor is going to have a hard time believing such deductions. They only invite questions about your honesty that good records are meant to prevent.

• False records. Another way to have "excellent" records become worthless is to show the IRS they are false.

Example: One client called me after giving the IRS meticulous records for meal expenses incurred in town for a period during which his travel records showed he was out of town.

Automobile records also often snag those who exaggerate driving deductions. The simplest way to deduct business driving expenses is the cents-per-mile method (currently 40.5 cents), which I recommend because it is near audit proof with an adequate driving log.

But larger deductions may be available using the "actual cost" method that entails recording all costs of car ownership and allocating a portion to business driving.

Trap: People who produce driving diaries that exaggerate deductions claimed under this method often are tripped up by inconsistencies between their diaries and their auto maintenance records, which the IRS can examine when this method of deduction is used.

Source: Martin S. Kaplan, CPA, 11 Penn Plaza, New York City 10001, *www.irsmaven. com.* He is author of *What the IRS Doesn't Want You to Know* (Wiley).

Index

A

Adjusted gross income (AGI), 386
Aging parents, supporting,
  300–304
Alimony, tax deductions for, 144,
  279
Alternative minimum tax (AMT),
  18, 30, 138
  for businesses, 238
  foreign tax credit in
    offsetting, 196–197
  limits for charitable
    deductions, 173–177
  protection for employees,
    266–267
Annuities, 132
  charitable gift, 168–169, 184
  fixed, 132
  nontransferable, 47–48
  tax-deferred, 132, 133
  variable, 48, 132, 330–331
Appreciated assets, transfer, to
  charitable remainder trust, 322
Appreciated property, donations
  of, 173–174
Appreciated securities
  donation to charities, 161–162,
    173,
  gift of, for tuition, 385
Archer medical savings accounts
  (MSAs), 202
Assets
  avoiding capital gains tax on
    inherited, 52
  deducting capital losses on
    inherited, 52
  deferred-income-type, 355–359
  division of, in divorce, 278–279
  exchanging, for private
    annuity, 323
  joint ownership of, 125–129
  protection of, 140–141
  stepped-up basis for inherited, 4
  transfer of appreciated, to
    charitable remainder trust,
    322
Audit risk for home-based
  business, 248
Automatic extension, asking for,
  366–367
Automobiles
  donating, to charity, 177, 369
  records on, for business, 194
  tax deduction for hybrid, 145

B

Bad debts
  for businesses, 194, 240
  tax deductions for, 361
Bankruptcy
  protection of IRA from
    creditors and, 73
Beneficiaries
  disclaimers of inheritance by,
    5, 7
  of IRA trust, 65
  naming
    for IRA, 16–17
    for tax-deferred retirement
      plans, 21
  naming trusts as, in estate
    planning, 7
  paying executors' fees to
    sole, 52–53
  splitting inherited IRA by, 45
Beneficiary forms, updating, 17
Bonds
  buying individual, 328
  savings, 325, 361
  transfer of, as result of merger
    or spin off, 323
Bond swap, 348
Bonus depreciation, 107
Burden of proof, independent
  contractors and, 260
Business. *See also* Small business
  accounting for simplifying,
    249–250
  bad debts for, 194
  buy-sell agreements in estate
    planning, 4–5, 7
  cash-flow planning for,
    106–107
  cutting building costs for,
    233–236
  electronic forms for, 251–252
  equipment purchases for, 107,
    192–193
  estimated taxes for, 193–194
  filing returns for, 252
  getting bigger tax refund for,
    212–215
  independent contractors and,
    194, 258–261
  information reporting for,
    216–219
  leasing versus purchase of
    equipment for, 205–208
  loans from, 256–258
  loans to, 254–256

  loss carryforward or carryback
    for, 194
  meal, entertainment, and
    automobile deduction records
    for, 194
  midyear tax-planning for,
    106–108
  on-line answers to tax
    questions, 224–228
  record keeping for, 250
  redeeming stock, 53
  retirement plan contributions
    for, 193
  setting up as LLC, 241–244
  sheltering income, 132, 380
  tax deductions for clubs and
    associations, 148–149
  tax deductions for employees'
    meals, 220–223, 392–393
  tax deductions for gifts, 394
  tax deductions for investment
    expenses, 350–351
  tax deductions for promotion
    costs, 199
  tax deductions for start-up
    costs, 396–400
  tax deductions for travel,
    101–102
  tax issues when selecting form
    of, 241–244
  tax payments for, 251
  tax-sheltered wealth for micro-,
    245–248
Business owners
  IRA withdrawal opportunities
    for, 72–73
  retirement plans for, 68–71,
    95–97
  tax return filing for, 191–194
  tax-savings tips for, 237–240

C

Cafeteria plans, 222–223
Capital gains and dividends, 274
  tax rates on, 361
Capital gains distributions,
    including from mutual funds,
    334–335
Capital gains taxes, 127–129
  avoiding, in selling company to
    employees, 10–13
  avoiding on inherited assets, 52
Capital losses
  deducting, on inherited assets, 52
  tax deductions for, 399–400

Cascading beneficiary plan for IRA tax deferral, 85–89
Cash, donating appreciable securities versus, 161–162
Cash transactions, information reporting for, 217–218
Catch-up payments, application to child support, 279–280
C corporations
  charitable contribution deduction for, 202
  compensation planning for, 239–240
Charitable donations, 161–187, 361–362
  automobiles as, 123, 177, 369, 376
  confining, to cash or check, 369
  from IRA and tax-deferred retirement accounts, 60–63
  making gift to, through will, 31
  protecting, 167
  tax deductions for, 202, 361–362
  valuation of, 370
  year-end strategies for, 173-177
Charitable foundation, setting up, 163
Charitable gift annuities, 168–169, 184
Charitable organizations
  dues for, 146–147
  mileage for, 147
  tax deductions for, 146–147
  unreimbursed expenses for, 147
Charitable remainder annuity trusts, 169–170
Charitable remainder trusts (CRTs), 164, 178–182
  leaving IRA and, 61–62
  transfer appreciated assets to, 322
Checks, appreciated securities versus, for charitable contributions, 121
Child care, tax deduction for, 103
Children
  as employees, 104, 150–151, 295–296, 381
  gifting of Roth IRAs to, 50–51, 151, 296
  making loans to, 290–294
Child support, 279–280
Child tax credit, 271–272, 275, 385
Classification settlement, independent contractors and, 260–261
Clothing, donating to charity, 123
Cohan rule, 116–119
Collectibles, donating to charity, 123
College
  tax-favored savings for, 282–285
College savings plans, 30, 133–134
  tax deduction for, 151–152, 296–297, 381–382
Company
  charitable remainder trust in selling, 178–182

selling to employees and avoiding capital gains tax, 10–13
Company stock in retirement plan account, 21–22
Compensation planning for businesses, 239–240
Compliance checks, independent contractors and, 260
Computers, donating used, 226
Conservation easement, tax deduction for, 166
Continuing education, tax deductions for, 104–105
Controlled corporations, transfers of assets to, 325
Corporate recapitalizations, 323–325
Corporations. See C corporations; S corporations
Coverdell Education Savings Accounts (ESAs), 124, 134, 151, 283–284, 296, 382
  funding, 137
Creditors
  protection of IRAs from, 73
Crummey letters in estate planning, 4

D

Deductible IRAs, 130–131
Deferral agreement in limiting taxes on lump-sum early retirement payment, 18
Deferred compensation plans, 385
  nonqualified, 203
Deferred-income-type assets, 355–359
Defined-benefit pension plans, 57, 107–108
  monitoring, 69
  tax deduction for, 381
Defined-contribution pension plans, 130
  in reducing adjusted gross income, 130
De minimis fringe benefit, 221
Dependency exemptions, 271, 286–287
Dependent care, 287
  for aging parents, 302–303
  use of flexible savings account for, 103–104
Dependents
  claiming exemptions for, 362–363
Depreciation
  for home offices, 140
  for leasehold improvements, 203
  in reducing taxable income, 213
Disclaimers of inheritances in estate planning, 5, 7
Dividend distributions for businesses, 237–238
Dividend income, tax on, 27
Dividend-paying stocks, 153–154, 298–299
Dividends, tax rate on, 383
Divorce
  child support versus alimony, 279–280

division of assets in, 278–279
  issues after, 281
  property transfer and settlement in, 323
  tax deductions for children, 362–363
  tax savings and, 269–272
Donations of intellectual property, 203
Donor advised funds, 122–123
  charitable contributions to, 122–123
Dynasty trusts, 317–321

E

Early withdrawal
  penalties on, 144
  from retirement plan, 32–35
Education. See also College
  deducting contributions to, for after-school programs, 162–163
  tax deductions for continuing, 104–105
  tax deductions for costs of higher, 144
  trusts for, 284
Education Savings Account (ESA), funding, 137
Electronic forms for businesses, 251–252
Employee benefit plan return, filing, 252
Employees
  alternative minimum tax protection for, 266–267
  children as, 104, 150–151, 295–296
  classification of, 225
  qualification of statutory, 370–371
  selling company to, and avoiding capital gains tax, 10–13
  tax deduction for entertaining, 394
  tax deductions for meals of, 220–223, 392–393
Employee stock ownership plan (ESOP)
  setting up, 10–13
  transfers, 325
  trust for business owners, 96–97
Employers
  match on 401(k) contributions, 29
  tax deductions for, 104
Employer-sponsored plans
  borrowing money from, 33
  life insurance in, 34
Entertainment
  records on, for business, 194
  tax deductions for, 392–393
Environment
  expensing of remediation costs, 202
Equipment
  tax deductions for businesses, 192–193, 381
Equipment purchases
  for businesses, 107, 238
Estate planning,
  business buy-sell agreements in, 4–5

Crummey letters in, 4
disclaimers of inheritances in, 5
for family business, 40–43
generation-skipping transfer
    tax exemptions in, 3–4
living trusts in, 5–6
stepped-up basis for inherited
    assets, 4
tax-free gifts in, 3
trust as beneficiary in, 5
Estate taxes
    delaying payment of, 54
    exemption threshold in estate
        planning, 3
    income tax deduction for, 53–54
    joint tenants with right of
        survivorship and, 127
    life insurance payment of by, 16
    rates for, in estate planning, 3
    state, 25–26
Estimated taxes, 367
    for businesses, 193–194
    evaluating, 135–136
    reclaiming overpaid, 214
Exchange-traded funds (ETFs),
    327–328
Executors' fees, paying, to sole
    beneficiaries, 52–53
Expatriates, taxes for, 211

F

Fair market value lease, 205
False records, 403
Family, protecting, with dynasty
    trust, 317–321
Family business, estate planning
    for, 40–43
Family limited partnership,
    shifting business into, 41–42
Fast track settlement for small
    business, 204
Federal high-low method in
    reimbursing employee travel
    expenses, 390
Federal Unemployment Tax Act
    (FUTA), 229–232
    annual filing of, 231–232
    depositing of taxes, 231
    50%/30%/20% rule, 394
Filing returns for businesses, 252
529 college savings accounts,
    137, 151, 296
Five-year carryback, 214–215
Fixed annuities, 132, 380
Flexible savings account (FSA) for
    dependent care, 103–104, 302
    for medical costs, 250
Foreign housing costs, 196
Foreign income exclusion, 195–196
Foreign tax credit, 196
Foreign taxes, payment of, 197
401(k) plans
    automatic enrollment in, 91, 92
    for business owners, 95
    employees included in, 68–69
    employer match on contributions
        to, 29
    fiduciary actions for, 93–94
    hardship withdrawals from,
        92–93
    matching contributions for, 93

nondiscrimination rules for,
    90–91
rule changes on, 90–94
Savings Incentive Match Plan
    for Employees (SIMPLE)
        retirement plans, 56, 58
savings opportunities for, 92
for small-business owners,
    38–39
solo, 36–37
taxation of distributions from,
    383–384

G

Gambling, tax deductions for,
    112–115
Generation-skipping transfer
    (GST) tax, 88–89, 319
    exemptions in estate planning,
        3–4
Gift annuities, charitable,
    168–169, 184
Gifts
    from grandparents, 284
    in kind, 226
    single-premium life insurance
        policy as, to charity, 183
    tax deductions for, 297–298
    tax savings on, 384–385
Gift taxes
    exemptions in estate planning, 3
    on joint accounts for unmarried
        couples, 126–127
    spousal, 126–127
Grandchildren, reviewing savings
    for, 29–30

H

Head of household status, 288
    filing as, 269–270
    in supporting aging parents,
        304
Health insurance
    self-employment, 145
    tax deductions for, 380
Health reimbursement
    arrangement (HRA), 250
Health savings accounts (HSAs),
    143, 202
Higher-education costs, tax
    deductions for, 144
Home
    short-term ownership of,
        139–140
    as tax shelter, 139–141
Home-based business, audit risk
    for, 248
Home entertainment, tax
    deductions for, 393
Home loans, pros and cons of,
    313–314
Home rental, tax deduction for,
    288–289
Home sales
    exclusion for, 139–140, 155–159
    division of real estate property,
        158–159
    home-office, 157–158, 310
    sale of multiple properties,
        156–157
    home-office deduction and,

157–158, 310
singles and, 310
tax deductions for, 360
tax-free gains on, 309–313
tax-free profit from, 155–159
Hybrid cars, tax deduction for, 145

I

Incentive stock options (ISOs),
    trap of, 253
Income
    sheltering from IRS, 130–134,
        378–382
    shifting of, 150–154, 288,
        295–299
Income taxes
    deduction for estate tax paid,
        53–54
    filing returns, 252
    on income-producing property,
        125–126
    states without, 23–25
Independent contractors
    information reporting on
        paying, 218–219
Individual retirement accounts
    (IRAs), 142–143. *See also* Roth
        IRAs
    audit guides for, 192
    beneficiaries naming for, 16–17
    bequeathing, to charities, 165
    buying real estate with, 79–82
    cascading beneficiary plan for
        maximum tax deferral, 85–89
    charity deductions from, 60–63
    opportunities for business
        owners withdrawal, 72–73
    protection of, from creditors, 73
    Savings Incentive Match Plan
        for Employees (SIMPLE)
            retirement plans, 58
    SIMPLE, 56–57
    taxation of distributions from,
        383–384
    tax break for inherited, 45
    tax deductions for, 363–364
    trustee-to-trustee transfer in
        executing rollover, 35
Individual retirement accounts
    (IRAs) trust
    revised, rules for, 64–67
Inheritances, disclaiming, 5, 53
Inheritance taxes, state, 25–26
Inherited assets
    avoiding capital gains tax on, 52
    deducting capital losses on, 52
    stepped-up basis for, in estate
        planning, 4
Inherited IRAs
    tax break for, 45
Innocent spouse relief, 280–281
Intellectual property, donations
    of, 203
Interest
    tax deductions for student-loan,
        143–144
Interest, tax on, 27
Interest-paying assets, shifting
    investments in stock to, 29
Internal Revenue Service (IRS),
    sheltering income from,
        378–382

Inventory write-downs for businesses, 240
Investments
carrying forward losses, 361
in low-income housing, 337–340
tax deductions for, 361, 383–384
Irrevocable trusts, 317

J

Job-hunting expenses, tax deduction for, 371
Joint ownership
of assets, 125–129
joint tenants with right of survivorship as form of, 98, 127
real estate tax return strategies and, 125–129
tenancy by the entirety as form of, 98
tenancy in common as form of, 98
Joint tenants with right of survivorship (JTWROS), 98
estate taxes and, 127

K

K-1 filings, 191–192
kinds of income reported on, 191–192
Keogh plan, setting up, 71
Kiddie tax, 152, 297

L

Last in, first out (LIFO) method inventory, adopting, in reducing taxable income, 212
Leasehold improvements, tax deductions for, 236
Leasing of business equipment, 205–208
Legal fees, overlooked deductions for, 386
Life insurance
donating policies to charity, 123, 183
in employer-sponsored plan, 34
exchange of one type for another type, 323
payment of estate taxes by, 16
permanent, 133, 381
in protecting business from death taxes, 42–43
variable, 331–332
Life insurance trust, creation of, 16
Lifetime gifts in estate planning, 41
Like-kind exchange, 344
tax deferrals in, 322
Limited liability company (LLC)
home-sale exclusion of, 158–159
setting up business as, 241–244
Limited use as reason for leasing business equipment, 206
Lincoln Trust, 80
Living trusts
in estate planning, 5–6

Loans
from business, 256–258
to business, 254–256
to children, 290–294
Long-term-care insurance, tax credit for, in New York, 24
Long-term gains, tax rate on, 383
Loss carryforward or carryback for business, 194
Loss deductions, 342–343
Lump-sum early retirement payment, deferral agreement in limiting taxes on, 18

M

Margin loans
pros and cons of, 314–315
risk of, 316
Marital deduction in protecting business from death taxes, 42
Marriage, timing, 28
Marriage penalty, 28, 362
relief for, 385
Meals
records on, for business, 194
tax deductions for, 220–223, 392–393
Medical expenses, 274
for aging parents, 303–304
tax deductions for, 287, 362
tax-free gifts for, 3
Membership dues, tax deduction for, 162
Midyear tax-planning for business, 106–108
Mortgages
not taking deductions, 370
refinancing, 27–28
Moving expenses, tax deductions for, 144
Multigenerational IRA planning, 87–88
Multiple homes, tax-free profit of selling, 156–157
Multiple support agreements for aging parents, 301–302
Mutual funds
buying and selling, 325–327
tax-sheltered alternatives to, 328–332

N

Net operating losses, 214–215
Nondeductible Individual Retirement Accounts (IRAs), 51
Nondiscrimination rules for 401(k) plans, 90–91
Non-load bearing partitions, tax deductions for, 234
Nonqualified deferred compensation plans, 203
Nonresident aliens, taxes for, 209, 210
Non-spouse beneficiaries for inherited retirement account, 46–49
Nontransferable annuity, 47–48

O

One-person 401(k) plans for self-employed, 74–78
On-line sales, collecting tax on,

262–265
Out-of-pocket costs, deduction for, for charity, 162

P

Parents
hiring as employees, 296
supporting aging, 300–304
tax deductions for, 103–104
Partial exclusion for home sale, 155–156
Pass-through entities, 191
advantages of, 242–243
alternatives, 241
differences among, 243–244
filing of schedule K-1 by, 191–192
Payroll tax returns, filing, 252
Pension funds, bequeathing, to charities, 165
Pension income, taxes on, 24
Permanent life insurance, 133
tax deduction for, 381
Personal income, 130–131
sheltering, 130–131, 378–379
Phantom income, transfer of, in divorce, 323
Prenuptial agreement, 71
Prepaid plans, 283
Private annuity, exchanging assets tax free for, 323
Profit from losses, 136
Profit-sharing plans, 57
Property owners, tax deductions for, 102–103
Property taxes, state, 25

Q

Qualified retirement plan, 107
information reporting on, 216–217
in reducing taxable income, 212–213
Qualified terminable interest property (QTIP) trust, 65
Questionable resale as reason for leasing business equipment, 206–207

R

Rapid depreciation write-offs, claiming, 215
Real estate, 329–371
business deductions for investment expenses, 350–351
buying with IRA, 79–82
pros and cons of home loans and margin loans, 313–316
retained interest gifts of, 172
subdividing, for home-sale exclusion, 158–159
swapping for bargains, 322–325
taking losses for future tax benefits, 333–336
tax breaks for real estate investors, 341–345
tax-free gains on selling home, 309–313
tax-sheltered alternatives to mutual funds, 328–332
wash-sale rules, 347–348

year-end tax moves for investors, 346–349

Reasonable compensation, 224

Records
need for, for tax deductions, 116–119
simplifying for business, 250

Refunds
for businesses, 193
for state tax, 363

Religious organization, deducting contributions to, for after-school educational programs, 162–163

Relocation, tax deductions for, 234

Resident aliens, taxes for, 209–210

Retained interest gifts of real estate, 172

Retired parents as employees, 151

Retirement, selection of state for, 23–26

Retirement accounts, 384
non-spouse beneficiaries for inherited, 46–49

Retirement plans
for business owners, 95–97
business owner sponsorship of, 68–71
changes in rules on, 363–364
contributions for businesses, 193
early withdrawal from, 32–35
maxing out, 135
midyear tax planning for, 106–108
for small-business owners, 36–39
tax deductions for, 363–364, 380

Revocable living trust for foreigners working in United States, 210

Rollover IRAs, establishing, for company stock, 21–22

Roth IRAs, 14–15
for children, 50–51, 151, 296
contributions to, 50, 142
conversion of traditional IRAs to, 35
distributions from, 50
holding Treasury Inflation Protected Securities (TIPS) in, 44–45
protection of, from creditors, 73
withdrawal penalties on, 15–16

S

Safe harbor rule, 136

Sales. See also Home sales
installment, 361
on-line, 262–265
split, 141
wash, 136, 327, 335–336, 347–348, 352

Sales taxes
collection of, 262–265
state, 25

Savings bonds
rollover from Series EE, to Series HH, 325
taxes on, 361

Savings Incentive Match Plan for Employees (SIMPLE) retirement plans, 107
for business owners, 95
creating, 135
401(k) plans, 56, 58
individual retirement accounts (IRAs), 58
IRAs, 56–57
for self-employed, 74

Savings plans, 283

S corporations
basis for businesses, 239
compensation planning for owners of, 240
home-sale exclusion of, 158–159
loans to, 254–256
tax laws affecting, 202–203

Securities, borrowing against your, 315–316

Self-directed IRA, 80

Self-employed individuals
health insurance for, 145
one-person 401(k) plans plan for, 74–78
SIMPLE plans for, 55
special write-offs for, 145

Separated individuals
tax deductions for children, 362–363
tax savings for, 269–272

Separate returns, filing, 273–276

Series EE bonds, rollover to Series HH bonds, 325

Simple IRAs, 37

SIMPLE plans, 229

Simplified employee pension (SEP-IRA) plans
for self-employed, 74
for small-business owners, 38
tax deduction for, 381

Small business. See also Business
retirement plans for owners, 36–39
tax deductions for, 401–404
unemployment taxes for, 229–232

Social Security, taxes on benefits, 24, 83–84

Social Security income, sheltering, 131–132, 379–380

Social Security taxes
overpaying, 371
working abroad and, 197

Sole practitioner, creation of market for practice, 42

Solo 401(k) plans, 36–37
for microbusiness, 246–247

Special write-offs for self-employed, 145

Split-dollar life insurance, 43

Sponsorship of athletic teams, tax deductions for, 198

State income tax rules for business, 213–214

States, selection of, for retirement, 23–26

State taxes, 30
unemployment rate and, 230–231

State tax refunds, 363
tax deductions for, 363

State unemployment tax (SUTA), 229–232

Statutory employees, qualification of, 370–371

Stepped-up basis, 97
for inherited assets in estate planning, 4

Stocks
buying individual, 328
of company, in retirement plan account, 21–22
dividend-paying, 153–154
investing in through tax-favored retirement accounts, 28–29
transfer of, as result of merger or spin off, 323

Student-loan interest, tax deductions for, 143–144

Substantiation of charitable deductions, 123–124
need for, for business reimbursements, 389

Succession planning, 12

T

Taxable income, reducing, for business, 212–213

Tax advisers, midyear tax planning and, 106

Tax deductions
for alimony, 144, 279
for bad debts, 361
for business promotion costs, 199
for business travel, 101–102
for capital gains and dividends, 361
for capital losses, 399–400
for charitable donations, 361–362
for charitable organizations, 146–147
for child care, 103
for circulation costs, 200
for clubs and associations, 148–149
for college savings plans, 151–152, 296–297, 381–382
for conservation easement, 166
for continuing education, 104–105
for defined-benefit pension plans, 381
for dependents, 362
in divorce, 362–363
for Dutch-treat meals, 394
for educator expenses, 145
for employees, 220–223, 39
for employers, 104
for entertainment, 392–393
for equipment, 192–193, 247, 381
for estate taxes, 53–54
for gambling, 112–115
for gifts, 297–298, 394
for health insurance, 380

for home offices, 140, 351, 366, 404
for home rental, 288–289
for home sales, 360
for hybrid cars, 145
for individual air-conditioning units, 234
for individual retirement accounts, 363–364
for installment sales, 361
for investment expenses, 350–351
for job-hunting expenses, 371
for leasehold improvements, 236
for life insurance, 381
for literature, 199
for loss leaders, 399
for meals, 220–223, 392–393
for medical expenses, 287, 362
for membership dues, 162
for moving expenses, 144
need for records and, 116–119
overlooked for legal fees, 386
for parents, 103–104
for relocation, 234
for retirement plans, 363–364, 380
for season tickets, 393–394
for shelf-space bonuses, 198
for simplified employee pension (SEP-IRA) plans, 381
for small business, 401–404
for sponsorship of athletic team, 198
for start-up costs, 396–400
for state tax refunds, 363
for student-loan interest, 143–144
for tax-deferred annuities, 381
for travel, 101–102, 370
for union dues, 148
for vacation home, 102–103
for vanity book, 198
for volunteer work, 162
for Web sites, 199
for worthless securities, 361
Tax-deferred annuities, 132, 133
tax deduction for, 381
Tax-deferred retirement plans
avoiding 50% penalty, 20–21
charity deductions from, 60–63
company stock in, 21–22
naming beneficiaries, 21
withdrawals from, 19–20
Taxes
cutting, by investing in low-income housing deals, 337–340
on Social Security benefits, 83–84

Tax-free cash flow, 341–342
Tax-free gains, on home sale, 309–313
Tax-free gifts
in estate planning, 3
for tuition in estate planning, 3
Tax-free profit, squeezing most, from home sale, 155–159
Tax liability, reducing for business, 213
Tax payments for businesses, 251
Tax returns
filing for business owners, 191–194
preparing, 365–367
strategies for joint ownership of assets, 125–129
Tax shelters
alternatives to mutual funds, 328–332
creation of, by microbusiness, 245–248
use of home as, 139–141
Tax traps, loans to kids and, 290–294
1099 information, reporting incorrect or missing, 365
Tenancy in common (TIC), 98
Term insurance, declining costs of, 42–43
Traditional IRAs
conversion to Roth IRAs, 14–15, 35
withdrawal penalties on, 15–16
Transfer taxes in estate planning, 41
Transportation costs, tax deductions for business related, 101–102
Travel
tax deductions for, 101–102, 370
Treasury Inflation Protected Securities (TIPS), 44–45
Trustee-to-trustee transfer in executing IRA rollover, 35
Trusts. *See also* Charitable lead trusts; Charitable remainder annuity trusts; Charitable remainder trusts (CRTs); Charitable remainder unitrusts
as beneficiary, in estate planning, 5, 7
for education, 284
income from, 64–65
individual retirement account, 64–67
Tuition
appreciated securities for, 137
gift of appreciated securities for, 385
paying for child, 29

tax-free gifts for, 3

U
Unemployment insurance (UD), 229
quarterly filing of, 232
Unemployment taxes for small business, 229–232
Unforeseen circumstances, 139
in home sales, 155–156, 311–312, 360
Uniform Gifts to Minors Act (UGMA) accounts, 284
Uniform Principal and Income Act (UPAIA), 64–67
Uniform Transfers to Minors Act (UTMA) accounts, 284
Union dues, tax deduction for, 148
U.S. savings bonds, transfer of Series EE to Series HH, 325
U.S. tax treaties with foreign countries, 210
Unitrust charitable remainder trusts (CRTs), 164
Unitrust provisions, 66

V
Vacation home, tax deductions for, 102–103
Variable annuities, 48, 132, 330–331, 380
Variable life insurance, 331–332
Volunteer work, tax deduction for, 162

W
W-2s, reconstructing missing, 365
Wash sales
avoiding, 327
rules for, 136, 335–336, 347–348, 352
Web sites, tax deductions for creating, 199
Will, make charitable bequest in your, 31, 163, 165
Withdrawals
penalties on, 15–16
from tax-deferred retirement plans, 19–20
Working abroad, 195–198
Work opportunity credit, tax credits only, 202
Worthless securities, tax deductions for, 361

Y
Year-end charitable strategies, 173–177